The Far Western Frontier

The Far Western Frontier

Advisory Editor
RAY A. BILLINGTON
Senior Research Associate
at the Henry E. Huntington Library
and Art Gallery

TEN YEARS IN OREGON

D[ANIEL] LEE AND J[OSEPH] H. FROST

ARNO PRESS
A NEW YORK TIMES COMPANY
New York • 1973

Reprint Edition 1973 by Arno Press Inc.

Reprinted from a copy in The State
Historical Society of Wisconsin Library

The Far Western Frontier
ISBN for complete set: 0-405-04955-2
See last pages of this volume for titles.

Manufactured in the United States of America

Publisher's Note: This volume was reprinted
from the best available copy.

Library of Congress Cataloging in Publication Data

Lee, Daniel, 1806-1895.
   Ten years in Oregon.

   (The Far Western frontier)
   Reprint of the 1844 ed.
   1. Oregon--Description and travel. 2. Indians of
North America--Missions. 3. Missions--Oregon.
4. Methodist Episcopal Church--Missions. I. Frost,
Joseph, H., joint author. II. Title. III. Series.
F880.L47   1973   917.95'0092'4 [B]   72-9457
ISBN 0-405-04985-4

TEN YEARS IN OREGON

TEN YEARS IN OREGON.

BY D. LEE AND J. H. FROST,
LATE OF THE OREGON MISSION OF THE METHODIST EPISCOPAL CHURCH.

The Albatross.

NEW-YORK:
PUBLISHED FOR THE AUTHORS: 200 MULBERRY-STREET

J. Collord, Printer.

"Entered according to Act of Congress, in the year 1844, by D. Lee & J. H. Frost, in the Clerk's Office of the District Court of the Southern District of New-York."

PREFACE.

THE American churches, and the public in general, have been anxiously waiting for correct information of a more extensive and particular kind, concerning the Oregon Territory, than they have hitherto been favoured with. And if the following work is in any tolerable degree calculated to furnish the information required, the authors will have secured the principal object for which they undertook the task of writing a book. If it is not, the usual excuses upon such an occasion are well known; and they may claim the benefit of them, in common with others.

If our work should appear upon examination to be in some respects disjointed, or disproportioned, it must be remembered that it has been our object not to make our volume so large as to put it out of the reach of hundreds who might not feel able to purchase a large work, and in so doing we have been under the necessity of abridging all its parts.

But we have endeavoured, as far as our

limits would permit, to lay before our readers all the most important particulars connected with the history of that country, from the time that the north-west coast was discovered by Capt. Cook, in the year 1792, until the present. And it becomes us to state here, that for the knowledge which we are enabled to communicate concerning that territory from the year 1792 down to the establishment of the Oregon Mission in the year 1834, we are principally indebted to the work entitled "Astoria," which is from the pen of our much-esteemed countryman, Washington Irving, Esq. And we have not hesitated to make use of the language of that accomplished author as far as it has suited our convenience. And we can freely vouch for the authenticity of that work, if this should be thought necessary; for we have had an opportunity of comparing it with the subject of which it treats, and also with the personal knowledge of several gentlemen who have resided for many years in that country.

Our knowledge of the face of that country was obtained by actual observation, having travelled through, and resided in, the most important portions thereof; and by information received from gentlemen of veracity who have resided there for many years, and travelled very extensively in almost every part of it.

PREFACE.

As one of us resided there for the space of ten years, and the other between three and four years, we had a sufficient opportunity to become acquainted with the climate, soil, and productions of the country; and as our residence was immediately and continually among the Indians, and as we had communications with them daily, we consider ourselves fully prepared to judge of their character and habits; and as it was our primary object while among them to labour as far as circumstances would permit for their spiritual welfare, and to observe the effects produced by the communication of religious truths to their dark understandings, as far as their very limited language would enable us to do so, we have been able to judge with reference to the prospects of bringing them into the enjoyment of the blessings of civilization and Christianity.

We were prepared to give more copious examples of their manners and customs; but presume that the examples we have given will be deemed satisfactory by the generality of readers, and feared that we might become tedious by dwelling at greater length upon this part of our subject. Their superstitions are exceedingly numerous, and deeply rooted, and it would require a volume to give anything like a full account of them, and after it was written it would be of no real service to the reader, so we have contented ourselves with giving an account of but a few of them.

By the perusal of our work the reader will get a tolerable idea of the toils, privations, and difficulties through which the missionary is called to pass, while labouring for the salvation of his fellow-men in heathen wilds; and we trust this view of things will lead the Christian, and all the friends of missions, to wrestle more earnestly with God in fervent prayer for the sustaining influences of the Holy Ghost to be poured out upon his servants and handmaidens, while thus, in their isolated situations, they forego all the blessings of a happy, Christian home, and spend their health and lives for the salvation of their wretched brethren; and that they will still be sustained by continual exertions in other respects.

And as the white population of that country has from the first shared in the labours of the missionaries, and are still sharing in their labours, we have endeavoured to show to what extent the Word of Life has proved effectual in bringing them from darkness to light, and from the power of Satan unto God.

CONTENTS.

CHAPTER I.

Captain Cook's voyage in the Pacific Ocean—Captain Gray, of Boston, enters Columbia River—Some of his ship's crew call at a native village, the inhabitants of which flee, never having seen white men before—Vancouver visits the River, and his Lieutenant, Broughton, explores it—Capt. J. Carver's projected exploration of Columbia River—Lewis and Clark's expedition—John Jacob Astor's trading scheme—Pacific Fur Company, ... Page 13

CHAPTER II.

Part of the company embark on board ship Tonquin for the purpose of establishing a trading post—Select a place, and call it Astoria—The Tonquin arrives at Vancouver's Island—Massacre of her crew by the Indians—Blown up by one of the survivors of the massacre—Others of them put to death by the Indians—Stratagem of Mr. M'Dougal to ensure himself and friends against their violence—Mansion completed—Schooner finished and launched—New-Year celebration, ... 18

CHAPTER III.

Departure of the land expedition—St. Louis—Missouri River—Missouri Fur Company—Daniel Boon, of Kentucky—Mad River—Travellers arrive at Mr. Henry's post, and take possession of huts deserted by him—A party of hunters leave for the purpose of trapping beaver—Man lost—Arrive at a terrific strait, and encamp—Separate into several detachments—Meet with Indians, and obtain some salmon and a dog for food—Mr. Hunt purchases a horse for an old tin kettle—The party abandon the river, and suffer from thirst—Meet with another party who are in a state of starvation—Kill two horses to satisfy the cravings of hunger—Celebrate New-Year on dogs and horse flesh—Arrive at Astoria, and meet with some of their old comrades, ... 26

CHAPTER IV.

Several expeditions depart from Astoria—Skirmish with the Indians—Arrive at Oakinagan—Set out on their return to Astoria—Encounter companions of a former expedition, who were supposed to be lost—Arrive at Astoria—Mr. Astor sends an agent to St. Petersburgh—He despatches a vessel to Oregon—She arrives at Astoria—Parties go out to establish new trading posts—A band separate from the main body on a journey across the Rocky Mountains—Meet four of their former companions, who join them—Their horses stolen by Indians—Encamp for the winter—Arrive at St. Louis, ... 39

CHAPTER V.

Agent sent to St. Petersburgh negotiates an agreement—Mr. Astor sends out another vessel to the settlement on the Columbia—Messrs. Stuart, Clark, and M'Kenzie establish new posts—Caches robbed by Snake Indians, who are attacked by the Blackfeet, who seize their booty—The Beaver departs on a coasting voyage—M'Kenzie breaks up his establishment, and returns to Astoria—He and others set out on a journey—Three of them enter a lodgment of Indians, and are in imminent danger—Arrives at his former station, and finds that his caches have been robbed—Mr. Clark causes an Indian to be hung—They return to Astoria, ... 48

CHAPTER VI.

The partners at Astoria agree to abandon the country—Action of the British and American governments in reference to the new settlement—Mr. M'Dougal, at Astoria, marries the daughter of an Indian chief—Anecdote—The Beaver makes her way to China, leaving Mr. Hunt on the Sandwich Islands—He returns to Astoria—Wreck of the Lark, and sufferings of her crew—The furs and merchandise belonging to Mr. Astor sold to the North-West Fur Company—Arrival of a British sloop of war, whose commander takes possession of the establishment at Astoria in the name of his British Majesty—Treaty between the United States and Great Britain as to the occupancy of Oregon—Reflections, . . . 59

CHAPTER VII.

Description of the country—Columbia River and its tributaries—Annual floods—Vancouver—Multnomah Island—Clatsop Plain—Walamet River and Falls—Valleys—Plains—Productiveness of the soil—Climate—Blackfish from fifteen to twenty feet in length—Whales—Epidemics, . 81

CHAPTER VIII.

Number of Indians in Oregon Territory—Their character—Wars among them—Personal appearance—Dress—Description of those inhabiting the lower country—Their heads flattened in infancy—Anecdote illustrative of their shrewdness—Slaves among them—Polygamy—They sell their daughters—Their moral character—Wild animals—Fish, . . . 95

CHAPTER IX.

Sand-bar at the mouth of the Columbia—Loss of the ship William and Ann—Of the Isabella—Of a vessel from Asia—Streams of the country possess petrifying qualities, trees and other things exposed to their action having been found in a petrified state—Japanese junk cast away—The epidemic ague—Indians' idea of its origin—Mr. David Douglass visits Oregon—A party of American traders under command of Captain Wyeth cross the Mountains, ... 106

CONTENTS.

CHAPTER X.

Causes which induced the establishment of the Oregon Mission—Dr. Fisk enlists in its favour—Rev. Jason and Daniel Lee appointed missionaries—Missionary meetings, in furtherance of the enterprise, held—Mr. Jason Lee goes to Boston to consult with Captain Wyeth as to the propriety of establishing the mission—Messrs. Lee set out for the west, and arrive at St. Louis—Join a party, who start for the Rocky Mountains—Description of the party, and of their method of travelling—Kanzas Indians—The antelope—Buffalo—A company of emigrants attacked by Indians, . 109

CHAPTER XI.

Rendezvous—Description of country—Hunting and battle ground of the Indians—The party take up their line of march—Soda Spring—Erect a fort—Procure buffalo meat—Accident—Fort Hall sold to Hudson's Bay Company—Missionaries join another party—Description of country and of Indians—Blue Mountains—Travellers arrive at Fort Wallah-wallah—Summary of travel—Arrive at Vancouver—Location for mission selected, ... 118

CHAPTER XII.

Claims of the Flathead Indians not sufficient to induce the missionaries to establish a mission among them—Mission commenced on the Walamet—Description of the incipient labours of the missionaries—A party from California arrives—Indian youth left with the missionaries to be instructed—A party of whites, who had been attacked by the Indians, arrives at the mission—Intermittent fever—Mr. Nuttall, the naturalist—Death of a trapper, and addition to the mission family—Mr. D. Lee embarks for the Sandwich Islands for the improvement of his health, . . . 127

CHAPTER XIII.

Voyage to the Sandwich Islands—Sea sickness—Arrival—Mr. Lee is cordially received by missionaries—Their mission—Arrival of a Quaker missionary from London—Return of Mr. Lee—Loss of a ship's crew—State of affairs at the mission during Mr. Lee's absence—Temperance Society formed—Mr. Lee engages in medical practice—Provision for mission family—First conversion of a white man in Oregon, ... 135

CHAPTER XIV.

Mission settlement receives a visit from Mr. Wm. A. Slocum—Petition to congress from people at the settlement, calling upon the American government to protect them by its laws—Mr. J. Lee procures cattle from California—Arrival of reinforcement to the misson, from the United States—An attempt to murder an Indian chief—Mission schools—Happy deaths—History of a sabbath in Oregon—Another reinforcement arrives—Attempt of missionaries to improve the condition of Calapooyas—Plans to extend the work formed, ... 144

CHAPTER XV.

Mission established at the Dalls—Visited by Mr. Jason Lee, on his way to the United States—Journeys of missionaries—Meetings among the Indians—Death of Mrs. J. Lee—Escape of Mr. Leslie and Mrs. White from imminent danger—Description of Mr. D. Lee's journey to and from Walamet—Carousals among the Dalls—Fire eater—Medicine men—Circumstances related, illustrative of the character of the Dalls, . . 151

CHAPTER XVI.

Mr. David Leslie has charge of Oregon Mission during the absence of Mr. J. Lee—His house burned—Glorious revival of religion at the Walamet station—One of the converts drowned—Happy deaths—Death of Mr. Cyrus Shepard, and extract from a letter written by him—Mr. and Mrs. Perkins return to the Dalls station—Farming operations—Statement by General Jackson—Description of Indian character and customs, . . 166

CHAPTER XVII.

Account of the "work of God" at the Dalls in 1839, '40—Specimen of an Indian prayer—Dancing-hall used as a meeting-house—Preaching of the missionaries, and formation of classes—Baptism of converts—Camp-meeting—Communion administered to several hundred Indians—Affairs at the Walamet station—Trip to Walamet and Chenook—Arrival of the Lausanne with a reinforcement to the mission, accompanied by Mr. J. Lee, ... 182

CHAPTER XVIII.

Description of the Columbia River, dike, rapids, rocky islands, &c.—Whirlpool, in which a party belonging to the Hudson's Bay Company were engulfed, and most of them perished—Indian mode of fishing—More than one thousand Indians employ a portion of their time in the salmon fishery—The Cascades—Indian hymn and translation, . . . 196

CHAPTER XIX.

Missions of the American Board and others—A monomaniac burned to death—Introduction of a printing press, and the publication of books in the native tongues—Children drowned—Indians form a civil compact—Hudson Bay Company's express—Catholics establish a mission—Two Scotch naturalists drowned—Mr. Pambeam thrown from his horse and killed—A body of emigrants settle in the country, ... 206

CHAPTER XX.

A reinforcement to the mission set out from New-York—Incidents of the voyage—Arrive at the Sandwich Islands—Occurrences there—Reach Astoria—Disappointed on finding that it consisted of but three or four houses—Voyage to Vancouver—Missionaries appointed to their various fields of labour—Marriage of Rev. D. Lee—A company of missionaries arrive at the Dalls—Trip to Vancouver—Dr. Richmond's journey—Two of the missionaries set out for Astoria—Return to Vancouver—Incidents of the journey, ... 216

CHAPTER XXI.

Account of the Dalls resumed—A cold-blooded murder committed—Encounter with Indians—Mission family suffer from sickness—Camp meeting—Mr. D. Lee's voyage from and to the Dalls—Journey to the Walamet station—Death of Mrs. Leslie—Birth—Marriages—Annual meeting—Building—Religious meetings—Death of Mrs. Jason Lee—Mr. and Mrs. D. Lee's voyage to and from Vancouver—Eruption of a volcano—Visit to Walamet Falls, and return—Religious state of the natives—Remarkable conversion—Mr. and Mrs. D. Lee sail for the United States, . . 241

CHAPTER XXII.

Voyage of Mr. Frost and family from Vancouver to Astoria—Murders committed—A body of Indians arrive to protect the settlement—One of the murderers is shot—Another of them is hung—Mr. Frost and others visit Mr. Smith at Clatsop Plains—Indian mother and her child—Mr. Frost visits Walamet Mission and returns—Barbarous act by the Indians—Indian trick—Mission family establish themselves—Extract from Mr. Frost's journal—His labours among the Indians—Salmon feast—Indian tradition, ... 266

CHAPTER XXIII.

Mr. Frost attends the yearly meeting at Walamet—Manual Labour School—The Oregon Institute—Visiters—Extract from Mr. Frost's journal—Exploring expedition—Messrs. Smith and Frost's journey to and from Walamet—Kilemook Indians—Mr. Kone and family return to the United States—Extracts from Mr. Frost's journal—Arrival of vessels—Immorality of seamen who visited Oregon—Reflections—Indians obtain ardent spirits, and proceed to murder one another—Some of the missionaries embark for the United States—Death of Rev. James Olley—Awful disaster—Return of missionaries to the United States, and conclusion, . . . 302

CHENOOK CANOE.

TEN YEARS IN OREGON.

CHAPTER I.

Captain Cook's voyage in the Pacific Ocean—Captain Gray, of Boston, enters Columbia River—Some of his ship's crew call at a native village, the inhabitants of which flee, never having seen white men before—Vancouver visits the River, and his Lieutenant, Broughton, explores it—Capt. J. Carver's projected exploration of Columbia River—Lewis and Clark's expedition—John Jacob Astor's trading scheme—Pacific Fur Company.

THAT truly renowned navigator, Captain Cook, while prosecuting his last voyage in the Pacific Ocean, became acquainted with the vast quantities of sea otter, beaver, and other valuable furs to be obtained on the north-west coast, and the immense prices to be obtained for those furs in China. When this knowledge was communicated to the civilized world it was, says Washington Irving, as if a new gold coast had been discovered. Individuals from many of the civilized nations engaged in this very lucrative traffic: so that in the year 1792 it is said there were twenty-one vessels under different flags plying along the coast, and trading with the natives. The greater part of these vessels were American, and owned by Boston merchants.

But little was known of the Columbia River, but the fact that it existed, except the vague and indefinite information gathered from Indian reports, up to the above date, when Captain Gray of Boston entered it, notwithstanding the sand-bar and breakers off its mouth, on board of the *Columbia*, and caused the American colours to wave over Baker's Bay, where she came to anchor.

The latitude of the mouth of the Columbia, according to the document now before me, is 46° 19″ north. A boat was well manned, and sent on shore, to a village on the beach, (the village referred to was that of the Chenook Indians ;) but all the inhabitants fled, except the aged and infirm. The kind manner in which these were treated, and the presents given them, gradually lured back the others, and a friendly intercourse took place. This was the first ship, and these the first white men, that those Indians ever saw. They entertained various conjectures relative to the vessel when in the distance, supposing her to be a floating island, then a monster of the deep ; but when they saw the boat pulling for shore with human beings on board, they decided that they were cannibals sent by some superior being to devour them, and ravage their country. And I imagine that I now see them all squatting together like so many frogs, consulting with reference to their future course, in a language full as melodious, and indicative of as much intelligence, as that of his frogship.

Capt. Gray ascended the river as far as the bay which bears his name to this day, a short distance above Astoria. After putting to sea, he fell in with the celebrated discoverer Vancouver, and informed him of his discovery, furnishing him with a chart which he had made of the river. Vancouver visited the river, and his lieutenant, Broughton, explored it by the aid of Capt. Gray's chart ; ascending it upward of one hundred miles, probably to where Vancouver, the principal depot of the Hon. Hudson's Bay Company, is now located.

In the years 1763 and '64, Capt. Jonathan Carver, who had been in the British provincial army, and an English gentleman of fortune, and a member of parliament, projected the enterprise of crossing the Rocky Mountains and exploring the Oregon, or River of the West, as the Columbia River was then called, to its exit into the Pacific. They were to take with them fifty or sixty men, artificers and mariners, in order to build forts on the Pacific coast for their protection, and vessels for the purpose of prosecuting more extensive discoveries by sea ; but the breaking out of the American revolution effectually defeated the undertaking.

In 1793 Sir Alexander Mackenzie crossed the continent to the Pacific Ocean, which he reached in lat. 52° 20′ 48″. His success once more suggested the possibility of linking together the trade of both sides of the continent. And as there might be a clashing of claims between the Hudson's Bay and North-west Companies, the one holding by right of charter, and the other by right of possession, it was proposed that the two companies should coalesce in this great undertaking. This scheme, however, proved abortive, in consequence of the long-cherished enmity or jealousy existing between the two companies, which would not allow them to listen to such counsel.

In the mean time the attention of the American government was attracted to the subject, and the memorable expedition under Messrs. Lewis and Clark fitted out. These gentlemen, in 1804, accomplished the enterprise which had been projected by Carver and Whitworth, in 1774. They ascended the Missouri; passed through the stupendous gates of the Rocky Mountains, hitherto unknown to the white man; discovered and explored the upper waters of the Columbia, and followed that river down to its mouth, where their countryman, Gray, had anchored about twelve years previously. Here they passed the winter, and I had the pleasure of seeing the spot where their hut stood, on a small river which enters Young's Bay, a short distance below Astoria, on the south side of the Columbia, called Lewis and Clark's River; and the Indians have often pointed out to me the trail by which a gang of their men went daily from their hut to the coast, probably to look out for vessels. Their hut had entirely disappeared at the time of my visiting the spot in 1842.

Messrs. Lewis and Clark returned across the mountains in the following spring. The reports published by them of their expedition, demonstrated the practicability of establishing a line of communication across the continent, from the Atlantic to the Pacific Ocean.

It was then that the idea presented itself to the mind of Mr. John Jacob Astor, of grasping with his individual hand this great enterprise, which for years had been dubiously yet desirously contemplated by powerful associations and fostering governments. The main feature of Mr. Astor's scheme was to establish a line of trading posts along the Missouri and the Columbia, to the mouth of the latter, where was to be founded the chief trading house or depot. Inferior posts would be established in the interior, and on all the tributary streams of the Columbia, to trade with the Indians; these posts would draw their supplies from the main establishment, and bring to it the peltries they collected. Coasting crafts would be built and fitted out, also, at the mouth of the Columbia, to trade, at favourable seasons, all along the north-west coast, and return, with the proceeds of their voyages, to this place of deposite.

Thus all the Indian trade, both of the interior and the coast, would converge to this point, and thence derive its sustenance.

A ship was to be sent annually from New-York to this main establishment with reinforcements and supplies, and with merchandise suited to the trade. It would take on board the furs collected during the preceding year, carry them to Canton, invest the proceeds in the rich merchandise of China, and return thus freighted to New-York.

Such is a brief outline of the mighty enterpise projected by Mr. Astor, but which continually expanded in his mind; and after obtaining the countenance of government, he prepared to carry his scheme into prompt execution, by procuring proper agents and coadjutors, habituated to the Indian trade and to the life of the wilderness. Among the clerks of the North-west Company were several of great capacity and experience, who had served out their probationary terms, but who, either through lack of interest and influence, or a want of vacancies, had not been promoted. They were consequently much dissatisfied, and ready for any employment in which their talents and acquirements might be turned to better account.

Mr. Astor made his overtures to several of these persons, and three of them entered into his views. One of these, Mr. Alexander M'Kay, had accompanied Mr. Mackenzie in both of his expeditions to the northwest coast of America, in 1789 and 1793. The other two were Duncan M'Dougal and Donald M'Kenzie. To these was subsequently added Mr. Willson Price Hunt, of New-Jersey. As this gentleman was a native-born citizen of the United States, and a person of great probity and worth, he was selected by Mr. Astor to be his chief agent, and to represent him in the contemplated establishment at the mouth of the Columbia.

On the 23d of June, 1810, articles of agreement were entered into between Mr. Astor and these four gentleman, acting for themselves and for the several persons who had already agreed to become, or should thereafter become, associated under the firm of " The Pacific Fur Company."

According to these articles, Mr. Astor was to be at the head of the company, and to manage its affairs in New-York. He was to furnish vessels, goods, provisions, arms, ammunition, and all other requisites for the enterprise at first cost and charges, provided they did not, at any time, involve an advance of more than four hundred thousand dollars.

The stock of the company was to be divided into a hundred equal shares, with the profits accruing thereon. Fifty shares were to be at the disposition of Mr. Astor, and the other fifty to be divided among the partners and their associates.

Mr. Astor was to have the privilege of introducing other persons into the connection, as partners, two of whom, at least, should be conversant with the Indian trade, and none of them to be entitled to more than three shares.

A general meeting of the company was to be held annually at the Columbia River, for the investigation and regulation of its affairs ; at which absent members might be represented, and might vote by proxy under certain specified conditions.

The association, if successful, was to continue for twenty years ; but the parties had full power to abandon and dissolve it within the first five years, should it be found unprofitable. For this term Mr. Astor covenanted to bear all the loss that might be incurred ; after which it was to be borne by all the partners, in proportion to their respective shares.

The parties of the second part were to execute faithfully such duties as might be assigned to them by a majority of the company on the north-west coast, and to repair to such place or places as the majority might direct.

An agent, appointed for five years, was to reside at the principal establishment on the north-west coast, and Mr. Hunt was the one chosen for the first term. Should the interest of the concern at any time require his absence, a person was to be appointed in general meeting to take his place.

Such were the leading conditions of this association. We shall now proceed to notice, as briefly as possible, some of the daring and eventful expeditions, by sea and land, to which it gave rise.

CHAPTER II.

Part of the company embark on board ship Tonquin for the purpose of establishing a trading post—Select a place, and call it Astoria—The Tonquin arrives at Vancouver's Island—Massacre of her crew by the Indians—Blown up by one of the survivors of the massacre—Others of them put to death by the Indians—Stratagem of Mr. M'Dougal to ensure himself and friends against their violence—Mansion completed—Schooner finished and launched—New-Year celebration.

IN prosecuting his great scheme of commerce and colonization, two expeditions were devised by Mr. Astor, one by sea, the other by land. The former was to carry out the people, stores, ammunition, and merchandise, requisite for establishing a fortified trading post at the mouth of the Columbia River. The latter, conducted by Mr. Hunt, was to proceed up the Missouri, and across the Rocky Mountains, to the same point; exploring a line of communication across the continent, and noting the places where interior trading posts might be established.

A fine ship was provided, called the Tonquin, of two hundred and ninety tons' burden, mounting ten guns, with a crew of twenty men. An assortment of merchandise, and all necessary supplies, were shipped in due season, and the command of the ship was intrusted to Jonathan Thorn, of New-York, a lieutenant in the United States Navy on leave of absence. Four of the partners were to embark in the ship, namely, Messrs. M'Kay, M'Dougal, David Stuart, and his nephew, Robert Stuart. Mr. M'Dougal was impowered by Mr. Astor to act as his proxy in the absence of Mr. Hunt, to vote for him, and in his name, on any question that might come before any meeting of the persons interested in the voyage.

Besides the partners, there were twelve clerks to go out in the ship, several of them natives of Canada, who had some experience in Indian trade, whose interests were to some extent identified with the company. Several artisans were likewise to sail in the ship, and also a number of Canadian "voyageurs." Thus armed and equipped, the Tonquin put to sea on the 8th of September, 1810: and as I do not design to give a history of the voyage, I will just remark that the Tonquin made the mouth of the Columbia River on the 22d of March, having, according to the best history that we have of the voyage, borne up a very unpleasant and ungovernable set of passengers, and a very straight-forward, stiff, and crusty captain, for the space of about six months. After losing two boats and eight men, the Tonquin crossed the bar and anchored in Baker's Bay. On the 5th of April, Mr.

M'Dougal and Mr. David Stuart set off for the southern shore, intending to be back by the 7th. After reaching that shore, they soon pitched upon a spot which appeared to them favourable for the intended establishment. It was on a point of land called Point George, having a very good harbour, where vessels of six hundred tons' burden might ride in safety.

After a day thus profitably spent, they recrossed the river, and after being detained for several days at the Chenook village, in consequence of bad weather, they reached the Tonquin in safety.

The old Chenook chief, or *King Comcomly*, as he was called, and his men, accompanied the two explorers to the Tonquin, where he and his people were entertained, and liberally rewarded for services rendered; after which they returned home highly satisfied, promising to remain faithful friends and allies of the white men. From the reports of the two exploring partners, it was determined that Point George should be the site of the general depot. Accordingly, on the 12th of April, the launch was freighted with all things necessary for the purpose, and sixteen persons departed in her to commence the establishment, leaving the Tonquin to follow as soon as the harbour could be sounded.

Crossing the wide mouth of the river, they soon reached the place of destination, and all hands set to work cutting down trees, clearing away thickets, and marking out the place for the permanent store-house and powder magazine, which were to be built of logs, and covered with cedar bark. The next thought was to give a name to the embryo metropolis. The one that naturally suggested itself was that of the projector and supporter of the whole enterprise. It was accordingly named ASTORIA.

The Tonquin, in the mean time, made her way through the intricate channel, and came to anchor in the little bay, and was saluted from the encampment with three volleys of musketry and three cheers. She returned the salute with three cheers and three guns.

After many unpleasant circumstances had transpired between Mr. M'Dougal and Captain Thorn, the necessary arrangements were made, and the Tonquin set out on her northward-bound coasting voyage on the 1st of June, from which voyage she was never to return.

Before the Tonquin left the Columbia, the captain procured an Indian interpreter by the name of Lamazee, (who was still living in 1843,) and in a few days after she set sail, she arrived at Vancouver's Island, and anchored in the harbour of Neweetee, very much against the advice of Lamazee, who warned the captain against the perfidious character of the natives of this part of the coast.

Numbers of canoes came off for the purpose of trade; but in consequence of the uncivil treatment which they received from Captain Thorn, the natives took offence, and determined on revenge.

Mr. M'Kay had been on shore, and returning soon after the Indians had left the ship, the interpreter who was with him, having been apprized of the threatening danger, begged him to prevail on the captain to make sail as soon as possible. Mr. M'Kay did as Lamazee had requested; but the captain, in a surly mood, pointed to his cannon and fire-arms as a sufficient safeguard against naked savages. On the following morning, at the dawn of day, while the captain and M'Kay were yet asleep, a canoe came alongside containing twenty Indians, headed by one of the chiefs. They appeared unarmed, and with aspects friendly, holding up otter skins, indicating a desire to trade. Although Mr. Astor had cautioned the captain in respect to the admission of Indians on board of the vessel, yet his advice had been for some time neglected; and the officer of the watch, at this time, perceiving those in the canoe to be, as he supposed, without weapons, and having received no orders to the contrary, readily permitted them to come on deck. Another crew soon followed the first, which was also admitted. In a short time Indians were clambering into the vessel on all sides.

The officer now became alarmed, and called for Captain Thorn and Mr. M'Kay. By the time they came on deck, it was thronged with natives. The captain was again advised to make sail; but he again made light of it. It was but a short time after this when the self-conceited captain became alarmed; but it was too late: for, while some of the crew were, in obeying his orders, weighing the anchor, and others aloft loosening sail, a scene of blood and carnage ensued, sufficiently horrid to appal the stoutest heart. At the appointed time a signal yell was given, which was followed by the brandishing of knives and war-clubs, which the treacherous natives had had concealed beneath their skin frocks, and with these weapons they rushed upon their victims. I need not attempt to describe what followed. Suffice it to say, that all of the officers and crew save four men were massacred on the spot. These four men succeeded in reaching the cabin; and after fastening the door, and breaking holes through the companion-way, and, with the muskets, opening a brisk fire upon the Indians, they soon cleared the deck. In the cabin they found Mr. Lewis still alive, but mortally wounded. Thus far the Indian interpreter described the scene. He had taken no part in the conflict, and having been spared by the natives as being of their race, when they left the ship he took his departure with them.

The survivors of the crew now sallied forth, and discharged some of the deck guns, which did great execution among the canoes, and drove all the savages ashore.

When the next day dawned, the Tonquin still lay at anchor in the bay, her sails all loose and flapping in the wind, and no one apparently on board of her. After a time, some of the canoes ventured forth to reconnoitre, taking with them the interpreter. While thus employed, one man appeared on deck, whom Lamazee recognized as Mr. Lewis. He made friendly signs, and invited them on board, and, after some delay, they complied. Finding no resistance, nor even a soul on deck, for Mr. Lewis had disappeared, others soon pressed forward to take the prize, so that the decks were soon crowded ; but in the midst of their exultation the ship blew up with a tremendous explosion. Arms, legs, and mutilated bodies, were blown into the air, and dreadful havoc was made in the surrounding canoes. The interpreter was in the main chains at the time of the explosion, from which he was thrown into the water, and succeeded in getting into one of the canoes. According to his statement, the bay presented an awful spectacle after the catastrophe.

The inhabitants of Neweetee were overwhelmed with consternation at this astounding calamity, which had burst upon them in the very moment of triumph. The warriors sat mute and mournful, while the women and children rent the air with the death-wail.

Their sadness and wailings, however, were suddenly changed into yells of fury at the sight of four unfortunate white men, brought captive into the village. Lamazee was permitted to converse with them, and they proved to be the four brave fellows who had made such desperate defence of the cabin. They told him that after they had cleared the ship, and finding it impossible to get her under way, they determined to leave her and endeavour to effect their escape in the ship's boat ; and as Lewis refused to accompany them, they left him to his fate ; who, after being alone, determined to revenge the blood of his shipmates by the awful method of decoying as many of the natives on board as possible, and then setting fire to the powder magazine, and terminating his life by a signal act of vengeance. How well he succeeded has been shown. His companions bade him a last and melancholy adieu, and laboured with might and main to get out of the bay, but found it impossible; for, being overpowered by the wind and tide, they were driven upon a point of land, where, after they had fallen asleep through fatigue, they were surprised by the Indians, and suffered a more painful and protracted death than their desperate companion who remained on board of the ship, being sacrificed by the savages to the manes of their friends with all the lingering tortures of savage cruelty. Some time after their death, the interpreter, who had remained a kind of prisoner at large, effected his escape, and brought the tragical tidings to Astoria.

Such was the fate of the Tonquin, her brave but headstrong captain, and her adventurous crew. How true it is that " in the multitude of counsellors there is safety." Had Captain Thorn's deportment been properly regulated, the insult which wounded the pride of the savage chieftain would never have been given; and had he attended to the directions of his employer in admitting but few of the natives at a time, they would not have been able to accomplish their treacherous designs. Yet it should be remembered, that throughout the whole voyage Captain Thorn showed himself to be loyal, single-minded, straight-forward, and fearless; and that he paid for his error with his life.

The tidings of the loss of the Tonquin, and the massacre of her crew, struck dismay into the hearts of the Astorians. They found themselves a mere handful of men, on a savage coast, surrounded by hostile tribes, who would doubtless be incited to deeds of violence by the late fearful catastrophe. In this juncture, Mr. M'Dougal, we are told, had recourse to a stratagem by which to avail himself of the ignorance and credulity of the savages; and, although such a course could scarcely be approved under any circumstances, it certainly does credit to his ingenuity.

The natives of the coast, and, indeed, of all the regions west of the mountains, had an extreme dread of the small-pox; that terrific scourge having, a few years previously, appeared among them, and almost swept off entire tribes. Its origin and nature were wrapped in mystery, and they conceived it an evil inflicted upon them by some superior being, or brought among them by the white men. The last idea was seized upon by Mr. M'Dougal. He assembled several of the chieftains whom he believed to be in the conspiracy. When they were all seated around, he informed them that he had heard of the treachery of some of their northern brethren toward the Tonquin, and was determined on vengeance.

"The white men among you," said he, "are few in number, it is true, but they are mighty in medicine. See here," continued he, drawing forth a small bottle, and holding it before their eyes, "in this bottle I hold the small-pox, safely corked up ; I have but to draw the cork, and let loose the pestilence, to sweep man, woman, and child from the face of the earth!"

The chiefs were struck with horror and alarm. They implored him not to uncork the bottle, since they and all their people were firm friends of the white men, and would always remain so ; but, should the small-pox be once let out, it would run like wild-fire throughout the country, sweeping off the good as well as the bad ; and surely he would not be so unjust as to punish his friends for crimes committed by his enemies.

Mr. M'Dougal pretended to be convinced by their reasoning, and promised that the vial of wrath should remain sealed up so long as they should manifest their friendship by a proper course of conduct. From this time, it is added, he was looked upon as holding their destiny in his hands, and was called, by way of preeminence, "the great small-pox chief."

All this time, the labours at the infant settlement went on with unremitting assiduity, and, by the 26th of September, a commodious mansion, spacious enough to accommodate all hands, was completed. It was built of stone and clay, as they had not discovered any calcareous stone in the neighbourhood from which lime for mortar could be procured. The schooner was also finished, and launched with the accustomed ceremony, on the 2d of October, and took her station below the fort. She was named the Dolly, and was the first American vessel launched on that coast.

On the 5th of October, a detachment from Mr. David Stuart's post on the Oakinagan arrived, bringing favourable accounts of the new establishment or interior trading post which had been formed at that place; but reported that, as Mr. Stuart feared that there might be a difficulty of subsisting the whole party throughout the winter, he had sent one half back to Astoria. Such is the hardihood of the Indian trader, determining to remain in the heart of a savage and unknown country, seven hundred miles from his associates, to spend a whole winter.

Nothing further of importance transpired up to the 1st of January, 1812. The partners made preparations for a New-year celebration, which was conducted as follows: At sunrise the drums beat to arms, the colours were hoisted, with three rounds of small arms and three discharges of cannon. The day was devoted to games of agility and strength, and other amusements; and grog was temperately distributed, together with bread, butter, and cheese. The best dinner their circumstances could afford was served up at noon. At sunset the colours were lowered, with another discharge of artillery. The night was spent in dancing, &c.

CHAPTER III.

Departure of the land expedition—St. Louis—Missouri River—Missouri Fur Company—Daniel Boone, of Kentucky—Mad River—Travellers arrive at Mr. Henry's post, and take possession of huts deserted by him—A party of hunters leave for the purpose of trapping beaver—Man lost—Arrive at a terrific strait, and encamp—Separate into several detachments—Meet with Indians, and obtain some salmon and a dog for food—Mr. Hunt purchases a horse for an old tin kettle—The party abandon the river, and suffer from thirst—Meet with another party who are in a state of starvation—Kill two horses to satisfy the cravings of hunger—Celebrate New-year on dogs and horse flesh—Arrive at Astoria, and meet with some of their old comrades.

Having followed up the fortunes of the maritime part of this enterprise to the shores of the Pacific, and the affairs of the embryo establishment to the opening of the new year, let us now turn back to the adventurous band to whom was intrusted the land expedition, and who were to make their way to the mouth of the Columbia, up vast rivers, across trackless plains, and over the rugged barriers of the Rocky Mountains.

The conduct of this expedition, as has been already mentioned, was assigned to Mr. Wilson Price Hunt, who was ultimately to be at the head of the establishment at the mouth of the Columbia River. The whole conduct of that gentleman proved him to be faithful and upright in his dealings, amiable in his disposition, and very accommodating in his manners. Mr. Hunt, and his associate, Mr. Donald M'Kenzie, who was well skilled in Indian trade and warfare, and who was renowned on the frontier as a "remarkable shot," repaired about the latter part of July, 1810, to Montreal, the ancient emporium of the fur trade, where everything requisite for the expedition could be procured. Here Mr. Hunt procured, as he supposed, a sufficient number of Canadian voyageurs to answer present purposes, and, having laid in a supply of ammunition, provisions, and Indian goods, embarked all on board of one of those great canoes at that time universally used by the fur traders for navigating the intricate and often obstructed rivers. The canoe was between thirty and forty feet long, and several feet in width; constructed of birch bark, sewed with fibres of the roots of the spruce-tree, and daubed with resin of the pine instead of tar. The cargo was made up in packages, weighing from ninety to one hundred pounds each, for the facility of transportation of portages. The canoe also could readily be carried on men's shoulders.

Being thus equipped, the expedition took its departure as usual from St. Ann's, near the extremity of the Island of Montreal, the great starting place of the traders to the interior. In consequence of the inefficiency of his crew, and the many obstacles to be overcome, Mr. Hunt did not arrive at Mackinaw (situated on the island of the same name, at the confluence of Lakes Huron and Michigan) until the 22d of July. Here the party halted for some time. Here the assortment of Indian goods was completed, and men of a more efficient character than those enlisted at Montreal were obtained. Here Mr. Hunt was also joined by Mr. Ramsay Crooks, a native of Scotland, who had been engaged as a partner, who had served in the North-West Company, and been engaged in trading expeditions upon his individual account, among the tribes of the Missouri. By this gentleman's advice, the party was considerably augmented; and after much delay, caused by the frolics and whims of the voyageurs, they left Mackinaw about the 12th of August, and pursued the usual route by Green Bay, Fox and Wisconsin Rivers, to Prairie du Chien, and thence down the Mississippi to St. Louis, where they landed on the 3d of September.

St. Louis is situated on the west bank of the Mississippi River, a few miles below the mouth of the Missouri; and was at that time a frontier settlement, and the last fitting-out place for the Indian trade of the southwest. Here Mr. Hunt secured to the interests of the association another of those enterprising men who had been engaged in individual traffic with the tribes of the Missouri. This was a Mr. Joseph Miller, a gentleman of a respectable family of Baltimore. This gentleman joined the company as a partner, and was considered a valuable acquisition to the same.

After enlisting several additional men, and making other necessary provisions, the party took its departure from St. Louis on the 21st of October, in three boats, with buoyant spirits, and soon arrived at the mouth of the Missouri. This vast river, three thousand miles in length, was of difficult navigation, in consequence of its strong current, and required all the skill and strength of the several crews to be brought into requisition in order to propel the boats forward. But by assiduous and persevering labour, they made their way about four hundred and fifty miles up the Missouri by the 6th of November, to the mouth of the Nodowa. As this was a good hunting country, and as the season was rapidly advancing, they determined to establish their winter quarters at this place.

Here the party was joined by Mr. Robert M'Lellan, another trader of the Missouri. This gentleman had been a partisan under General Wayne, in his Indian wars, and many marvellous stories were told of his exploits. Another recruit that joined the camp at Nodowa deserves equal mention. This was John Day, a hunter from the backwoods of Virginia.

After the party was fairly settled for the winter, Mr. Hunt left the encampment in charge of the other partners, and set off on foot on the 1st of January, 1810, for St. Louis. At Nodowa he procured horses; and arrived at St. Louis on the 20th of January. Here he, as he formerly had, met with opposition from the Missouri Fur Company, by which his plans were considerably impeded; and as the Missouri Company was at that time fitting out a party to cross the mountains, under the conduct of Mr. Manuel Lisa, for the purpose of searching for some of their men, who they feared had been cut off by the savages, it became more difficult for Mr. Hunt to raise necessary recruits, and more especially to procure a Sioux interpreter. There was but one man to be met with at St. Louis who was fitted for the purpose; he was a half-breed, named Pierre Dorion, the son of Dorion, the French interpreter who accompanied Messrs. Lewis and Clark in their expedition across the Rocky Mountains. By good management, Mr. Hunt succeeded in securing Pierre, who had, during the preceding year, conducted the traders of the Missouri Company in safety through the different tribes of the Sioux.

After Mr. Hunt had got everything ready for his departure, and had prevailed on two out of five of his men who had returned in a state of dissatisfaction from winter quarters, to return with him, and agreed to take the squaw and two children of Dorion on board, he entered the boat and set out, being accompanied by two other gentlemen, whose names deserve to be noticed.

The one was Mr. John Bradbury, under the patronage of the Linnean Society, of Liverpool, to make a collection of American plants. The other was Mr. Nuttall, likewise an Englishman, who has since made himself known by two scientific works.

The wife of Pierre Dorion was still living in the Walamet Valley, in the year 1843. She was in the habit of visiting the missionaries at the Walamet; and it is said she could speak pretty good English, and was quite polite in her address.

As this reinforcement passed up the river, they touched at Charrette, where they met with the renowned Daniel Boon, of Kentucky, leading a hunter's life, though now in his eighty-fifth year. He was said to flourish several years after this meeting; and died, full of sylvan honours and renown, in 1818, in his ninety-second year.

The next morning they met with another hero of the wilderness, named John Colter, who had accompanied Lewis and Clark across the mountains, and had just accomplished a voyage alone, in a small canoe, of three thousand miles, from the head waters of the Missouri to St. Louis, in thirty days.

The party proceeded up the river, and arrived at Fort Osage on the 8th of April. Here they remained until the 10th, when they again embarked, and after much exposure and hardship they arrived at the station near the Nodowa River, where the main body had been quartered during the winter. As soon as the spring rains subsided, Mr. Hunt broke up the encampment, and resumed his course up the Missouri. The party now consisted of nearly sixty persons. They embarked in four boats, and they succeeded in reaching the mouth of the Platte River on the 28th; and on the 10th of May they arrived at the Omaha village, about eight hundred and thirty miles from the mouth of the Missouri. On the 15th of May they took their departure from the village of the Omahas, and on the 11th of June they encamped about six miles below the Arickara village, and Mr. Lisa, of whom we have already made mention, encamped at no great distance. At this Indian village Mr. Hunt left his boats, and after the necessary provisions were made, they took up their line of march by land; and on the evening of the 23d of July they encamped on the bank of what was then termed Big River. At the above place they continued about two weeks, when they again pursued their perilous journey. On the 13th of August, Mr. Hunt varied his course, and inclined westward, in hopes of falling in with three of the party who had been missing for a number of days, namely, Pierre Dorion, Carson, and Gradpie. Soon after the party reached the Little Missouri, the three lost ones came lagging into the camp, themselves and horses being worn down by their wanderings in the wilderness. (And I will here observe that Carson lived to reach the Columbia in safety, and after trapping for some time on the west side of the mountains, and residing for about three years in the Walamet Valley, he was murdered by an Indian about the year 1837.) The party now pursued their journey with renewed vigour; and after meeting with parties of the Crow, Shoshonies, and Flathead Indians, they reached the north branch of the Bighorn River on the 9th of September.

After pursuing their journey until about the 22d, they fell in with a party of Snake Indians, from whom they purchased a quantity of jerked buffalo meat, which, in addition to what had been killed by their hunters, constituted an abundant supply. All things being in readiness, Mr. Hunt broke up camp on the 24th; and a march of fifteen miles over a mountain ridge brought them to one of the head waters of the Columbia. The party took up their line of march along the banks of this river (Hoback's River) until it was joined by a river of greater magnitude: these two uniting formed an impetuous stream, which had received the name of Mad River.

On the banks of the Mad River Mr. Hunt held a

consultation with the other partners as to their future course. And after much deliberation it was determined to manufacture canoes, and pursue the remainder of their journey by water. And at this point the first interior trading post was established, or rather a party of trappers was left here, with all necessary supplies for the purpose of collecting furs; and when they should obtain a full cargo, they were to make their way to the mouth of the Columbia, or to the next trading post. The party left here consisted of Carson, of whom mention has already been made, St. Michel, Detaye, and Delaunay. The party now set to work at constructing canoes, and, while thus employed, two Snake Indians made their appearance, and gave them to understand that their labour would be in vain, as the Mad River down which they proposed to pass was not navigable. This information being confirmed by the scouting party which had been sent out for the purpose of ascertaining the character of the river, for some distance, they employed the two Indians as their guides, and shaped their course by land for Mr. Henry's post, or fort, on another branch of the Columbia, down which they hoped to be able to navigate canoes; and on the evening of the 8th of October they reached that post, which had been deserted by Mr. Henry in the course of the preceding spring.

The weary travellers gladly took possession of the deserted log huts which had formed the post, and which stood on a stream upward of a hundred yards wide, on which they intended to embark. There being plenty of suitable timber in the neighbourhood, Mr. Hunt immediately proceeded to construct canoes. As he would have to leave his horses and accoutrements here, he determined to make this a trading post, where the trappers and hunters, to be distributed about the country, might repair; and where the traders might touch on their way through the mountains, to and from the establishment at the mouth of the Columbia.

At this place another detachment of hunters prepared to separate from the party for the purpose of trapping beaver. This party consisted of Robinson, Hoback, and Rezner. Afterward another hunter by the name of Cass was associated with them, and previous to their departure upon their expedition, Mr. Miller, one of the partners, determined to accompany them; and being amply fitted out, they were to bring in all the peltries they should collect, either to this trading post, or to the establishment at the mouth of the Columbia.

By the 18th of October fifteen canoes were completed, and the following day the party embarked with their effects; intrusting their horses with the two Snake Indians, their former guides.

After encountering many difficulties, the party fell in with some Shoshonies on the 24th, the first human beings seen by them since they had left their comrades at Fort Henry. Shortly after leaving this camp, they met with three of the Snake Indians; but could not bring them to a parley. Soon after this one of their canoes was wrecked, and one man by the name of Clappine was lost. They now arrived at a terrific strait, that forbade all further progress. This strait received the name of "the Caldron Linn."

Mr. Hunt and his companions encamped on the bank of this whirling and tumultuous stream, and the next morning seven men were despatched along the banks of the stream, to ascertain its character for some distance below, and, after exploring the banks for forty miles, they returned, and reported the passage to be exceeding difficult. The party, however, who had explored the south side of the river, found a place, about six miles from the camp, where they thought it possible the canoes might be carried down the bank, and launched upon the stream, and from whence they might make their way with the aid of occasional portages. Four of the best canoes were accordingly selected for the experiment, and sixteen men bore them upon their shoulders to the place. At the same time four men were detached to explore the river further down. The party sent with the canoes returned on the following day, having found it impracticable to pursue their onward journey. After a little anxious but bewildered counsel, says the author before me, they determined that several small detachments should set off in different directions; and after the necessary provisions were made, the several bands departed, Mr. M'Lellan heading one, Mr. Crooks another, and Mr. M'Kenzie a third. The first was to keep down along the bank of the river, the second was to retrace their steps up it, and the third was to strike to the northward across the desert plains, in hopes of coming upon the main stream of the Columbia. Mr. Hunt, with the remainder of the party, prepared *caches*, in which they deposited their surplus baggage and merchandise. After this work was accomplished, which had employed about three days, Mr. Crooks and his party returned, having despaired of reaching Fort Henry, and determined to share the fate of their comrades.

At length two of the companions of Mr. Reed returned, bringing also a discouraging report, in consequence of which the hope of being able to prosecute their journey by water was totally abandoned.

The resolution of Mr. Hunt and his companions was now taken, to set out immediately on foot. As to the other detachments that had in a manner gone forth to seek their fortunes, there was little chance of their return; they would probably make their own way through the wilderness. And as they were yet a thousand miles from Astoria, the winter approaching, and all kinds of perils awaiting them, they made all necessary preparations, and commenced their doubtful journey, keeping along the course of the river, where they would always have water at hand, and would be able occasionally to procure fish, and might perchance meet with Indians from whom they could obtain provisions. They divided into two parties: Mr. Hunt with eighteen men, besides Pierre Dorion and his family, proceeded down the north side of the river; while Mr. Crooks and eighteen men kept along the south side. It was on the morning of the 9th of October that the parties set forth on their several courses.

On the second day after they left the Caldron Linn, Mr. Hunt fell in with some Indians, who, by exhibiting a knife, gave evidence that some of the advance party had passed that way. Here they obtained some salmon and a dog, a very timely supply of food. In their progress they met with more of the natives, all of whom behaved very friendly. On the 15th of November they met with more natives, who spoke of Mr. Reed's party having passed through that place. On the 17th, Mr. Hunt succeeded in purchasing a horse for an old tin kettle, which was very acceptable as a pack horse, his men being much worn down with fatigue; and on the 19th he succeeded in obtaining another horse. He now, by the advice of the Indians, abandoned the river; but soon had cause to repent the change, as the road led across a dreary waste, without verdure, fountain, pool, or stream, in consequence of which their sufferings were extreme, having no water to quench their parching thirst. The second day, however, brought with it a refreshing rain, and the writer knows, by having experienced something of the same nature in the wilderness of Oregon, as will be hereafter shown, how our way-worn travellers appreciated this blessing. On the next day they arrived at a beautiful little stream running to the west. Here they also fell in with Indians; here they encamped and obtained fish and dogs from the natives; and here an Indian laid claim to one of Mr. Hunt's horses, saying that it had been stolen from him; and as the fact could not be disproved, Mr. Hunt relinquished the horse to the claimant. The next day two of the men were fortunate enough to purchase a horse: one of them was Pierre Dorion, to whose poor wife and family this horse was a most timely acquisition; his wife, as I have before stated, was still living in the Walamet Valley in the latter part of 1843. At the time the above horse was obtained, Madam Dorion was far advanced in her pregnancy, and had two children to take care of, one four, and the other two years of age. The latter of course she had frequently to carry on her back, in addition to the burden usually imposed upon the squaw by her inhuman husband; yet, throughout this weary and painful journey, she had borne all her hardships without a murmur, and kept pace with the best of the pedestrians! And it is said that in the course of the enterprise, she displayed a force of character which won the respect and applause of the white men.

On the 27th they obtained intelligence again of the advance party, and, as the natives informed them that they had a live dog in their possession, it was conclusive that they had not been reduced to the extremity of hunger. Here Mr. Hunt could obtain no provisions, and they proceeded forward on their now very painful journey, while the month of December set in drearily, and after accomplishing four hundred and seventy-two miles of their dreary journey since they left Caldron Linn, on the 6th of December they discovered Mr. Crooks and his party, on the opposite bank of the river. As soon as they could be heard they made known their deplorable condition, which was that of starvation. No time was lost on the part of Mr. Hunt to furnish them with a portion of his remaining supplies, and as soon as Mr. Crooks had appeased his hunger, he gave Mr. Hunt some account of his wayfaring. He had been three days' journey further down the river, where he found further progress to be impossible; and, being destitute of provisions, he turned back, hoping to reach the Indians again previous to arriving at the point of starvation; but it was evident when he met with Mr. Hunt's party that, in consequence of fatigue and hunger, they could not have proceeded much further. In view of the forbidding prospects ahead, Mr. Hunt and party determined next morning to retrace their steps to the place where they last obtained provisions from the Indians. On their return they fell in with a party of natives, from whom they obtained some horses; after killing two of them, with which they satisfied their hunger, and leaving two more with Mr. Crooks and John Day, one of his men, who was unable to proceed but at a very slow rate, Mr. Hunt proceeded up the river in order to join the main party, and succeeded in coming up with them in the evening. Here he purchased another horse, and after twenty days of ineffectual toil to find a passage down the river, they reached a little willowed stream, which they had crossed on the 26th of November, and here they camped. Not far from this place Mr. Hunt suceeded in obtaining a guide, and on the 21st of December they set out again with spirits somewhat elated. They prosecuted their formidable journey with as much despatch as possible, many interesting particulars of which I cannot mention; but one circumstance should not be passed over unnoticed. Early on the morning of the 29th the wife of Dorion, who had hitherto kept on without flinching or murmuring, was suddenly taken in labour, and enriched her husband with another child. Dorion remained in the camp with his family, in order that his faithful spouse might recruit, with the promise that he would soon join the party again; and he was as good as his word; for in the course of the next morning but one, the whole Dorion family appeared in the camp in very good health and spirits!

The next morning ushered in the new year, (1812.) Mr. Hunt was about to resume his march, when his men requested to celebrate the day; this request was granted, and the day passed away amidst singing and dancing, and feasting most sumptuously upon dogs and horse flesh. So, after two days of welcome rest, the travellers addressed themselves once more to their painful journey; and after much hard travelling and hard fare they reached the Columbia River not far from the influx of the Wallah-wallah, on the 21st of January. Two hundred and forty miles had they marched, through wintry wastes and rugged mountains, since leaving Snake River; and six months had elapsed since their departure from the Arickara village on the Missouri. Their whole route by land and water, from that point, had been, according to their computation, seventeen hundred and fifty-one miles.

After travelling down the banks of the Columbia for about sixty miles, Mr. Hunt obtained from the Indians vague, but deeply-interesting intelligence of that part of the enterprise which had proceeded by sea to the mouth of the Columbia. The Indians spoke of a number of white men who had built a large house at the mouth of the great river, &c. On the 31st of January, they arrived at a fall of the Columbia, and encamped at the village of Wish-ram. Here they obtained intelligence of the loss of the Tonquin. They could obtain no canoes in which to descend the river until they arrived at the " Cascades," the last rapid to be met with in their downward voyage. Here Mr. Hunt obtained the necessary canoes, and on the 15th of February they swept around " Tongue Point," and came in sight of the establishment at Astoria. Among the first to greet them on their landing were some of their old comrades and fellow-sufferers, who, under the conduct of Reed, M'Lellan, and M'Kenzie, had parted from them at Caldron Linn. These had reached Astoria nearly a month previously, and, judging from their own narrow escape from starvation, had given up Mr. Hunt and his party for lost. I need not say their greetings were warm and cordial. When the first burst of feeling was over, the different bands interchanged accounts of their several wanderings after separating at Snake River; but to notice these particulars would swell this volume to too great a size. Suffice it to say, that the whole wound up with the firing of guns, hoisting colours, feasting on fish, beaver, and venison, a distribution of grog, and a dance at night by the Canadians.

Thus, all the leading men of Mr. Hunt's expedition were once more gathered together, except Mr. Crooks, of whose safety they entertained but little hope, considering the feeble condition in which they had been compelled to leave him in the heart of the wilderness.

CHAPTER IV.

Several expeditions depart from Astoria—Skirmish with the Indians—Arrive at Oakinagan—Set out on their return to Astoria—Encounter companions of a former expedition, who were supposed to be lost—Arrive at Astoria—Mr. Astor sends an agent to St. Petersburgh—He despatches a vessel to Oregon—She arrives at Astoria—Parties go out to establish new trading posts—A band separate from the main body on a journey across the Rocky Mountains—Meet four of their former companions, who join them—Their horses stolen by Indians—Encamp for the winter—Arrive at St. Louis.

TRANQUILLITY had prevailed at Astoria. The apprehensions of hostilities from the natives had subsided : indeed, at the close of the salmon season, the Indians, for the most part, disappeared from the river, so that, for want of their aid, the Astorians had at times suffered considerably for want of provisions. There were some deer and some black bears to be found in the vicinity, and elk in great abundance on the adjacent mountains and hills ; but the country was so rough, and the forests so dense, that it was almost impossible for any but the Indians to beat up the game. The quantity of game, therefore, brought in by the hunters was very scanty, and it was frequently necessary to put all hands upon allowance. Toward spring, however, the fishing season commenced—the season of plenty on the Columbia.

As the spring opened, the little settlement at Astoria was in agitation, and prepared to send forth various expeditions. The task of supplying the trading post of Mr. David Stuart, at Oakinagan, was assigned to Mr. Robert Stuart. The seeking out of the *cache* at Caldron Linn, made by Mr. Hunt, was assigned to two clerks named Russell Farnham and Donald M'Gilles, to be conducted by a guide, and accompanied by eight men, to assist in bringing home the goods. The despatches, to go across the mountains to Mr. Astor at New-York, were confided to Mr. John Reed; and, as it was still hoped that Mr. Crooks might be in existence, and that Mr. Reed might meet with him, he was charged with goods and provisions to aid that gentleman on his way to Astoria. Mr. M'Lellan also joined Mr. Reed's party. As the route of these several parties would be the same for nearly four hundred miles, they all set off together, on the 22d of March, to the number of seventeen men, in two canoes; and early in the month of April they arrived at the long narrows. Here they were obliged to make a portage, and, in so doing, the Indians stole some of their goods, and the tin box in which were deposited the despatches. Mr. Reed, the bearer of the box, was severely wounded. After making the portage they proceeded up the river: but as the Indians had lost two of their number, who were shot during the skirmish at the portage, they killed two horses, drank the hot blood to give firmness to their courage, performed the dead dance round the slain, and raised the war-song of vengeance; then mounting their horses to the number of four or five hundred, they succeeded in getting some distance above the canoes undiscovered, and were crossing the river to post themselves on the side along which the party was coasting, when they were fortunately discovered. Finding that the Indians had the advantage of the ground, the party halted, made a fire, prepared their arms for action, dressed Mr. Reed's wounds, lashed their canoes to the shore, and there awaited the menaced attack.

The Indians, seeing their white neighbours so well prepared to receive them, offered to negotiate, and peace was finally restored for the consideration of a blanket to cover the dead, and some tobacco to smoke by the living. The tin case, however, containing the important despatches for New-York, was irretrievably lost. As the object of Mr. Reed's overland journey was thereby defeated, the whole party repaired with Mr. Stuart to Oakinagan. After remaining here two or three days, they all set out on their return to Astoria, accompanied by Mr. David Stuart. This gentleman had a large quantity of beaver skins at his establishment, but left them for fear of being robbed by the way.

On their way down, they were hailed one day in English. Looking around, they descried two wretched men, entirely naked. They pulled to shore; and, to their surprise and joy, they proved to be Mr. Crooks and John Day, whom Mr. Hunt was obliged to leave, in the month of December, on the banks of the Snake River. They had been wandering on the mountains and over desolate wastes much of the time; but were at last providentially led to the Wallah-wallah tribe of Indians, who treated them kindly, and directed them to the Columbia, and they reached the falls of that river; but here they were stripped of everything, and compelled to depart immediately, at the peril of their lives. In this forlorn plight they sought to find their way back to the hospitable Wallah-wallahs, and had advanced eighty miles along the river, when fortunately, on the very morning they were going to leave the river, and strike inland, the canoes of Mr. Stuart hove in sight.

It is needless to attempt to describe the joy of these poor men, or the hearty welcome with which they were received by their old associates. The whole party now continued down the river, and arrived in safety at Astoria on the 11th of May.

Having given a brief account of the two expeditions by sea and land to the mouth of the Columbia, and presented a view of affairs at Astoria, we will turn for a moment to the master spirit of the enterprise, who regulated the springs of Astoria, at his residence at New-York.

A part of Mr. Astor's plan was to furnish the Russian fur establishment on the north-west coast with regular supplies, so as to render it independent of those casual vessels which cut up the trade, and supplied the natives with arms. This plan had been countenanced by our own government, and likewise by Count Pahlen, the Russian minister at Washington. But Mr. Astor was desirous of establishing a complete arrangement on the subject with the Russian American Fur Company, under the sanction of the Russian government. For this purpose, in March, 1811, he despatched a confidential agent to St. Petersburgh, with full powers to enter into the requisite negotiations.

A passage was given to this gentleman by the government of the United States in the John Adams, one of its armed vessels, bound to Europe. Mr. Astor now despatched the annual ship, contemplated in his general design, not having heard of the previous expeditions, but presuming all to be well. This vessel was called the Beaver, four hundred and ninety tons' burden, and was freighted with a valuable cargo. A reinforcement was also shipped, consisting of a partner, five clerks, fifteen American labourers, and six Canadian voyageurs. His agents being principally British subjects, experienced in the Canadian fur trade, henceforth it was his intention to select, as far as possible, Americans, to secure a preponderance of their influence in the management of the company, and to make it decidedly national. Accordingly, the present partner, who took the lead in the present expedition, was a native of the United States. Most of the clerks were young gentlemen of good connections in the American cities.

Mr. Astor instructed Captain Sowle, the commander of the Beaver, to touch at the Sandwich Islands, inquire about the fortunes of the Tonquin, and whether an establishment had been formed at the Columbia. If so, he was to take as many Sandwich Islanders as the ship would accommodate, and proceed thither. From that he was to proceed to New-Archangel, with the supplies for the Russian post at that place, where he could receive peltries in payment, return to Astoria, by trading along the coast, take in the furs at that place, and proceed to Canton.

The Beaver sailed from New-York on the 10th of

October, 1811, and reached the Sandwich Islands without any occurrence of moment. Here a rumor was heard of the fate of the Tonquin. Doubts were entertained with respect to the success of the former expeditions; but after much deliberation, the captain took twelve Sandwich Islanders on board, and proceeded on his voyage.

On the 6th of May he arrived off the mouth of the Columbia. After firing guns, and having been answered by the Astorians, a white flag was discovered waving on Cape Disappointment, and on the 9th the vessel came to anchor in Baker's Bay.

The arrival of the Beaver, with men and supplies, gave new life and vigour to affairs at Astoria. Two parties were immediately set on foot to proceed severally under the command of Messrs. M'Kenzie and Clark, for the purpose of establishing posts above the forks of the Columbia, at points where most rivalry and opposition were apprehended from the North-West Company. Mr. David Stuart was to repair with supplies to his post on the Oakinagan; and Mr. Robert Stuart was chosen to head a fourth party for the purpose of conveying despatches to Mr. Astor, at New-York. In this expedition he was accompanied by Mr. M'Lellan and Mr. Crooks. These several parties all set off in company, on the 29th of June, under a salute of cannon from the fort.

Soon after they left Astoria, John Day became insane. His companions saw him back in safety to Astoria, where he died within a year. Nothing further of importance occurred previous to the parties reaching Wallah-wallah, except their success in recovering the rifles of Mr. Crooks and John Day, of which they had been robbed on their way down the river, as before observed. At Wallah-wallah the party met with a cordial reception; and Mr. Stuart purchased a sufficient number of horses for the prosecution of his journey across the mountains. All things being in readiness, he and his little band mounted their steeds on the

31st of July, took leave of their associates, who gave them three cheers, and shaped their course for the Rocky Mountains; and on the 20th of August they reached the main body of Woodpile Creek, where Mr. Hunt had separated from Mr. Crooks in the preceding year.

On the 21st they arrived at Snake River. On the second evening, as they were passing up the river, they were visited by a Snake Indian, who informed them that a white man resided at an encampment of the tribe; but they found him not. They soon fell in with some Shoshonies, who said there were some white men residing with their people, on the opposite side of the river; but this proved to be an *Indian* story.

Not far distant they fell in with an Indian who engaged to be their guide, and acted as such for a day or two; but was among the missing one morning, in company with Mr. Stuart's horse.

On the 25th of August one of the men scrambled down the bank of the river to drink, and what was his surprise to behold a white man, by the side of the river, fishing! This proved to be John Hoback, one of their long-lost companions. They had scarcely exchanged greetings, when three other men came out from among the willows. They were Joseph Miller, Jacob Rezner, and Robinson, the scalped Kentuckian, the veteran of the Bloody Ground. After these wanderers had recounted their perilous adventures and hair-breadth escapes, they joined the party, resolving to give up the life of trappers, and return with Mr. Stuart to St. Louis. They pursued their journey, and on the 29th arrived at Caldron Linn. They now proceeded to the spot where Mr. Hunt and his party had made the caches, and found all open and rifled but three. From these Mr. Stuart took what things were necessary for his journey, deposited all surplus baggage, and closed all up again. And here it is worth time and paper to record the indomitable spirit of the western trapper.

No sooner did the trio of Kentucky hunters, Robinson, Rezner, and Hoback, find that they could once more be fitted out for a campaign of beaver trapping, than they forgot all that they had suffered, and determined upon another trial of their fortunes, preferring to take their chance in the wilderness, rather than return home ragged and penniless. As to Mr. Miller, he determined to go with the party, being satisfied with the novelty of the woods.

The three hunters were accordingly fitted out as fully as the caches would permit, and after taking leave of their companions, and receiving their good wishes, they set out in pursuit of the beaver; and on the 1st of September, Mr. Stuart and his party resumed their journey, and after passing many dangers, and being nearly robbed by a band of Crows, they reached Mad River on the 18th of September. On the 19th they rose early in the morning, and began to prepare for a departure. Mr. Stuart was on the bank of the river, at a short distance from the camp, when he heard the cry of "Indians! Indians! to arms! to arms!" A mounted Crow galloped past the camp, bearing a red flag. He halted on the summit of a neighbouring knoll, and waved his red banner. A diabolical yell now broke forth on the other side of the camp, beyond where the horses were grazing, and a small troop of savages came galloping up, whooping and making a great clamour. The horses took fright, and dashed across the camp, in the direction of the standard-bearer, attracted by his waving flag. He instantly put spurs to his steed, and scoured off, followed by the panic-stricken herd, their fright being increased by the yells of the savages in the rear. The reserve party of savages now came up, whooping and yelling in triumph and derision, the last of whom proved to be their leader, who had previously failed to obtain Mr. Stuart's excellent horse. As he passed Mr. Stuart and his comrades, he exhibited the most insulting gestures, and uttered some jeering words, which they could not understand. The rifle of Ben Jones was levelled in an instant, and the bullet had well nigh flown. "Not for your life!" exclaimed Mr. Stuart, "you will bring destruction on us all!"

It was hard to restrain Ben, when the mark was so fair. "O, Mr. Stuart," exclaimed he, "only let me have one crack at the rascal, and you may keep all the pay that is due me."

"If you fire," cried Mr. Stuart, "I'll blow your brains out."

By this time the Indian was far out of reach, and had joined his men, who were scampering off with the horses, their red flag flying in triumph over their heads. Thus were our travellers in a moment deprived of the means of conveying themselves or baggage, while a wide mountain region was left for them to traverse, which region was everywhere infested with bands of marauders like unto their last visiters.

For a few moments the whole party were disheartened and dismayed, but they soon recovered their wonted fortitude, and set to work with promptness to fit themselves for the change in their condition. They selected from their baggage such articles as were indispensable to their journey, and deposited the rest in caches; but as they were preparing for their departure, they discovered two heads peering over the edge of an impending cliff, which evidently belonged to Indian spies, who were watching the movements of the camp; and lest they should enrich themselves with more booty, by rifling the caches, they were torn up, and all the articles not needed were collected together and burned.

They now shouldered their packs, and set off on their pedestrian wayfaring. Nothing but what must be expected on a journey of such a description befell them, until they reached one of the head waters of the Platte River, and after pursuing it for some distance they pitched their camp for the winter, it being impossible to reach the Missouri before spring, in consequence of the cold and snow, which had already rendered their journeying very painful.

It was now the 2d of November, and the first work

was to secure provisions, then a house, deer-skins for moccasins, garments, and other purposes; and these things were all secured in due season, for here were abundance of buffalo and deer, and plenty of timber. In a few days they were comfortably housed, and abundantly supplied with all that was deemed necessary for a very comfortable winter's residence. But they had not enjoyed their comforts long before they were convinced—by the approach of an Arapahay war party, who were in pursuit of a party of Crows who were said to be encamped to the north, and who had recently robbed the Arapahays of their horses and squaws— that their retreat was not a very safe one. Consequently they determined to shift quarters with all despatch. Accordingly, on the 13th of December, they bade adieu to their comfortable quarters, where for several weeks they had been indulging in the sweets of repose, of plenty, and of fancied security. And after a dreary journey down the river, they determined once more to set up their winter quarters. New-year's day dawned, when, as yet, but one wall of their cabin was completed: the day, however, was not permitted to pass uncelebrated. The choicest of the buffalo meat was forthcoming; and boiling, and roasting, and eating, such as would astonish any one that has not lived among hunters or Indians, made up the labours of the day; and as an extra regale, having no tobacco, they cut up an old tobacco pouch, still redolent with the potent herb, and smoked it in token of brotherly love and unfading friendship.

The next day they resumed their labours, and by the 6th of the month the cabin was completed. They soon killed abundance of buffalo, and again laid in a stock of winter provisions. Here they were permitted to remain in quiet, plenty, and health, until the 8th of March, when they resumed their journey.

When they arrived at Grand Isle, they met with an Otto Indian, by whom they learned that war had existed for a whole year between the United States and

England. This Indian conducted them to his village, where they met with two white men, Messrs. Dornin and Rio, Indian traders, recently from St. Louis.

Mr. Dornin furnished them with a canoe, and provisions for their voyage to St. Louis. On the 16th of April they commenced their downward passage, and arrived at Fort Osage. Here Lieutenant Brownson furnished them with an ample supply of provisions, for the continuance of their voyage; and on the 30th of April they arrived, in perfect health, and fine spirits, at St. Louis. Their arrival caused quite a sensation at the place, bringing the first intelligence of the fortunes of Mr. Hunt and his party, and of the new establishment at Astoria.

CHAPTER V.

Agent sent to St. Petersburgh negotiates an agreement—Mr. Astor sends out another vessel to the settlement on the Columbia—Messrs. Stuart, Clark, and M'Kenzie establish new posts—Caches robbed by Snake Indians, who are attacked by the Blackfeet, who seize their booty—The Beaver departs on a coasting voyage—M'Kenzie breaks up his establishment, and returns to Astoria—He and others set out on a journey—Three of them enter a lodgment of Indians, and are in imminent danger—Arrives at his former station, and finds that his caches have been robbed—Mr. Clark causes an Indian to be hung—They return to Astoria.

THE agent sent by Mr. Astor to St. Petersburgh, to negotiate in his name, as president of the American Fur Company, had, under sanction of the Russian government, made a provisional agreement with the Russian Company. By this agreement, which was ratified by Mr. Astor in 1813, the two companies bound themselves not to interfere with each other's trading and hunting grounds, or to furnish arms and ammunition to the Indians. They were to act in concert, also, against all interlopers, and to succour each other in case of danger. The American Company was to have the exclusive right to supply the Russian post with goods and necessaries, receiving peltries in payment, at stated prices. They were also, if requested by the Russian governor, to convey the furs of the Russian Company to Canton, sell them on commission, and bring back the proceeds, at such freight as might be agreed on at the time. This agreement was to continue in operation four years, and to be renewable for a similar term, unless some unforeseen contingency should render a modification necessary. By other arrangements, in connection with the above, Mr. Astor hoped gradually to make Astoria the great emporium of the American fur trade in the Pacific, and the nucleus of a powerful American state. But while he was entertaining these sanguine expectations, and before he had ratified the agreement, as above stated, war broke out between the United States and Great Britain.

The prospect now became exceedingly discouraging, but in the midst of all, notwithstanding he had received no intelligence of the first expedition, in consequence of Mr. Reed's mishap in losing the tin box at the falls of the Columbia, and the unhorsing of Mr. Stuart by the Crows among the mountains, Mr. Astor determined to send another ship to the relief of the settlement. He selected for this purpose a vessel called the Lark, remarkable for her fast sailing. But previous to her departure he learned that the North-West Company were preparing to send out an armed ship of twenty guns, called the Isaac Todd, to form an establishment at the mouth of the Columbia. These tidings gave much uneasiness. A considerable proportion of the persons in his employ were Scotchmen and Canadians, and several of them had been in the service of the N. W. Company. Should Mr. Hunt have failed to arrive at Astoria, the whole establishment would be under the control of Mr. M'Dougal, of whose fidelity he had received very disparaging accounts from Capt. Thorn. The British government might also deem it worth while to send a force against the establishment, having been urged to do so some time previously, by the N. W. Company. Under all these circumstances, Mr. Astor wrote to Mr. Monroe, then secretary of state, requesting protection from the government of the United States. He received no reply to his requests up to the month of March, when he ordered the Lark to put to sea. The officer who was to command her shrunk from his engagement, and in the exigency of the moment she was given in charge to Mr. Northrop the mate. Mr. Nicholas G. Ogden, a gentleman of probity and talents, sailed as supercargo. The Lark put to sea in the beginning of March, 1813.

By this opportunity Mr. Astor wrote to Mr. Hunt, as head of the establishment at the mouth of the Columbia; for he would not allow himself to doubt of his welfare. "I always think you are well," said he, "and that I shall see you again, which Heaven I hope will grant." Mr. A. further observed, "*Our enterprise is grand, and deserves success, and I hope in God it will meet it.*" And in view of the threatening troubles, he further remarked, "If my object were merely gain of money, I should say, Think whether it is best to save what we can, and abandon the place; *but the very idea is like a dagger to my heart.*" This extract is sufficient to show the spirit and the views which actuated Mr. Astor in this great undertaking.

Weeks and months passed away without any tidings by which the painful incertitude that hung over every part of this enterprise might be dispelled. But as Mr. Astor was sitting one gloomy evening at his window, revolving over the fate of the Tonquin, and fearing lest something equally as tragical might have befallen the party of Mr. Hunt while crossing the Rocky Mountains, he received a newspaper; and the first paragraph that caught his eye announced the arrival of Mr. Stuart and his party at St. Louis, and also that Mr. Hunt had effected his perilous journey to the mouth of the Columbia. This gleam of sunshine for a time dispelled every cloud, and he looked forward with some hope to the accomplishment of his plans.

The course of our narrative now takes us back to Wallah-wallah, to the parties whom Mr. Stuart left there, when he commenced his land journey across the mountains to St. Louis. The three parties left there separated from each other soon after Mr. Stuart's departure. Mr. David Stuart proceeded with his men to his post at the mouth of the Oakinagon. Having furnished this with goods and ammunition, he proceeded three hundred miles up that river, where he established another post. Mr. Clark conducted his little band up Lewis River to the mouth of a small stream coming in from the north, called, by the Canadians, Pavion. Here he found an encampment of *Nez Percés*, or Pierced-nose Indians, whose character will be spoken of hereafter. Here Mr. Clark laid up his boats in a sheltered place under the promised protection of the Nez Percé chief, purchased horses from the Indians, and proceeded across hill and dale until he arrived at a point of land where the Pointed Heart and Spokan Rivers meet. Here he established a trading post, and here we leave him for the present.

Mr. M'Kenzie, who was at the head of the third party, navigated for some days up the south branch of the Columbia, commonly called Lewis River, in honour of the first explorer. Having arrived at the mouth of the Shahaptan, he ascended it some distance, and established his trading post upon its banks. He now detached a small band under the command of Mr. John Reed to visit the caches made by Mr. Hunt at Caldron Linn, and to bring the contents to that post; as he depended in some measure on them for his supplies of goods and ammunition. They had not been gone a week, when two Indians arrived of the Pallatapalla tribe, who lived upon a river of the same name. These communicated the unwelcome intelligence that the caches had been robbed. They said that some of their tribe had, in the course of the preceding spring, been across the mountains, which separated them from Snake River, and had traded horses with the Snakes in exchange for blankets, robes, and other goods; that these articles the Snakes had procured from caches to which they had been guided by some white men who resided among them, and who afterward accompanied them across the Rocky Mountains. This perplexing intelligence was confirmed by the Indians, who exhibited an English saddle and bridle, which had formerly belonged to Mr. Crooks. The secret of the caches was revealed after the following manner, as ascertained by Mr. Reed, when he arrived at the Snake River. Here, in an encampment of the natives, he met with six white men, wanderers from the main expedition of Mr. Hunt, who, after their many wanderings and misfortunes, had fortunately come together at this place. Three of these men had left Mr. Crooks in February in the neighbourhood of the Snake River, being dismayed by the increasing hardships of the journey, and fear of starvation. They had returned to a Snake encampment, where they passed the residue of the winter.

Early in the spring, being utterly destitute, and in great extremity, and having worn out the hospitality of the Snakes, they determined to avail themselves of the buried treasure within their knowledge. They communicated their designs to the Snake chieftains, who pledged their honour as great *chiefs* and *Snakes*, that if they would conduct them to this hid treasure, they should be rewarded with horses and provisions for their homeward-bound journey. So, being elated with the fair prospect of wealth on the part of their Snakeships, and of once more reaching the land of civilization on the part of the whites, they set off for Caldron Linn. Who can describe the delight of the savages when the caches began to disgorge the blankets, the robes, and brass trinkets, and the perfect ecstasy when the strips of scarlet cloth made their appearance! This treasure rendered the Snakes absolutely rich, and once more placed our Canadians in very enviable circumstances, inasmuch as their friends the Snakes had most faithfully fulfilled their promise in supplying them with horses to ride, and with arms from the treasures of the caches. The Snakes now determined on a hunting match on the buffalo prairies, to lay in a supply of beef, that they might live in plenty, as became men of their improved condition; and our newly-mounted cavaliers determined to accompany them in this expedition. They crossed the mountains, and reached the head waters of the Missouri in safety, and made great havoc among the buffaloes. But in the midst of their feasting and rejoicing, and hopes of future abundance, their camp was surprised by the Blackfeet, when they were obliged to drop all, and after beholding several of their party slain on the spot, the remainder, with their Canadian allies, scampered off for the mountains, like so many mice scudding to their holes, on being surprised by puss, while in the very act of devouring a fine piece of stolen cheese. Our heroes succeeded in returning to the old encampment on Snake River, as poor as they were before they obtained the treasure from the caches. They had not been long there when they were cheered with the arrival of Carson and other trappers, who had been left by Mr. Hunt to trap beaver, in the preceding month of September. They had departed from the main body well armed, and provided with horses to ride and to carry their furs, if they should collect any. But having fallen in with the Crows, and after being overpowered by numbers, and stripped of all they possessed, they were obliged to turn back, and were fortunate enough to reach their old friends, the Snakes, and their old companions in tribulation, as ragged and as destitute as the latter, who had been surprised by the Blackfeet, as before mentioned.

When Mr. Reed arrived at the encampment, where these forlorn adventurers had accidentally met, they were making arrangements once more to cross the mountains. After Mr. Reed heard their several stories, he took them all into his party, and set out for the Caldron Linn, in order to secure the goods in the two or three caches which had not been discovered to the Indians. At that place he met with Robinson, the Kentucky veteran, who, with his two comrades, Rezner and Hoback, had remained there when Mr. Stuart went on. Robinson had been trapping higher up the river, but had come down in a canoe, to wait the expected arrival of the party, and obtain horses and equipments.

Mr. Reed took up the remainder of the goods from the caches, and returned in safety to M'Kenzie's post, on the Shahaptan.

After the departure of the different detachments, or *brigades*, as they are called by the fur traders, the Beaver prepared for her voyage along the coast, and her visit to the Russian establishment at New-Archangel, where she was to carry supplies. It had been determined in the council of partners at Astoria, that Mr. Hunt should embark in this vessel for the purpose of transacting certain business with the commander of the Russian post, and to acquaint himself with the coasting trade, and be returned in October, at Astoria, by the Beaver, on her way to the Sandwich Islands and Canton.

The Beaver put to sea in the month of August. Her departure, and that of the various brigades, left the little fortress of Astoria but slightly garrisoned. This was soon perceived by some of the Indian tribes, and the consequence was, increased insolence of deportment, and a disposition to hostility. Fortunately, the Chenooks and the other adjacent tribes manifested a more pacific character. Old Comcomly, who held sway over them, was a shrewd calculator. He was aware of the advantage of having the whites as neighbours and allies, and of the benefit to be derived from acting as intermediate traders between them and the more remote tribes. He was, therefore, a firm friend of the Astorians, and formed a kind of barrier between them and the hostile intruders of the north.

The summer of 1812 passed away without bringing with it any hostilities; and, at the close of the salmon season, the Neweetees and other dangerous visiters left the neighbourhood, and returned to their own lands.

To provide against the scarce season, the shallop was sent up to the Walamet, where her crew secured an abundance of dried meat, which was sent to Astoria for the supply of the garrison. Thus October passed away, but without the return of the Beaver. November, December, and January followed, and still no tidings were received of her. Fearing that she might have been wrecked in her coasting voyage, or that she had been surprised by the savages, like the Tonquin, M'Dougal became despondent, condemned the whole enterprise, magnified every unfortunate circumstance, and prophesied nothing but evil.

While in this state of gloom and fearful forebodings, M'Kenzie made his unexpected appearance, with his very countenance presenting an index to a whole volume of misfortunes. He had been sadly disappointed at the post assigned him on the Shahaptan, finding the beaver too scarce in that vicinity to warrant the continuance of the establishment; he therefore repaired to the post of Clark to hold consultation. While the two partners were in conference in Mr. Clark's wigwam, Mr. John George M"Tavish, a partner of the North-West Company, who had charge of the rival trading post in that vicinity, is said to have come bustling in upon them. He was the bearer of unwelcome tidings. Having been to Lake Winnepeg, and obtained an express from Canada, containing the declaration of war between the United States and Great Britain, and President Madison's proclamation, he handed the last document to Messrs. Clark and M'Kenzie. He also told them that he had received a fresh supply of goods from the other side of the mountains, for the purpose of carrying forward, with greater vigour, his opposition to their establishment; and to crown the burden of his warlike intelligence, he assured them that the Isaac Todd, an armed vessel, was to be at the mouth of the Columbia in March, to secure the trade of the river, and that he was ordered to join her there at that time.

The receipt of this intelligence determined M'Kenzie. He immediately returned to the Shahaptan, broke up his establishment, deposited his goods in caches, and set off without delay for Astoria.

The intelligence which he brought completely overcame M'Dougal. He held a council with M'Kenzie, and it was determined to abandon the establishment in the course of the following spring, and return across the Rocky Mountains. Consequently, all trade with the natives was suspended, and the stock of goods on hand was reserved for their contemplated journey. But, lest the men should become uneasy and disobedient, this new project was kept a secret.

In the mean time, M'Kenzie was despatched for the purpose of apprizing the Messrs. Stuart and Clark of their determination, that they might be in readiness to take their departure at the same time, and to get his goods from the caches, and buy horses with them, and procure provisions and other necessaries for the tour. M'Kenzie was accompanied by two of the clerks, John Reed, and Mr. Alfred Seton, of New-York. They embarked in two canoes, manned by seventeen men, and ascended the river in safety until they arrived at the rapids, where Mr. Reed had been formerly wounded, and robbed of the *tin box* of despatches. It was known that Reed's rifle was still in possession of these freebooters, and M'Kenzie offered to cross the river and demand it, if any one would accompany him; and, notwithstanding the imminent danger attending such an attempt, two of the men stepped forward. In a few moments they were on the other side of the river, and entered the principal lodge. The passage into the same was immediately filled after them by a rush of Indians, who had, previously to this moment, kept out of sight. At the head of the lodge sat the old chief, and on either side sat a large number of Indians wrapped in their buffalo robes. A single glance convinced them that they had found their way into a dangerous den, and that a retreat was impossible. The chief pointed them to a seat; they sat down: a pause ensued; while the keen-eyed warriors gazed in astonishment upon their unwelcome visiters. Feeling the peril of their situation, M'Kenzie directed his associates to keep their eyes on the chief while he addressed him, and, if he should give any sign to his band, to shoot him and make for the door. He advanced, and offered the pipe of peace to the chief; but it was refused. He then explained the object of their visit, and proposed to give, in exchange for the rifle, two blankets, an axe, some beads, and tobacco.

When he had done, the chief arose, and made a speech in his turn, in which he manifested great passion; at the conclusion of which it was evident that the savages waited only a signal from their head, when they would pounce upon and devour their prey. M'Kenzie and his comrades, having risen to their feet during the speech of the old man, cocked their rifles, and advanced toward the door: the savages, being thus taken by surprise, fell back to the right and left: they passed out, and reached their camp in safety, without the least desire to repeat their visit to their grim neighbours.

The next day, while pursuing their voyage, they descried two canoes, filled with white men, coming down the river, to the full chant of a set of Canadian voyageurs. This proved to be a brigade of North-Westers, headed by John G. M'Tavish, bound to the mouth of the Columbia River, to await the arrival of the Isaac Todd. Both parties halted, and camped together for the night. It was said that they separated next morning on the best of terms, having renewed their former acquaintance and friendship.

M'Kenzie arrived in safety at his former station, but found, to his chagrin, that his caches had been discovered and rifled by the Indians. He was now in a dilemma; for his whole dependance had been placed on these stolen goods to purchase horses from the Indians. He sent men in all directions for the purpose of discovering the thieves, and despatched Mr. Reed with letters to the Messrs. Clark and David Stuart.

The resolution announced in these letters was rejected by both Clark and Stuart, and the design of M'Dougal to abandon an enterprise of so much cost and promise, on the first difficulty, they considered both rash and pusillanimous. They made no arrangements, therefore, for leaving the country, but continued to act with a view to the maintenance of their new and prosperous establishments.

When the regular time arrived when the parties of the interior posts were to rendezvous at the mouth of the Wallah-wallah, on their way to Astoria with their collections of peltries, Mr. Clark packed all his furs on twenty-eight horses, and, leaving a clerk and four men to take charge of the post, departed on the 25th of May with the residue of his force. On the 30th he arrived at the confluence of the Pavion and Lewis Rivers. Here he found his boats, which he had left in charge with the Nez Percé chief, in tolerable repair; but while the necessary repairs were making, Mr. Clark's silver goblet, out of which he drank, was stolen. This enraged the gentleman to that degree that he threatened to hang the chief if it was not restored. The succeeding night an Indian was caught in the act of bearing away a load of goods, who was, on the morning following, tried, and promptly executed, notwithstanding the intercessions of his friends, and the advice of Mr. Clark's own associates. This rash act of Clark proved to be very impolitic, and was strongly censured by Messrs. Stuart and M'Kenzie, whom he met at the mouth of the Wallah-wallah, on their way down to Astoria. Pursuing their journey in company, they arrived at Astoria on the 12th of June.

About two days previously, the brigade which had been quartered in the Walamet had arrived with numerous packs of beaver, the results of a few months' trapping on that river: these were the first-fruits of the enterprise, gathered by men who were as yet mere strangers in the land; but which gave substantial proof that the facilities afforded, in that country, for the accumulation of wealth were very abundant, and that it required only time and proper management to accomplish all that had been fondly anticipated.

CHAPTER VI.

The partners at Astoria agree to abandon the country—Action of the British and American governments in reference to the new settlement—Mr. M'Dougal, at Astoria, marries the daughter of an Indian chief—Anecdote—The Beaver makes her way to China, leaving Mr. Hunt on the Sandwich Islands—He returns to Astoria—Wreck of the Lark, and sufferings of her crew—The furs and merchandise belonging to Mr. Astor sold to the North-West Fur Company—Arrival of a British sloop of war, whose commander takes possession of the establishment at Astoria in the name of his British Majesty—Treaty between the United States and Great Britain as to the occupancy of Oregon—Reflections.

THE partners found Mr. M'Dougal in all the bustle of preparation; having about nine days previously announced, at the factory, his intention of breaking up the establishment, and fixed upon the 1st of July for the time of departure. Messrs. Stuart and Clark were highly displeased with his rash and precipitate conduct, especially in coming to such an important conclusion without their knowledge or consent, when he knew at the same time that their arrival could not be far distant. Indeed, the whole conduct of M'Dougal was such as to awaken strong doubts of his loyal devotion to the cause. His old sympathies with the North-West Company seemed to have revived. He had received M'Tavish and his party as friends and allies, who came as spies to reconnoitre the state of affairs at Astoria, and to await the arrival of a hostile ship.

They might have been obliged to leave the ground for want of provision, and the Chenooks wanted only a signal from the factory and they would have driven them away as intruders and enemies. But M'Dougal, on the contrary, supplied them from the stores of the garrison, and had gained them the favour of the Indians by treating them as friends. M'Dougal was sorely disappointed when he found that Messrs. Stuart and Clark had determined not to co-operate with him in his unmanly project; and because horses and provisions had not been provided, it was then too late to carry forward his plans until another year.

In the mean time, the non-arrival of the annual ship, and the apprehensions entertained of the loss of the Beaver and of Mr. Hunt, had their effect upon the minds of Messrs. Stuart and Clark. They began to listen to the desponding representations of M'Dougal and M'Kenzie, who inveighed against their situation as desperate and forlorn : left to shift for themselves, or perish upon a barbarous coast ; neglected by those who sent them there, and threatened with dangers of every kind. In this way they were brought to consent to the plan of abandoning the country in the ensuing year.

About this time M'Tavish applied at the factory to purchase a small supply of goods wherewith to trade his way back to his post on the upper waters of the Columbia, having waited in vain for the arrival of the Isaac Todd. This proposition of M'Tavish brought on a consultation among the partners, and it was finally determined that they should give up to M'Tavish the post on the Spokan, and all its dependencies, in consideration of which they were to receive horses and such other articles as might be most acceptable to them in their contemplated journey across the mountains. The merchandise sold to him amounted to eight hundred and fifty-eight dollars.

This agreement being concluded, the partners formed their plans for the year to come, which were as follows : Mr. M'Dougal was to continue in charge of Astoria with forty men. David Stuart was to return to his former post on the Oakinagan, and Mr. Clark was to spend his time among the Flatheads, and they were all to engage in collecting as many furs as their diminished means would allow.

Mr. M'Kenzie was to winter in the abundant valley of the Walamet, from whence an abundant supply of provisions could at all times be sent to Astoria. As there were more clerks on hand than the circumstances required, three of them were permitted to engage in the service of the North-West Company. Having completed these arrangements, the four partners, on the 1st of July, signed a formal manifesto, stating the alarming state of their affairs, from the non-arrival of the annual ship, the apprehended loss of the Beaver, their want of goods, &c., &c. And as, by the 16th article of the company's agreement, the enterprise might be abandoned within five years, if it was found unprofitable, they now formally announced their intention to do so on the 1st of June of the ensuing year, unless in the interim they should receive the necessary support and supplies from Mr. Astor or the stockholders, with orders to continue.

This instrument, accompanied by private letters of similar import, was delivered to Mr. M'Tavish, who departed on the 5th of July. He engaged to forward the despatches to Mr. Astor by the usual winter express sent over land by the North-West Company. The manifesto was signed with great reluctance by Messrs. Clark and D. Stuart, whose experience by no means justified the discouraging account given of the internal trade, and who considered the main difficulties of exploring an unknown and savage country, and of ascertaining the best trading and trapping grounds, in a great measure overcome. They were overruled, however, by M'Dougal and M'Kenzie, who, having resolved upon abandoning the enterprise, were desirous of making as strong a case as possible to excuse their conduct to Mr. Astor and to the world.

While difficulties and disasters had been gathering about Astoria, the mind of the projector of the enterprise at New-York was a prey to great anxiety. The ship Lark had been despatched only a fortnight when he received intelligence, which justified all his apprehensions of hostilities on the part of the British. The North-West Company had presented a second memorial to that government, representing Astoria as an

American establishment, stating the vast scope of its contemplated operations, magnifying the strength of its fortifications, and expressing their fears that, unless crushed in the bud, it would effect the downfall of their trade.

Influenced by these representations, the British government ordered the frigate Phœbe to be detached as a convoy for the armed ship, Isaac Todd, which was ready to sail with men and munitions to form a new establishment. They were to proceed together to the mouth of the Columbia, capture or destroy whatever American fortress they should find there, and plant the British flag on its ruins.

Informed of these movements, Mr. Astor lost no time in addressing a second letter to the secretary of state, communicating this intelligence, and requesting it might be laid before the president : as no notice, however, had been taken of his previous letter, he contented himself with this simple communication, and made no further application for aid.

Awakened now to the danger that menaced the establishment at Astoria, and aware of the importance of protecting this foothold of American commerce and empire on the shores of the Pacific, the government determined to send the frigate Adams, Captain Crane, upon this service. On hearing of this determination, Mr. Astor immediately proceeded to fit out a ship called the Enterprise, to sail in company with the Adams, freighted with additional supplies and reinforcements for Astoria.

About the middle of June, while in the midst of these preparations, Mr. Astor received a letter from Mr. R. Stuart, dated at St. Louis, confirming the intelligence of his safe arrival, and of Mr. Hunt's safe arrival at Astoria, and of the former prosperity of the enterprise.

This flattering intelligence almost overpowered Mr. Astor. "I feel ready," said he, "to fall upon my knees in transports of gratitude."

At the same time he heard that the Beaver had succeeded in her voyage from New-York to the Columbia: this was an additional ground of hope for the welfare of the little colony. The post being thus relieved, and strengthened with an American at its head, and a ship of war about to sail for its protection, the prospect for the future seemed full of encouragement, and Mr. Astor proceeded with fresh vigour to fit out his merchant ship.

Unfortunately for Astoria, this bright gleam of sunshine was soon obscured. Just as the Adams had received her complement of men, and the two vessels were ready for sea, news came from Commodore Chauncey, commanding on Lake Ontario, that a reinforcement of seamen was wanted in that quarter. The demand was urgent, the crew of the Adams was immediately transferred to that service, and the ship was laid up.

Although this was a most discouraging circumstance, yet Mr. Astor determined to send the Enterprise to sea alone, and let her take her chance of finding her unprotected way across the ocean. Just at this time, however, a British force made its appearance off the Hook; and the port of New-York was effectually blockaded. The Enterprise was, consequently, unloaded and dismantled, and Mr. A. was obliged to comfort himself with the hope that the Lark had reached Astoria in safety, and that, aided by her supplies, and the good management of Mr. Hunt and his associates, the little colony might be able to maintain itself until the return of peace.

We will now return to Astoria; and here we find Mr. M'Dougal, as usual, engaged in a new project. He had sought the hand of one of the native princesses, a daughter of the one-eyed potentate Comcomly, who swayed his sceptre over the fishing tribe of Chenooks, and was in fact the most popular and powerful chief ever known upon the Columbia River from the time of its first discovery by white men.

M'Dougal's suit prevailed, and after the preliminaries were all adjusted, Comcomly, with his fleet of canoes, bearing the royal family, and his band of warriors, crossed over to Astoria, on the 20th of July, and M'Dougal was put in possession of his greasy bride.

The writer cannot refrain from relating an anecdote concerning M'Dougal and his princess. Some time after their union had taken place, Mrs. M'Dougal, on seeing, from the window of her room in the fort, a large swine rolling in the mire, and basking in the sun, and being at the same time, according to outward appearances, entirely destitute of care and perplexity, called out to her loving husband, who immediately obeyed the summons, and entered the presence of his beloved ; when, having inquired after her commands, she said to him, "You profess to be a great chief; but I see you hard at work every day, behind the counter and at the desk, and your time is so fully employed that you have scarcely time to eat your food, or to enjoy the society of your wife a moment;" upon this she pointed to the swine in the puddle, and said, " See there, that is the true chief; he has no labour to perform, like a slave ; when hungry, his food is served up, he fills himself, he then lies down in the soft mud, under the influence of the warming rays of the sun, sleeps and takes his comfort." " That," she repeated, "is the true chief."

The above anecdote was related to me by my old and tried friend, Mr. James Birnie, who has charge of the Hudson's Bay trading post at Astoria. This gentleman also informed the writer, that Mrs. M'Dougal was still living, but her glory had departed, as she was subsisting upon the hospitality of her Indian friends, some distance up the Columbia.

But a short time after M'Dougal had consummated the above-mentioned matrimonial contract, and, as it has been said, before the honeymoon had begun to wane, about the 20th of August, one of the sons of Comcomly hurried into the fort, and announced a ship at the mouth of the river. This was the Albatross, which Mr. Hunt had chartered at the Sandwich Islands to bring him, with a few supplies, to the mouth of the Columbia.

The circumstances which led him to charter this vessel I will now briefly relate. After leaving Astoria, on the 4th of August, 1812, as before related, the Beaver reached New-Archangel on the 19th, having met with nothing worthy of note on her voyage. After being detained at this port for some time, they sailed to St. Paul's, in the vicinity of Kamschatka, for the purpose of obtaining a cargo of seal-skins. Here the vessel was standing off and on, while the skins were being brought off in skin boats; but one night, while Mr. Hunt was on shore, a gale arose, and the ship was obliged to put to sea, and did not reappear until the 13th of November. Mr. Hunt now hurried the remainder of the cargo on board, and because of the injury which the rigging had received during the gale, and the fact that there is great danger in approaching the bar at the mouth of the Columbia after the winter storms commence, Mr. Hunt was induced to run down to the Sandwich Islands, and arrived at Oahu in safety, where the ship underwent the necessary repairs, and again put to sea on the 1st of January, 1813, leaving Mr. Hunt on the Islands. The Beaver made the port of Canton, in China, according to directions, where the captain received the letter of Mr. Astor, giving him information of the war, and directing him to convey the news to Astoria.

He wrote a reply, refusing to comply with his orders; but said to Mr. Astor that he would remain there until the return of peace, and then return home. While here, Captain Sowle was offered one hundred and fifty thousand dollars for the furs he had taken on board at St. Paul's; but, unfortunately, he refused this offer, hoping to realize more. While thus holding on, the furs fell so much in value, that he borrowed money on Mr. Astor's account, at eighteen per cent., and laid up his ship for the return of peace.

While Mr. Hunt was anxiously awaiting the return of the Beaver, the Albatross arrived at the Islands from China, which brought the first tidings of the war. Mr. Hunt was no longer in doubt as to the reason of the non-appearance of the annual ship; and in order that Astoria might not be left destitute, he chartered the Albatross, as before observed, to convey him to the Columbia.

When he arrived at Astoria, he was surprised and astonished to learn that the partners had resolved to abandon the establishment; and soon found that matters had gone so far that it would be of no avail to oppose their plans. And being beset, too, with all the disparaging accounts which had been communicated to Mr. Astor concerning the interior trade, and the doubtful prospects of the whole concern, and as his own experience had been full of perplexities and discouragements, he was brought, by degrees, to acquiesce in the step taken by his colleagues, as perhaps advisable in the exigencies of the case. His only care was to wind up the business with as little further loss to Mr. Astor as possible. A large stock of furs was collected at the factory, which it was necessary to get to a market. There were twenty-five Sandwich Islanders, who were, according to contract, to be returned to the Islands; and as the Albatross was bound to the Marquesas, and thence to the Sandwich Islands, it was resolved that Mr. Hunt should sail in her in quest of a vessel, and, if possible, return by the 1st of January, bringing with him a supply of provisions.

Should anything, however, occur to prevent his return, an arrangement was to be proposed to Mr. M'Tavish to transfer such of the men as were so disposed from the service of the American Fur Company into that of the North-West, the latter becoming responsible for the wages due them, on receiving an equivalent in goods from the storehouse of the factory. As a means of facilitating the business, Mr. M'Dougal proposed that, in case Mr. Hunt should not return, the whole arrangement with Mr. M'Tavish should be left with himself. This proposition was assented to. All these matters being arranged, Mr. Hunt sailed in the Albatross on the 26th of August, and, without accident, arrived at the Marquesas just before Porter made that port in the frigate Essex, with a prize of London whalers.

From Commodore Porter he received the intelligence that the British frigate Phœbe, with a store-ship, mounted with battering pieces, calculated to attack forts, had arrived at Rio Janeiro, where she had been joined by the sloops of war Cherub and Racoon, and that they had all sailed in company on the 6th of July for the Pacific, bound, as it was supposed, for the Columbia River.

Mr. Hunt considered this the death-warrant of unfortunate Astoria; and, in much perplexity of spirit, endeavoured to make an arrangement with the commodore to bring off the property of Mr. Astor, but without success. He obtained this officer's promise, however, that, if possible, he would intercept or anticipate the enemy.

In this state of suspense, Mr. Hunt was detained at the Marquesas until the 23d of November, when he proceeded in the Albatross to the Sandwich Islands. He had still hoped that the annual ship would be found here; but alas for the Lark! for, notwithstanding she reached, in safety, within a few degrees of the Sandwich Islands, here a gale sprang up, in the fury of which she "broached to," when two waves completely upset her. The masts and rigging were cut away, but she was left a mere hull, full of water. After the gale had measurably subsided, they rigged a temporary stage, on which the crew raised themselves above water, and in this way, suffering beyond description from exposure, hunger, and thirst, and after losing the first mate and four seamen, on the 21st they descried, to their great transport, a canoe approaching, managed by natives. From them they obtained a very welcome supply of potatoes. The second mate went on shore in the canoe to procure help to tow the wreck into harbour, but neither help nor men returned. The next day ten or twelve canoes came alongside, but rendered no aid. They all now abandoned the ship, got into the canoes, and reached the land at no great distance. As soon as they touched the beach they were surrounded by natives, who stripped them almost naked. The name of this inhospitable island was Tahoorowa.

In the course of the night the wreck came drifting to the strand, with the surf thundering around her, and shortly afterward bilged. The natives would not allow the seamen to help themselves to the provisions which floated on shore, neither were they allowed to go on board of the wreck. Mr. Ogden made his way to the Island of Owyhee, and endeavoured to make some arrangements with Kamáhamáha, the king of the Sandwich Islands, for the relief of his companions in misfortune. The king agreed to furnish the crew with provisions during their stay in his territories, and to return to them all their clothing that could be found; but he stipulated that the wreck should be abandoned to him as a waif cast by fortune upon his shores. With these conditions Mr. Ogden was fain to comply. Upon this the great Tomahamaha deputed his favourite John Young, the tarpaulin governor of Owyhee, to proceed with a number of the royal guards, and take possession of the wreck on behalf of the crown. This was done accordingly, and the property and crew were removed to Owyhee. The royal bounty appears to have been but scanty in its dispensations. The crew fared but meagerly; though, on reading the journal of the voyage, it is singular to find them, after all the hardships they had suffered, so sensitive about petty inconveniences as to exclaim against the king as a "savage monster," for refusing them a "pot to cook in," and denying Mr. Ogden the use of a knife and fork which had been saved from the wreck.

Such was the unfortunate catastrophe of the Lark. Had she reached her destination in safety, affairs at

Astoria might have taken a different course. A strange fatality seems to have attended all the expeditions by sea, and those by land were not much less disastrous.

Captain Northrop was still at the Sandwich Islands when Mr. Hunt arrived on the 20th of December. The latter immediately purchased, for ten thousand dollars, a brig called the Pedlar, and put Captain Northrop in command of her. They set sail for Astoria on the 22d of January, intending to remove the property from thence to the Russian settlements on the north-west coast, to prevent it from falling into the hands of the British. Such were the orders of Mr. Astor sent out by the Lark.

We will now leave Mr. Hunt on his voyage, and return to see what has taken place at Astoria during his absence. On the 2d of October, about five weeks after Mr. Hunt had sailed in the Albatross from Astoria, Mr. M'Kenzie set off with two canoes and twelve men for the posts of Messrs. Stuart and Clark, to apprize them of the new arrangements determined upon in the secret conference of the partners at the factory.

He had not ascended the river a hundred miles when he met a squadron of ten canoes sweeping merrily down under British colours, the Canadian oarsmen, as usual, in full song. This proved to be an expedition fitted out by Mr. M'Tavish, with Mr. Stuart, another partner of the North-West Company, and a number of clerks. They had heard of the Phœbe and the Isaac Todd being on the high seas, and were on their way to await their arrival. In one of the canoes Mr. Clark came passenger, the alarming intelligence having brought him down from his post on the Spokan.

M'Kenzie determined to return to Astoria with them. So, veering about, the two parties camped together for the night. The leaders, of course, observed a due decorum; but some of the subalterns could not restrain their chuckling exultation, boasting that they would soon plant the British standard on the walls of Astoria, and drive the Americans out of the country. In a secret conference held between Clark and M'Kenzie, they agreed to steal a march on the other party, and get down in time to apprize M'Dougal of the approach of these North-Westers. The latter, however, were completely on the alert: just as M'Kenzie's canoes were pushing off, they were joined by a couple from the North-West squadron, in which was M'Tavish, with two clerks and eleven men. With these he intended to push forward and make arrangements, leaving the rest of the convoy, in which was a large quantity of furs, to await his orders.

The two parties arrived at Astoria on the 7th of October. The North-Westers encamped under the guns of the fort, and displayed the British colours. The young men in the fort, " native Americans," were on the point of hoisting the American flag, *but were forbidden by M'Dougal!* The young men were astonished at this prohibition, and were exceedingly galled by the tone and manner assumed by the clerks and retainers of the North-West Company, who ruffled about in that swelling and braggart style which grows up among these heroes of the wilderness. They, in fact, considered themselves lords of the ascendant, and regarded the hampered and harassed Astorians as a conquered people.

On the following day M'Dougal convened the clerks, and read to them an extract of a letter from his uncle, Mr. Angus Shaw, one of the principal partners of the North-West Company, announcing the coming of the Phœbe and the Isaac Todd, "to take and destroy everything American on the North-West coast."

This intelligence was received without dismay by such of the clerks as were " native Americans." They had felt indignant at seeing their national flag struck by a Canadian commander, and the British flag flying, as it were, in their faces. They had been stung to the quick, also, by the vaulting airs assumed by the North-Westers. In this mood of mind they would willingly have nailed their colours to the staff, and defied the frigate.

She could not come within many miles of the fort, as they supposed, and any boats she might send could be destroyed by their cannon. The cool and calculating spirits, however, at the head of affairs, felt nothing of the patriotic spirit of indignation which characterized these young men, and every true American, when an insult is offered by the retainers of any foreign despot. The extract of the letter had, apparently, been read by M'Dougal merely to prepare the way for a preconcerted stroke of management. On that same day M'Tavish proposed to purchase the whole stock of goods and furs belonging to the company, both at Astoria and at the interior posts, at cost and charges. M'Dougal undertook to comply, assuming the whole management of the negotiation in virtue of the power vested in him in case of the non-arrival of Mr. Hunt. That power, however, was limited and specific, and did not extend to such an extensive operation. No objection, however, was made to his assumption; and he and M'Tavish soon made a preliminary arrangement, perfectly satisfactory to the latter.

Mr. Stuart and the reserve party of North-Westers arrived shortly afterward, and encamped with M'Tavish. The former exclaimed loudly against the terms of the arrangement, and insisted upon a reduction of the prices. New negotiations had now to be entered into; and to say no more of the peremptory tone assumed, and the insults offered, by the North-Westers, notwithstanding they were completely at the mercy of the inmates of the fort, the terms of sale were lowered by M'Dougal to the standard fixed by Mr. Stuart, and an agreement executed on the 16th of October, by which the furs and merchandise of all kinds in the country belonging to Mr. Astor passed into the possession of the North-West Company, at about a third of their real value.

Not quite $40,000 were allowed for furs worth upward of $100,000. Beaver was valued at two dollars per skin, though worth five dollars; land otter at fifty cents, though worth five dollars; sea otter at twelve dollars, worth from forty-five to sixty dollars; and for several kinds of furs nothing was allowed. The goods and merchandise for the Indian trade ought to have brought three times the amount for which they were sold.

The North-West Company also guarantied to such as did not choose to enter into the service of that company, a safe passage through all their posts in the interior, and the amount of wages due them was to be deducted from the price paid for Astoria.

M'Dougal did not satisfy Mr. Astor in reference to the integrity of his conduct, in thus abandoning the enterprise, and disposing of the property, as will appear by an extract from a letter written by that gentleman to Mr. Hunt. " Had our place and our property," said he, " been fairly captured, I should have preferred it. I should not feel as if I were disgraced."

Shortly after concluding the above agreement, M'Dougal became a member of the North-West Company, and received a share productive of a handsome income.

On the morning of the 30th of November a sail was descried doubling Cape Disappointment. It came to anchor in Baker's Bay, and proved to be a ship of war; and, for fear that it might prove to be an American vessel, M'Tavish loaded two barges with all the packages of furs bearing the mark of the North-West Company, and made off for Tongue Point, three miles up the river.

In the mean time M'Dougal, who still remained nominal chief at the fort, on his way to the ship instructed his men, who were recently in the employ of the American Fur Company, to pass themselves off for Americans or Englishmen, according to the exigencies of the case.

The vessel proved to be the British sloop-of-war Racoon, of twenty-six guns, and one hundred and twenty men, commanded by Captain Black. This vessel had sailed from Rio Janeiro in company with the Phœbe and Cherub, as a convoy to the Isaac Todd. Mr. John M'Donald, partner of the North-West Company, had taken passage on board of the Phœbe, to profit by the anticipated catastrophe at Astoria.

But as the convoy had been separated by stress of weather off Cape Horn, and as nothing had been heard of the Isaac Todd afterward, and as intelligence was received of the mischief that Commodore Porter was doing among the whale ships, Commodore Hillyer ordered the Racoon to the Columbia, while the other two went in search of Porter.

The officers of the Racoon were in high spirits. The agents of the North-West Company, in instigating the expedition, had talked of immense booty to be secured by the fortunate captors of Astoria. Mr. M'Donald had kept up the excitement during the voyage, so that there was not a little midshipman on board but was ready to burst with hopes of obtaining sacks of prize-money, nor a lieutenant but felt his importance, if possible, more than ever, when he dreamed of the treasures which they would bear home to old England, and throw down at the feet of their wives and sweethearts. But when there is not a sufficient allowance made for "*shrinkage,*" as one observed, we are apt to shrink in our dimensions when we fail in realizing a consummation of our fond and long-cherished hopes. It was so in this case with the " lieutenants" and " middies," when they learned that their warlike attack upon Astoria had been forestalled by a snug commercial arrangement, and that their anticipated booty had become British property in the regular course of traffic; and that all this had been effected by the very company which had been instrumental in getting them sent on what they now stigmatized as a fool's errand. The captain himself felt so indignant on finding that they had been so completely duped and fooled by a set of shrewd men of traffic, that we may reasonably conclude that he shrunk away to the common size of an ordinary "*Jonathan.*"

In a word, M'Dougal found himself so ungraciously received by his countrymen on board the ship, that he was glad to cut short his visit and return to shore. He was busy at the fort, making preparations for the reception of the captain of the Racoon, when his one-eyed father-in-law made his appearance, with a train of Chenook warriors, all painted and equipped in warlike style.

Old Comcomly had beheld with dismay the arrival of a " big war canoe," displaying the British flag; and having learned something of politics by his daily visits at the fort, he knew of the war existing between the nations, but knew nothing of the arrangements between M'Dougal and M'Tavish. He trembled therefore for the power of his white son-in-law, and the glory of his daughter, and assembled his warriors in all haste. "King George," said he, " has sent his great canoe to destroy the fort, and make slaves of all the inhabitants. Shall we suffer it? The Americans are the first white men that have fixed themselves in the land. They have treated us as brothers. Their great chief has taken my daughter to be his squaw. We are therefore as one people."

His warriors all determined to stand by the Americans to the last, and to this effect they came painted and armed for battle. Comcomly made a spirited war speech to his son-in-law; and offered to kill every white man from King George's ship that should attempt to land, which would be an easy matter, as the ship could not reach the shore by a considerable distance ; and as the crew would be obliged to land in boats, the old chief could lay concealed in the thicket on shore, and cut them all off as soon as they landed.

But what must have been the astonishment of the old warrior when M'Dougal advised him and his men to lay aside their arms and war dress, and wash off the paint from their faces and bodies, and appear like clean and peaceable savages to receive the strangers courteously; for notwithstanding the ship belonged to King

George, her crew would not injure the Americans or their Indian allies.

This was so contrary to the old chieftain's notions of receiving a hostile nation, that it was only after M'Dougal repeated in the most positive manner the assurances of the amicable intentions of the strangers, that he was induced to lower his fighting tone. He said something to his warriors explanatory of this singular posture of affairs, and in vindication, perhaps, of the pacific character of his son-in-law. They all gave a shrug, and an Indian grunt of acquiescence, and returned in a sulky mood to their village, to lay aside their weapons for the present.

As soon as the proper arrangements were made, Captain Black caused his boats to be manned, and landed with befitting state at Astoria. From the talk that had been made by the North-West Company of the strength of the place, he expected to find a place of some importance. When he beheld nothing but stockades and bastions calculated for defence against naked savages, he felt an emotion of indignant surprise, mingled with something of the ludicrous. "Is this the fort," cried he, "about which I have heard so much talking?" "Why," said he, adding an oath, "I'd batter it down in two hours with a four-pounder." But when he heard of the amount of rich furs that had been passed into the hands of the North-West Company he was outrageous, insisting that an inventory should be taken of all the property purchased of the Americans, with a view to ulterior measures in England for the recovery of the value from the North-Westers. As he grew cool, however, he relinquished the idea of preferring such a claim; and reconciled himself, as well as he could, to the idea of having been forestalled by his bargaining coadjutors.

On the 12th of December the fate of Astoria was consummated by a regular ceremonial. Captain Black, attended by his officers, entered the fort, caused the British standard to be erected, broke a bottle of wine, and declared in a loud voice that he took possession of the establishment and of the country in the name of his Britannic Majesty, changing the name of Astoria to that of Fort George.

Although this was explained to the Indian warriors as being a friendly arrangement and transfer, yet they shook their heads grimly; and could not be persuaded that their ancient allies were not all subjugated to a state of slavery, until they beheld the Racoon depart without taking away any prisoners.

As to Comcomly, he no longer prided himself upon his white son-in-law; but, whenever he was asked about him, he shook his head, and replied, that his daughter had made a mistake, and, instead of getting a great warrior for a husband, had married herself to a squaw.

On the 28th of February, the brig Pedlar anchored in Columbia River. This was the vessel which Mr. Hunt had purchased at the Sandwich Islands, to take off the furs collected at the factory, and to restore the Islanders to their home. Mr. Hunt expressed his indignation in the strongest terms when he learned in what manner M'Dougal had disposed of the whole establishment, and determined to make an effort to get back the furs. As soon as his wishes were known in this respect, M'Dougal came to sound him on behalf of the North-West Company, intimating that he thought the furs might be purchased at an advance of fifty per cent. This overture was not calculated to sooth the angry feelings of Mr. Hunt, and his indignation was complete when he discovered that M'Dougal had actually been a partner of the North-West Company since the 23d of December. He had, notwithstanding, retained the papers of the Pacific Fur Company in his possession, and had continued to act as Mr. Astor's agent; besides divulging to his new associates all Mr. Astor's plans of operation, and copying his business letters for their perusal! Mr. Hunt, with some difficulty, obtained possession of the papers of the concern, and brought the business to a close; remitted the drafts of the North-West Company in Mr. Astor's favour to him by some of his associates who were about to cross the mountains, and embarked on board of the Pedlar on the 3d of April, and bade a final adieu to Astoria.

The next day, April 4th, Messrs Clark, M'Kenzie, and David Stuart, and such of the Astorians as had not entered into the service of the North-West Company, set out to cross the Rocky Mountains.

These return parties from Astoria, both by sea and land, experienced on the way as many adventures, vicissitudes, and mishaps, as the far-famed heroes of the Odyssey. They reached their destination at different times, bearing tidings to Mr. Astor of the unfortunate termination of his enterprise.

At the return of peace, Astoria, with the adjacent country, reverted to the United States by the treaty of Ghent, on the principle of *status ante bellum*, and Captain Biddle was despatched in the sloop of war Ontario to take formal repossession.

For various reasons, the most important of which being the supineness of the American government to act in the premises, when solicited to do so by Mr. Astor, he made no further efforts to reoccupy Astoria.

The British government soon began to perceive the importance of this region, and to desire to include it within their territorial domains. A question has consequently risen as to the right of the soil, and has become one of the most perplexing now open between the United States and Great Britain. In the first treaty relative to it, under date of October 20th, 1818, the question was left unsettled, and it was agreed that the country on the north-west coast of America, westward of the Rocky Mountains, claimed by either nation, should be open to the inhabitants of both for ten years, for the purposes of trade, with equal right of navigating all its rivers. When these ten years had expired, a subsequent treaty, in 1828, extended the arrangement to ten additional years. *So the matter stands at present.*

Having recorded all the leading events in the history of the Oregon Territory, from the time that the northwest coast was discovered by Capt. Cook until the overthrow of Mr. Astor's bold and enterprising scheme to colonize, and call into requisition the resources of that wilderness region, I will pass on without any further reflections upon the subjects just treated, except recording my regrets, with those of Washington Irving and others, that our government should have neglected the overture of Mr. Astor, and suffered the moment to pass by when full possession of this region might have been taken quietly, as a matter of course, and a military post established, without dispute, at Astoria. The second period of ten years has elapsed, during which the powerful, because very wealthy, British Fur Company has monopolized all the trade, with a very small exception, (and, consequently, an untold amount of wealth, arising therefrom,) of that vast country, from California, nay, of California itself, to a great extent, and from that to Kamschatka. What profits the Americans have derived from that country have been procured by great toil; because, when they reached that coast, they found themselves unprotected, and goaded on every side by this powerful monopoly, which possesses a sinking fund of two millions sterling, if the writer has been correctly informed, for the express purpose of competing with every vessel that may come on the coast for the purpose of trade. And they possess not only the means, but also the men, qualified in every respect for the accomplishment of the several duties assigned them. And the object of this "Honourable Company" is, to control the destinies of the whole country, as far as they may be permitted so to do, and to drain it of its last farthing of wealth; and if at any time it should become necessary for them to take up their traps, and vast herds and flocks, they can accomplish this as expeditiously, and with but little more loss than M'Tavish sustained when he packed the furs, purchased at so fine a lay from "*Comcomly's white son-in-law,*" into his barges, and scud away for Tongue Point. For they have their anticipated head quarters ready for occupancy at any time, on Vancouver's Island, a little above the 49th degree of north latitude. Their vessels are ready at short notice, by which to convey their peltries, goods, &c., and their Canadians, ever most obedient to their superiors, can very soon drive the flocks and herds through to Nasqually, (Puget Sound,) and from thence to head quarters. And what will they be obliged to leave behind? Why nothing but a few miserable buildings, the best of which consist of posts set up, which are then filled in with slabs from the saw-mill, sealed up in the inside, in a very rough and cheap manner. And if there should be a more important location, such as that at the Walamet Falls, for instance, the best water privilege in the country, then *individuals* of the Honourable Hudson's Bay Company mark out their claims, as Doctor John M'Laughlin, the "principal agent of the company west of the Rocky Mountains," has done, at the above-named falls; where he claims a mile square on the east side of the river, embracing that side of the falls which is, by far, the most important side. There he has a saw-mill in operation; and there a company of Americans have, also, a saw-mill and flouring-mill in operation, (which are, however, claimed by the doctor, until some *government* shall take it in hand, and settle the dispute between them; the two mills being located, as the doctor will have it, upon his mile square.)

Upon that claim the above-named gentleman is building a city, and was selling off small city lots at *one hundred dollars a piece,* to "*native Americans,*" too, and gives them a good warrant deed! Does not this argue that British subjects actually possess the right of soil in that territory? The writer was credibly informed in the spring of 1843, while at the Walamet Falls, that the doctor had just sold twenty lots at the above-named price. And how will these claims be disposed of if our government should recover full possession there? Why, all that these *individuals* would have to do would be simply to " hoist the American colours," and proclaim themselves American citizens, and then " they would be all right," and might continue as agents of the Hudson's Bay Company, in carrying forward their lucrative operations still. Thus the reader may perceive that the country is not only being drained of its wealth by the removal of its furs and skins, and wheat and other grains, and butter, and lumber, to England and other foreign markets, but even the *soil itself* is being disposed of, *and that to Americans too,* in order to fill the already overflowing coffers of that vast trading establishment.

And are the gentlemen of that company blameworthy because they are engaged, heart and hand, in this money-getting business? No, not in the least. They are, on the contrary, worthy of ten thousand praises; for a kinder and more hospitable company of gentlemen, I doubt, cannot be found on the globe. Never will the poor wanderer be turned from their doors unfed or unclothed; and their many acts of kindness bestowed upon the writer and his family will ever lay him under obligations to love and respect them. But, if there is any blame to be attached to any one because of the course that has been, and is being, pursued there, at whose door must it lie? No doubt it must lie at the door of our government at Washington. There " Uncle Sam" has been smoking and dozing over the subject, like his " worthy predecessor," " Peter Stuyvesandt," since the time that Captain Biddle was despatched in the sloop of war Ontario to take repossession of Astoria. And if, at any time, he has been aroused from his sweet repose, it has only been effected by a hunch from " John Bull's" elbow, reminding him that the term of treaty had expired, and that, in order that " John" might apply his " *muck rake,*" as Bunyan said, with renewed energy, in scraping the remaining wealth out of the country, it would be necessary to renew it. But we will leave this topic to be discussed by the able politicians of the day, and will now proceed to give a description of the face of the country.

CHAPTER VII.

Description of the country—Columbia River and its tributaries—Annual floods—Vancouver—Multnomah Island—Clatsop Plain—Walamet River and Falls—Valleys—Plains—Productiveness of the soil—Climate—Blackfish from fifteen to twenty feet in length—Whales—Epidemics.

The whole of the north-west coast is exceedingly mountainous and rugged, with dense forests of fir, hemlock, spruce, white-cedar, cotton-wood, ash, elm, dogwood, black alder, crab, Norway pine, and a species of maple, called green-maple, or "devil wood," remarkable for its toughness. This is the principal variety of timber to be found on the coast; but as we pass into the interior, the white oak, and white ash, and a very inferior quality of soft maple, may be added to the above; the white and yellow pine are also to be found in the interior. The red fir constitutes the greater part of the timber in the country, which is a very inferior quality of timber, being of no more value than our hemlock. Its growth, however, is immense. One of these trees, the dimensions of which were taken by some gentleman of the exploring expedition which visited the Columbia in 1841, measured forty-eight feet in circumference, consequently sixteen feet in diameter.

The face of the country, in general, is very broken and mountainous; and many of the mountains are of such altitude, that, when in the valley of the Walamet, the eye may behold them in every direction, and during every season of the year, towering above the clouds; and, being covered with perpetual snow, they present the scowling aspect of changeless winter.

4*

The country abounds in rivers and creeks, and as the Columbia and the Walamet Rivers are to be found in the immediate vicinity of all the missionary stations in the country, and as the greater part of the produce of the country is floated down upon their bosoms, they demand a more particular description. The Columbia originates in the Rocky Mountains, being augmented, as it pursues its downward course, by many tributaries, which also commence their devious courses in the same mountainous region. The most important of these tributaries, among which are the M'Gillivray's, Flathead, Oakinagan, Spokan, and Snake Rivers, disgorge their waters into the Columbia before it reaches Wallah-wallah, about three hundred miles from its mouth, in a direct line, or nearly due east. The banks of the Columbia are generally very high and precipitous, studded in many places with gigantic pillars of basaltic rock, all giving evidence of having passed the ordeal of fire in ages past. There are to be found, at intervals, narrow strips of low land on the banks of the river, which are, however, in general of but little value, when considered with reference to agricultural purposes, as they are mostly overflowed by the swelling of the river in the months of May and June—in that time of the year when a flood must inevitably destroy the crops. These annual floods are caused by the melting of the snows in the mountainous regions through which the Columbia and her tributaries pursue their serpentine course, as the reader may discover by referring to the map which accompanies this work. The flats in the vicinity of Fort Vancouver, and on the Multnomah Island, which island lies on the Columbia between the upper and lower mouths of the Walamet, are the most important; and a considerable portion of these are also overflowed.

Vancouver is situated about five miles above the upper mouth of the Walamet, and nearly one hundred miles from the coast on the north side of the river. The lower mouth of the Walamet is from twelve to fifteen miles below the upper mouth: between these two mouths, as before observed, lies the Multnomah Island. From this to the coast there is but very little land that is fit for the plough, unless some of our "down-easters" should see fit to leave the mountain homes of their fathers, perform the toilsome journey across the continent, and then turn to and clear up a farm more mountainous than those they left. At Astoria, now called by the Hudson's Bay Company Fort George, the original Astorians, or their successors, have had from fifteen to twenty acres cleared off, and under cultivation, which is now however all overgrown with young trees, shrubs, and briers, except the gardens of the gentleman in charge of that trading post. Immediately upon the coast, on the south side of the Columbia, there is a plain, which extends to Cape Lookout, about twelve miles in length, and about two and a half miles wide in the widest place. This is called Clatsop Plain, of which more particulars will be given hereafter. On the north side of the river there is another small plain, bounded partly by the Chenook River and Bay. This river empties into the Pacific, a little to the north of Cape Disappointment.

The Columbia River is about three miles in width at the mouth, between Cape Disappointment on the north side and Point Adams on the south; and about the same width across from Astoria to Chenook Point. At Vancouver, according to the measurement of Mr. Gardner, a physician, formerly in the employ of the Hudson's Bay Company, it is 1670 yards in width; and the width continues nearly the same until its junction with the Snake River. The channel is remarkably crooked, and at some places quite narrow; and is from five to nine fathoms deep until you reach Vancouver.

A more accurate description of the Columbia may be expected in the journal of the United States exploring expedition, who took surveys of that region in the year 1841, if "Uncle Sam" should happen to wake up, and *keep awake* long enough to publish it, before our readers are all dead and forgotten.

The Walamet River heads in about 43° of north latitude, and empties into the Columbia about ninety-five miles from the coast; and its direction is in general from south-east to north-west. Its greatest width, near the Multnomah Island, is a full half-mile; but as you ascend it, the width diminishes rapidly. The tide flows up it within about two miles of the falls, and the channel is sufficiently deep to admit of shipping to the head of tide water; and during the annual freshets the swollen waters of the Columbia set up the Walamet to that degree that vessels have ascended as high as the falls, thirty miles from its junction with the Columbia. These falls are about twenty-five feet in height; which, as before observed, constitutes the most important water privilege in the country. After this obstacle is overcome, which might be effected by a canal and locks, the river would be navigable for a small-sized steamboat until we arrive at Champoeg, which is a little above the commencement of the Walamet settlement, and about twenty-five miles above the falls. Above this the river becomes shoal, and more rapid, so that, unless during the time of a freshet, this would be the head of navigation for a craft of any considerable size.

The valleys, of which the Walamet is the most important, constitute that part of the country which is best adapted to agricultural purposes. This valley is about one hundred and fifty miles in length, and about sixty miles wide in the widest part, through which the Walamet River winds its devious way, whose transparent waters reflect the various objects on its banks as perfectly as their originals.

The valley next in importance is that through which the Cowalitz River passes. This is a small river that heads in about 46° 30′ north latitude, and empties itself into the north side of the Columbia, about fifty miles from the coast. On this river, which can be navigated only with flat-bottomed boats and Indian canoes, the Hudson's Bay Company has an extensive farming establishment, about fifty miles from its junction with the Columbia. This valley is considered very productive, and of considerable extent.

The valley of the Columbia is of less importance as a farming region, unless, as before observed, the rugged mountains and hills were divested of their majestic forests, and the most of these, even, would be found unmanageable. This valley is about fifteen miles wide in the vicinity of Vancouver. The other valleys which have come under our observation are of small dimensions, being simply narrow strips on the margins of the rivers and creeks which pass through deep cuts in the mountains.

In giving a description of the soil, we will commence with those plains which lie upon the coast, at the north and south of the Columbia. The Clatsop Plain is evidently *alluvial*. When digging a cellar, the writer discovered a tree, one foot and a half in diameter, at the depth of five feet below the surface of the earth, which had lain there sufficiently long to become entirely decayed, yet preserving its form perfectly. This entire plain is composed of a light-coloured sand, covered to the depth of from four to twenty-four inches with a composition of sand and decayed vegetation, which assumes a black colour. It is not probable that this soil will be durable; but the plain in its natural state is covered with a most luxuriant growth of the best quality of grasses, such as red clover, a species peculiar to that country; and timothy, precisely such as we cultivate in this country; and a kind of cane grass, which grows in some places to the height of from four to six feet. Horses and cattle are very fond of it when young, and in taste it resembles the young stalks of corn. On the ridge next the ocean, the plain being formed of ridges and valleys running parallel with the ocean, the wild pea abounds, which nearly resembles the *tare*. The writer having made the experiment, found them to answer a very good substitute for *green peas!* They come forward early, and are much sought after by the cattle. In addition to the above, there are various other species of wild grasses, and one which resembles the red-top of the States. Strawberries, raspberries, whortleberries, several species of which we have never met with elsewhere; and blackberries, sallal berries, service berries, gooseberries, Scotch caps, and cranberries abound on this plain and in the adjacent marshes. This catalogue embraces all the wild fruits in this vicinity, with the exception of the crab-apple, which is very much used by the Indians, and with which some of our ladies have made very agreeable tarts. There is, also, a berry which grows upon a small shrub, a species of laurel, about the size of a large pea, of a red colour, very stringent, and containing hard seeds. These are also used by the Indians as food, being prepared; as are the crab-apples, by being boiled, or roasted under the ground or under the ashes. The leaves of this kind of laurel are dried, and mixed with tobacco by the natives for smoking.

This soil, as will hereafter appear, when under cultivation, yields sufficiently to satisfy the husbandman for all his toils.

The soil of the plain on the north side of the river is very like to that of the one just described; but the ridges and mountains immediately in the rear of the plains which are bounded by the Pacific are, as before stated, covered with dense forests, and present a soil composed mostly of gravelly clay, which is a stronger and more durable soil; and judging by the abundant crops of most excellent potatoes and garden vegetables produced by Mr. Birnie, at Astoria, it may be put down as being very productive. The soil of the valley of the Columbia, in the vicinity of Vancouver, is, on the margin of the river, alluvial; but as you leave ths stream it assumes the character of a mixture of sand, gravel, and loam. This produces abundant crops of wheat, oats, barley, buck-wheat, flax, and tolerable corn and potatoes, and garden vegetables of all kinds. Fruit trees, such as apples and peaches, thrive and bear abundantly. The peach, however, is frequently destroyed, in consequence of putting forth its blossoms too early, which are cut off by the succeeding frosts. A species of grape is also cultivated with success by Dr. M'Laughlin, and also the English gooseberry and currant; but not any of the tropical fruits, such as the orange, &c., as one writer would have it. The Cowalitz Valley the writer has no personal acquaintance with; but from the description given by those who have visited it, and from the fact that the Hudson's Bay Company has an extensive farming establishment there in successful operation, where they grow thousands of bushels of wheat and other grains annually, we conclude that the soil is decidedly fruitful. There are also a number of settlers in this valley, consisting of Canadians whose time of service in the company having expired, they have been permitted to settle here with their Indian wives. They secure their subsistence by cultivating the earth, and also furnish a number of hundreds of bushels of wheat, and other articles of food, for the Vancouver market. This settlement is about thirty miles from the Columbia. In the vicinity of all the above-named places, except at Astoria, there are extensive *prairies* or *natural meadows*, which produce an abundance of pasture for vast flocks and herds, both summer and winter.

We will now enter the Walamet Valley, which, as stated above, is the most important portion of the territory when viewed in respect to farming operations. The river, between its junction with the Columbia and the falls, is interspersed with several beautiful islands, the soil of which, and of the adjacent shores, is a kind of loam, producing abundance of grass; but, unfortunately for the farmers, this land, which would no doubt be very productive, is generally rendered unfit for cultivation in consequence of the annual floods, which would destroy any crop that might be put upon it. One farmer, however, by the name of Johnson, an American, discovered a location sufficiently extensive for a farm, on the west side of the river, about fifteen miles from the Columbia, where he was residing, and tilling the ground, and attending his flocks, &c., when we left the country. There was another settler between this and the falls at that time, by the name of M'Cary, who had selected a high rocky promontory, on the east side of the river, where he had made a residence, in the rear of which he said there was a very good plain. The writer called to see him for a few moments, in the spring of 1843, when he found that his Indian wife had, in addition to several former heirs, just presented him with a pair of twins. So that the reader may discover that Oregon is destined to be populated, even if the strange " *Oregon fever,*" which has been and is still raging in the United States, should subside.

The next place worthy of note is the Clackamus Plains, quite an extensive prairie, or it rather embraces a number of prairies, interspersed with groves of trees, and underwood, and the hazel-nut, which abounds in this valley, and is the only kind of *nut* to be found in the country, unless the *acorn* can be thus denominated, which also abounds here and elsewhere in the interior. The soil on this plain is chiefly composed of clay, gravel, and sand, and is considered productive. We will allude to this place again when we come to speak of the missionary operations. At the falls there is but very little soil of any kind. What is there is sandy, and is chiefly to be found on the east side of the river, running down in a narrow strip, bounded by the river on the west, and by a high rocky ridge on the east side, increasing in width as you descend from the falls to the Clackamus River, which descends through the Clackamus Plains and enters the Walamet about two miles below the falls. The west side of the river, at the falls, and for some distance above and below, is joined by a high rocky ridge, where there is but very little soil of any kind. On ascending the river we find the country on both sides in its native state, being clothed in its forest dress; so much so, that where once the populous Indian village covered the bank, and from whence the forest warrior sallied forth upon his foe, now the willow and the cotton-wood trees hold possession of the spot, and no traces of humanity are to be seen, except the trophies of death, such as old kettles and pans, which were the property of the former inhabitants, elevated upon sticks over the canoes or holes in the earth wherein their former owners were deposited; and the last death-wail has long since passed away upon the floating breeze.

This is the state of things until we arrive at a place on the east bank of the river, called the Bute, two miles below Chumpoeg, where the Walamet settlement proper commences: and the settlement extends from this, up the east side of the river, to the mission saw-mill, the distance of twenty-four miles, which is one continued prairie, being crossed at intervals by groves of timber and streams of water, upon which are also found a number of small lakes or stagnant ponds.

The soil of this prairie is a deep, strong clay, producing abundant crops of wheat, oats, barley, potatoes, tolerable corn, and garden vegetables of all kinds, and pastures for flocks and herds to almost any extent. The natural fruit of this valley is much the same in kind and quality as that upon the Clatsop Plain and in its neighbourhood, with the addition of wild cherries, red and black, and the thorn-apple. The natural flowers upon this extensive plain are the most beautiful that our eyes ever beheld.

Upon the Tualatin Plains, which lie to the west of the river and falls, there is also a settlement, though of much smaller dimensions and of more recent date than that on the east side; yet it was in a prosperous state, enjoying the productions of a rich and luxuriant soil. And there is also a settlement on the west side of the river opposite to Chumpoeg, in the Chehalim Valley, which bids fair to succeed; and there are settlers scattered along on the west bank of the river from this until you reach the Yam-hills, opposite to the first missionary establishment. From this point the writer crossed the plain and mountains to the coast. A more particular description of this journey will hereafter be given, "if the Lord will." The Yam-hill country presents an entirely different soil from that part of the valley already described. It was a loose gravel, and to all appearance quite productive, inasmuch as it was covered with a stiff sward, and abundance of grass of a good quality, especially through the valley bordering on each side of the Yam-hill River; which is a stream of pure water taking its rise in the mountains which bound the Pacific, and pursuing a north-easterly direction, empties itself into the Walamet below the missionary post spoken of above. This part of the valley is inhabited by a small remnant of the Yam-hill clan of Indians only; but as it is the most inviting portion of the Walamet Valley, the time is not far distant when the poor Indian will feast for the last time upon the " savoury meat" which the God of nature provides for him in such abundance, and when, instead of the antic deer, and the bounding elk, and growling bear, the lowing cow, and prancing horse, and bleating sheep, will be seen, in vast herds, engaged in stripping the plains of their carpets of green. And where shall the spirits of the original proprietors of the soil have found a lodgment? In the motley charnel-house, where eternal death prevails— that death which shall never issue into life? Or shall they rise in judgment and condemn many thousands of those of us who have had our lives and education given us in a land of Bibles and ministers, and sermons and prayers? O, reader, stop and reflect.

The Walamet Valley, above the Yam-hills on the west, and the mission saw-mill on the east side, is uninhabited save by a remnant of the Calapooyas. The average crop of wheat in that country has been estimated, by a very good judge, to be about fifteen bushels from one bushel of seed; but there have been instances where one acre has produced forty bushels. My neighbour on Clatsop Plain gathered five hundred bushels of potatoes from a little over thirty bushels of seed. This was the first crop which was raised upon that plain. And forty bushels of peas have been gathered from one acre in the Walamet. Other grains do well, and garden vegetables are produced in great abundance.

Having thus briefly described the face of the country, soil, and productions, we will now say something of the climate. The climate of the coast is temperate, resembling, in many respects, that of the island of Great Britain. The year is made up of the dry and rainy seasons. The dry season commences, generally, about the 1st of May, and continues until the 1st of November. During this period we have but very few showers, which are seldom, if ever, accompanied with thunder and lightning. But vegetation seldom suffers on this account; for the mighty fogs from the Pacific supply the place of gentle showers to all the country bordering on the coast.

But not so in the interior. There the earth, and the clay soil especially, becomes exceeding dry, and in some places it may be found baked almost to the consistency of a brick; consequently, in those regions, in midsummer, the grass is entirely dried upon the fields, and the herds feed upon it as ours do upon hay during winter, with the addition of some green grass obtained along the streams and in the swales. In the Walamet Valley there are heavy dews, which in some measure atone for the lack of showers; but when you reach the region of the Dalls, even these are denied, and those highland plains are like unto the "mountains of Gilboa," upon which the dews of heaven were never to descend.

There are but few days upon the coast so warm during summer as to require a man, unless in active employment, to lay aside his coat, the atmosphere being most delightfully tempered by the breeze from the ocean, which comes in with the morning tide, and generally continues through the day. This is the most healthy portion of the lower country during summer. The winter rains commence about the 1st of November, and continue, in general, with many bright and sunny intermissions, until May. But the winter of

1842 was an exception to this general rule. Never did rain descend in such torrents, and never did a storm continue for such a length of time, as it did there, at least so the writer thought, while he spent that dreary winter in loneliness, as the reader will hereafter discover, on the banks of the Columbia; and he was exceedingly thankful whenever he could see the face of the stranger sun, and be permitted, for a few moments, to bask in his genial rays. But during the other two winters which he spent there, the storms from the southward would generally endure for from two to four days, and then there would be intermissions of a week, during which the weather would be as pleasant as was ever enjoyed during the month of May in the state of New-York. The reader will feel safe in receiving the above statement as truth, when the writer assures him that on the 25th of December, 1840, he plucked a strawberry blossom near his cabin on Clatsop Plain.

There is but little snow in this region. During the winter of 1840 there was a fall of snow which measured seven inches on the level, but it did not remain upon the ground as many days as it was inches in depth. During the two following winters of the writer's sojourn there, there was scarcely snow enough to whiten the ground. The storms from the southward, which prevail during the wet season, are accompanied with tremendous blows, so that if a whale or black-fish gets into the eddy which is formed by Cape Lookout, at the southern extremity of Clatsop Plain, he is pretty sure to come ashore. This fact was exemplified during the month of November, 1840, when forty black-fish came ashore upon the Clatsop beach, measuring from *fifteen* to *twenty* feet in length. And in the month of January following, two large hump-back whales were driven ashore in the same vicinity. And during the winter of 1842, a part of a whale came on shore: this was of sufficient size to permit Mr. Solomon Smith, my neighbour, to stand in a stooping posture within his abdomen, and cut out pieces of fat as large as he was able to dislodge. These are times of rejoicing and fat living among the Indians, as will hereafter more fully appear. In consequence of the repeated and protracted rains, the climate, from November until May, is exceedingly humid, and in addition to the rain there is a continual vapour arising from the earth, and much of the time a dense fog being blown in from the ocean; which renders the climate unfavourable for persons afflicted with chronic diseases. But the intermittents, so prevalent in the interior, never originate here, and cases of the kind are unknown in this vicinity, with the exception of such as visit the interior during the prevalence of the epidemic. Ploughing can be done during any of the winter months, as a general thing, and potatoes may be planted in the month of March.

I must here relate a circumstance, which was, to us, quite strange; the next summer after the first crop of potatoes were raised on the plain, my neighbour found his field being covered with young potato tops, which proved to have sprung from the seeds, or potato apples, as they are sometimes called, which had dropped into the ground the preceding year. The writer knows not what yield these spontaneous vines produced, as he left the country before the next potato harvest. The young grass on this plain is frequently as fresh, green, and forward, on the plain in February and March, as it is in New-York on the 1st of May. After the rainy season passes away, and the month of May sets in, all nature puts on a smiling aspect, and life and vigour pour through every vein of animated nature.

The climate of the interior is quite different in many respects. At Vancouver and the Walamet, the dry and rainy seasons prevail, and during the former, or dry season, it is, some of the time, say from the 1st of June until September, hot some days almost to suffocation, the thermometer having risen to nearly one hundred degrees of Fahrenheit; and the nights would be so cool that one or two blankets were found to be by no means unwelcome companions. These sudden changes from heat to cold were brought about, no doubt, by the influence exerted upon the atmosphere, as soon as the sun disappears, by the everlasting snows which perpetually crown the lofty mountains, with which this region is surrounded, as before observed. The above changes, connected with the facts, that when the annual floods subside, they deposite a vast amount of decayed and decaying vegetation upon the shores of the rivers and the tributaries, up which the waters back for miles, which vegetable matter sends forth a noxious miasma; and also, that that region abounds with stagnant lakes and pools, which, as the waters diminish or evaporate during the dry season, emit their unhealthy vapours, and the breaking of the soil, cause the annual epidemics to prevail, from which but few of the inhabitants escape.

At the approach of winter these diseases, with which the atmosphere was loaded, now begin to disappear, and then the poor man who is affected with chronic pains must pay tribute to the "Esculapian," or "*medicine man*," as the Indians say. And now it becomes every honest citizen to haul on his sea boots, if he is so fortunate as to possess a pair, for moccasins are of no further avail, for the earth, which was, during the heat of summer, as hard as a brick, now becomes, in consequence of the protracted southerly rains, which prevail here as well as upon the coast, like unto a bed of mortar. And upon some portions of the Walamet Plains, which, during summer, are perfectly solid, a horse will, during the rainy season, sink in up to his belly, when his rider must dismount in the mire, and allow his nag to find his way out to "terra firma" the best way he can, where he remounts and gallops off until he meets with another disaster of the kind, or a worse one.

In this region they have some more snow than upon the coast, and the weather during the winter is colder; yet not so much snow and cold as to prevent the horses and cattle procuring a sufficiency of food, with the exception of a very few instances, when cattle have been known to die because of the inclemency of the weather, and want of food.

In the region of the Dalls, and further in the interior, the country is generally more healthy.

CHAPTER VIII.

Number of Indians in Oregon Territory—Their character—Wars among them—Personal appearance—Dress—Description of those inhabiting the lower country—Their heads flattened in infancy—Anecdote illustrative of their shrewdness—Slaves among them—Polygamy—They sell their daughters—Their moral character—Wild animals—Fish.

We now proceed to give, as accurately as possible, the number of Indians in the Oregon Territory, their character, and manners and customs.

The Rev. Samuel Parker, whose "Journal of an Exploring Tour beyond the Rocky Mountains" is now before us, estimates the number of natives in that territory in the lower country, between California and the forty-seventh degree of north latitude, at 50,000, and those of the upper country at 32,585, and then observes that "we might more than double this" (the last) "number, and probably still come below the population of the upper country."

Doctor Bangs, in his History of Methodism, supposes their numbers to amount to, probably, 150,000.

And Mr. Thomas J. Farnham, *professedly*, gives "an extract from the report of Lieutenant Wilks, to the secretary of the navy," in which the numbers of the Indians in the Oregon Territory are estimated at 19,199. What a contrast! And yet this last number is the most accurate, being, as the writer believes, not many hundreds wide of the mark; but in this estimate there are, to his certain knowledge, two errors. He passed through the Killamook country, while the exploring squadron, under the command of Lieutenant

Wilks, was in the Columbia, and ascertained the number of the Killamook clan to amount to no more than two hundred, whereas, in this "extract" it is estimated at four hundred. And the numbers of the Dalls Indians are underrated at least one half. This last statement the writer makes upon the authority of a gentleman who resided there for the space of five years, which embraced the time when the above-mentioned squadron made their surveys in the country.

And now, with these very different and contradictory statements, the writer will leave the world to guess at the exact number of Indians in that territory, while he will proceed to give a brief description of their character, manners, and customs; and in so doing he will have occasion to refer, once more, to the Journal of the Rev. Mr. Parker. When speaking of the character of "the Indians of the plains or upper country," this gentleman states, that "they are scrupulously honest in all their dealings, and lying is scarcely known." And says, "They fear to sin against the great Spirit and therefore, have but one heart, and their tongue is straight, and not forked." And further adds, "And so correctly does the law written upon their hearts accord with the written law of God, that every infraction of the seventh commandment of the decalogue," that is, the commandment which prohibits the commission of adultery, "is punished with severity!"

I know not how to apologize for these misstatements, only by stating, which is no doubt the fact, that this gentleman was not in the country a sufficient length of time to become acquainted with the Indian character. With reference to their honesty and integrity our readers may judge, when we assure them from personal observation, and from information received from gentlemen and ladies who have resided among those Indians, that they are both *thieves* and *liars*; and they will also judge of their virtuous dispositions, when they learn that in two instances attempts were made upon *white* ladies who resided among them. Surely these were *virtuous* Indians !

This gentleman further states : " The Indians west of the great chain of mountains have no wars among themselves, and appear to be averse to them, and do not enter into battle except in self-defence, and then only in the last extremity." See Journal, p. 236. Now the facts in the premises lie upon the opposite side of the "*trail*." There are perpetual feuds existing between the different clans. They do not often come forth in battle array, as did the armies of the kings of Israel and Philistia ; but whenever they get a sly chance, they pounce upon their foe like the panther upon his prey, and as many of their enemies as do not fall before the arrow, the rifle-ball, or the knife, are driven away, and sold into perpetual slavery.

The Chenooks who reside on the north side of the Columbia, in plain sight and hearing of the writer, while he resided on the south side of the river, during the summer of 1842, were at war among themselves, and they were not at peace when he left the country. During the summer referred to, you could hear the muskets and rifles firing, some days, from morning till night ; and that clan will soon be in the condition of the Kilkenny cats, of whom it is reported that they continued to fight until they devoured each other all but the tails.

This dispute and consequent war arose among them in precisely the same way that the most irreconcilable disputes and exterminating wars have arisen in other hereditary monarchies among their *Christian* neighbours. Chenamus, their chief, was called upon by death to abdicate the ancient throne upon which Comcomly once sat in dignity and pomp when his white son-in-law bore rule at Astoria : and now, as it generally goes, his son, the " heir apparent," would needs ascend this seat of ancient honour ; but in this he found a rival, for another salmon-eater, who perhaps felt a drop of " royal blood" running through *his* veins, would be chief also, which was, of course, a sufficient cause of war.

After enumerating a number of vices to which these Indians are addicted, such as gambling, &c., he adds: "It is not to be supposed that their virtue, any more than that of other tribes, would be invulnerable if exposed to temptation." No; for actual experiment has long since proved to a demonstration, that the slightest temptation has completely overcome their long-cherished virtuous principles.

But still the writer is very much inclined to join with his Christian brother in saying: "The moral disposition," that is, the natural disposition, " of these Indians is very commendable, certainly as much so as any people," in their natural state, " that can be named." For, since he has reached his own Christian nation, he finds it important and absolutely necessary to keep things under lock and key to prevent them from taking to themselves legs and walking away.

Perhaps, before dismissing these Indians, it should be observed, that, in general appearance, they resemble each other from the Dalls to the Rocky Mountains. The men are generally above the middling size, and the women of common stature, and both are well formed. Their complexion may be a little lighter than other Indians. Their hair and eyes are black, their cheek bones high, and very frequently they have aquiline noses. Their hands, feet, and ankles are small and well formed, and their movements are easy, if not graceful. They wear their hair long, part it upon their foreheads, and let it hang in tresses on each side or down behind.

Their dress is much the same throughout the different clans, which consists of a shirt, worn over long, close leggins, with moccasins for the feet. These are of dressed skins of the deer, antelope, mountain-goat, and sheep. They use many ornaments, such as feathers, beads, buttons, and painted porcupine quills. The dress of the women and men is much the same, except, instead of the shirt, the women wear a kind of frock, which comes down nearly to the feet. Many of them wear a large cap made of dressed skins, ornamented with beads. They have abundance of horses, and are excellent horsemen. Their arms consist of the bow and arrow, musket, rifle, and knife.

We will now dismiss the Indians of the upper country, and when we come to speak of the missionary operations at the Dalls we will exhibit some more particular traits in their character.

The character of those which inhabit the lower country, between the Dalls and the coast, now demands our attention.

The Chenooks inhabit the north side of the Columbia, their summer residence being immediately on the banks of the river during salmon season, and upon the Chenook River a few miles to the north, where they take a second run of salmon, which are of an inferior quality. These are preserved for their winter food.

To the north of the Chenook we meet with the Checaldish clan, who also reside on the Columbia during summer in times of peace. And to the north of these is another clan called the Quiniutles. These sometimes visit the Columbia, but not generally. The Cawalitz are the next to be met with on the north side of the river, and between them and the Dalls it is inhabited by scattering bands of Chenooks and Clickatats. The south side of the Columbia, immediately on the coast, is inhabited by the Clatsops, and to the south of them is the Killemook country. A clan called the Claskanios lived upon the streams which empty into the head of Young's Bay, which clan is very nearly extinct. Further up the river we meet with a remnant of a clan called the Ne Coniacks. From this to the Dalls again we meet with only a few wandering bands of Clickatats and Chenooks.

The natives of the Walamet Valley consist principally of the Calapooyas; and here we are under the necessity of correcting another mistake recorded in the

Journal of the Rev. Mr. Parker. This gentleman represents the Calapooyas as being "divided into seventeen different tribes, under their respective chiefs, and number about eight thousand seven hundred and eighty persons, who speak the same language, radically, with only a little difference in dialect," &c. See page 262, third edition. Now the fact is this: there never was but one tribe of Calapooyas, and of that tribe there are only a few most miserable remnants left, (which is the condition of all the Indians in the lower country,) and these remnants, consisting of but a few families each, are scattered over the most part of the Walamet Valley, and will not number more than from five to eight hundred. To prevent mistake, I will here observe that the Yam-hills, of whom previous mention has been made, are a remnant of this nation; which band consists of two or three families, and is, perhaps, one of Mr. P's tribes.

As it regards the Umbaquas, of whom Mr. P. says "they are divided into six tribes," it will be well for the reader to understand, that, in the year 1840, the Rev. Messrs. J. Lee and G. Hines made a tour through their country for the purpose of selecting a location for a missionary post among these supposed "six tribes;" but, after passing through their country from the Walamet Valley, through deep, dark ravines, and over high, rugged, and precipitous mountains, and finally down the rapid, whirling Umbaqua River to the coast, they found a few miserable fish-eaters, who were as savage as the bears, their neighbours, from among whom, as they were informed by their guide and guardian, an Indian woman, the wife of the man who had charge of the company's trading post in that region, they did well to escape with their lives; for, while there, she had watched their movements all night, while the missionaries slept, and had expected an attack from them before morning. The brethren decided that it was "not expedient to establish a missionary post there," in which decision the writer most heartily concurred.

These Indians of the lower country resemble each other in person and manners, and, with some slight exceptions, in dress also, and the exceptions must be *very slight*, unless it be this, that some have a very little covering, and others none at all, and the best have but three changes, as it is said, that is, to put on, put off, and go without, and the latter change is frequently preferred. The writer dares not attempt a particular description of their wardrobe; but he will venture to say that the men wear a shirt, and when it is cold, a blanket if they can get it; but there are a few immediately on the river who dress as Europeans *sometimes*, which clothes they obtain from trading vessels and the Hudson's Bay Company for salmon and furs. The dresses of the females are entirely inexpressibles, except that they sometimes wear a blanket over their shoulders, made of small skins sewed together with the sinews of the elk or deer, or such as are obtained from the traders.

They are very fond of ornaments, such as beads, rings, bracelets, feathers, and shells. One kind of shells in use among them are obtained on the northwest coast, which is a small, white, spiral shell, called by them the "Ta-cópe-ta-cópe," or "Hiaqua." A fathom of these, when strung upon a string, are worth a good three point blanket, and these are their currency. It is not unfrequently the case that you may meet with an Indian with a bunch of these, say ten or fifteen, tied together, and hung in each ear, and one sticking through a hole in the ligament which divides the nostrils, with face and parts of the body daubed with a kind of red clay, and a rude cap, adorned with feathers, upon his pancake-shaped head, with long hair queued up behind, upon which must be suspended a bunch of shells and some feathers, and a short dirty shirt. After spending much time in thus richly and genteelly attiring himself, he comes out a "*perfect beau.*" And it can easily be ascertained when their young ladies are considered fit for market, by the profusion of the like ornaments with which their persons are adorned. And yet it is with them as with other nations, ornaments do not constitute beauty, for neither sex can boast of this gift of nature Their noses are generally broad and rather flat at the top, and fleshy at the end, with large nostrils. They have wide mouths, thick lips, with very good teeth: they are frequently, however, in aged persons, worn away to the gums by eating so much sand with their food. The men carefully eradicate every vestige of beard, which they consider a deformity, except a few individuals, who leave what is called, by some of their politer neighbours, a "*goaty*" under the chin. Their hair is black and coarse, and both sexes wear it at full length. In size they are generally below five feet five inches, with crooked legs and thick ankles; a deformity caused by their passing so much of their time sitting or squatting upon their heels in the bottom of their canoes—a favourite position, which they retain even when on shore. The women increase the deformity by wearing tight bandages round the ankles, which prevent the circulation of the blood, and cause a swelling in the muscle of the leg.

While in infancy their heads are flattened, by compressure, from the eye-brows to the crown, and the flatter they can be made the more beautiful they are in their estimation. One of their females came into the house of the writer one day with a child, the head of which was exquisitely flat. On being asked how she succeeded in making it so flat, the woman said that she had put a bag of sand on it in the first instance, but as that proved too light, she removed it, and put the axe in its place, which effected the work to perfection. The slaves, however, are not allowed to enjoy the benefit of this strange deformity; consequently their heads are left in their natural state.

The following anecdote will show that they are not wanting in intellect, or, at least, shrewdness. When the Rev. J. Lee visited the United States in 1839, he brought with him two boys of the Chenook nation. One of these being asked, by a gentleman of the States, the reason why their people flattened their heads, asked, in return, "Why do your ladies make themselves so small about the waist?" And now, having committed myself by mentioning "*slaves*," I shall be under the necessity of saying something more on this subject. Their slaves and their women constitute the greatest part of their property. What! their *women?* Yes; but hold, I must speak of slavery first. Their slaves are such as are taken prisoners in time of war, or, perhaps, more properly, such as are stolen from other tribes. For instance, a band of Killemooks go to the south, and falling in with a weaker clan of their southern neighbours, they make no further ado, but fall upon them, gun and knife in hand; some they kill, the remainder they take prisoners, and convey them to the north, and sell them to their Clatsop, Chenook, or Checalish neighbours, when they become slaves for life, and their children after them. What they call a good man slave is worth as much as a horse, that is, from ten to twelve blankets, and so on, according to their size and qualifications. The female slaves are worth less, from the fact that they are not able to perform so much drudgery. But in what sense are their *women* their property? Why, the more wives a man has, the more work he can have done; and every man has a right, according to their view of things, to have as many wives as he is able to purchase. And do the parents sell their daughters? Yes, in the following manner. When a *young* beau or an *old* beau—and the latter circumstance is just as likely to happen there as in the civilized world—makes overtures for the hand of one of his neighbours' daughters, he in the first place approaches the parents, or, in case the girl has no parents, the proposals are made to her nearest relative. The parent or relative then breaks the subject to the girl, and if the suit proves favourable, the terms are settled, which may require the swain to produce so many canoes, horses, blankets, kiaquas, or other articles of property, upon the day when the nuptials are to be celebrated. This property is divided among the relatives of the bride; and after the ceremony—marriage ceremonies, however, have become nearly if not quite obsolete in the lower country—the bridegroom receives the bride's dowry, which is generally of much less value than the goods paid down by him.

One girl of the Clatsop clan refused to tender her much desired hand to a Chenook of some rank, alleging as a reason for her denial that her relatives would require a very high price for her, and as but little would be given in return, if she conceded to the proposition, she would be obliged to work very hard to make her husband's heart good; so, embracing a favourable opportunity, she hid herself in the woods until the storm of love had measurably subsided, when she returned to enjoy the bliss of a single squaw's life.

In respect to their *moral character*, I cannot, in justice to them, and to myself, say that it is blacker than that of thousands and tens of thousands of their white brethren in the civilized world. And for a full description of both I will refer the reader to the first chapter of Paul's Epistle to the Romans, from the 19th verse to the close of the chapter.

Their superstitions are almost endless and very deeply rooted, and are manifested more and more as we become better acquainted with them. To enumerate and describe which, would require a considerable labour, and such a description would necessarily take up a number of our pages, and when done, the benefit derived therefrom to our readers would not quit cost; consequently we deem it our duty to pass this subject by, and proceed to notice those things in connection with the history, which will be calculated to render this work more valuable.

These Indians are the most degraded human beings that we have met with in all our journeyings, taking them as a whole. There is not one among them that can be considered *virtuous*. And, in consequence of disease, which cleaves to them from their birth, and the many murders committed among them, they are rapidly wasting away, and the time is not far distant when the last deathwail will proclaim their universal extermination. It is truly heart-rending to see, as we have, how the "last enemy" chases them "from the cradle to the grave."

The wild animals of that country demand our notice. They consist of elk, deer, black and grizzly bear, (the latter, however, does not inhabit the lower country,) the wolf, small and large, panther and catamount, fox, racoon and rabbit, porcupine, polecat, squirrel and weasel, beaver, otter, both land and sea, and mountain sheep.

The wild-fowl may be enumerated as follows. The swan, goose and duck, of every variety, and in great abundance; the pelican, cormorant, and gull; all the above are eaten by the Indians; the eagle, crow, hawk, raven, pigeon, robin, lark, swallow, buzzard, owl, jay, yellow-bird, and humming-bird; besides some others of the smaller tribes. So that game is very abundant, especially in the spring and fall.

The forests and plains are no more profuse in presenting man with stores of food, than the rivers and streams, which abound in the finny tribes. The Columbia and Frazier's Rivers, at the north, to mention no more, produce vast numbers of salmon; those of the Columbia, however, are far superior to any others. Of these the writer obtained one which weighed 45lbs., and this was by no means a rare specimen. The salmon season commences about the 1st of April and continues until August. The common price for a salmon is five charges of ammunition, or one common cotton shirt for ten. The Indians take them in the lower part of the river with the seine and spear. The seine is manufactured by themselves out of a native hemp, and the bark of a species of willow: the spear is also their own manufacture. At the falls they take them with what is sometimes called a scap-net, and spear. Hundreds of barrels are purchased from them annually by individuals and the Hudson's Bay Company. And yet many thousands are found completely worn out with fatigue at the very head of the river and its tributaries.

In the month of November they have another run of salmon, of a very inferior quality, which come in from the ocean at the smaller rivers, which the Indians take in great abundance, and prepare them by cutting them in very thin parts and drying without salt, for their winter food.

Besides the salmon they have abundance of sturgeon of an excellent quality, and a great variety of smaller fish, such as salmon trout, trout, and what they call "calahtubbah," and crabs, clams, and mussels.

Having thus briefly described the face of the country; the soil, climate, and productions; the natives, with some of their manners and customs; the animals and fishes, we will now return to the time of the abandonment of Astoria by Mr. Hunt and his friends, and follow down the stream of time until the next party of Americans cross the Rocky Mountains.

CHAPTER IX.

Sand-bar at the mouth of the Columbia—Loss of the ship William and Ann—Of the Isabella—Of a vessel from Asia—Streams of the country possess petrifying qualities, trees and other things exposed to their action having been found in a petrified state—Japanese junk cast away—The epidemic ague—Indians' idea of its origin—Mr. David Douglass visits Oregon—A party of American traders under command of Capt. Wyeth cross the mountains.

THE sand-bar at the mouth of the Columbia has been mentioned heretofore, as being dangerous to those who are not well acquainted with the channel. In consequence of this obstruction, in the year 1828 the ship William and Ann was cast away a little within the bar; and as all on board perished, (being twenty-six in number,) the circumstances of the catastrophe, so lamentable in its character, could never be ascertained. And on the 23d of May, 1830, the ship Isabella was cast away upon a bar projecting from Sand Island opposite to Baker's Bay. As soon as she struck the men all deserted her, and without stopping at Fort George, made their way to Vancouver. It is thought that if they had remained on board until the tide served, she might have been saved; most of her cargo was saved. About thirty or forty miles to the south of the Columbia are the remains of a vessel which was sunk in the sand near shore, probably from the coast of Asia, laden, at least in part, with bees-wax. Great quantities of this wax have been purchased from the Killemook Indians by the Hudson's Bay Company and individuals; the writer also obtained a number of pounds of the same article from them while there, and was informed by them, that whenever the south-west storms prevail, it is driven on shore. While living on the banks of the Columbia, an Indian girl who lived in the family brought in a piece one day which had drifted around with the tide, and lodged upon the beach of the river; this was as large as a man's fist, and having been lodged in the mouth of some small stream, which enters the ocean somewhere to the south of the river, and stuck between stones, or wood, as was evident from the prints remaining in it, it was completely petrified. The writer presented it to Rev. Dr. Richmond when he left the country, in the autumn of 1842. And, perhaps, it may not be considered out of place if I here state, that many of the streams of this country possess petrifying qualities, insomuch, that whole trees have been found in a state of perfect petrifaction. And the writer has now in his possession a piece of bark of the fir tree, which retains its natural appearance, but will, notwithstanding, emit sparks when smitten with steel, like the flint.

In March, 1833, a Japanese junk was cast away fifteen miles to the south of Cape Flattery. Out of seventeen men, only three were saved. In the following

May, Captain McNeil, of the Lama, brought the three survivors to Fort Vancouver; and from thence they were, in the following October, sent to England, to be forwarded to their own country.

From this wreck the writer has a beautiful China flower-pot, and a tea-cup, which were obtained from the Indians, having been in their possession since the time of the wreck.

In the same year eleven Japanese in distress were drifted in a junk to Oahu, Sandwich Islands.—Was this the way in which the American continent and the Islands of the Ocean became peopled?

The epidemic *ague*, which has already been mentioned, and of which more will be said hereafter, which has swept away great numbers of the natives, and proved an annual scourge to the white man, commenced, according to the best authorities, in 1830. Before that time it had never been known in the country, not even a single case. The Indians account for the origin of this scourge in the following manner. The writer will state it just as he received it from one of them. At the time of its commencement there was an American vessel in the river, commanded by Captain Domanis, for the purpose of trading for furs. This, of course, brought on a competition between Domanis and the Hudson's Bay Company; and as the captain of the vessel paid a high price for furs, the Indians professed to bring him all the beaver, &c. But as the captain gave more for small skins than the company, they brought him all the small ones, and took all the large ones to the company. But, say they, when Captain Domanis became acquainted with this fact, he was "hias silix," that is, great angry; and that he might be revenged on them for deceiving him thus, he hung up some bad sail in a tree, and then opened, or uncorked, a small vial, and let out the ague and fever upon them, which has carried off thousands, and continues its ravages still. The writer laboured to reason them out of their folly, but it was of no avail, for they said that there were *whites* in the country at the same time that told them it was all true!

About this time a gentleman from Scotland, Mr. David Douglas, visited Oregon, under the patronage of the London Horticultural Society, for the purpose of scientific researches; and after fulfilling his mission returned to the Sandwich Islands, where he unfortunately lost his life. Some more particulars connected with his death will be given hereafter.

The next party of American traders which crossed the Rocky Mountains after the abandonment of Astoria, was under the command of Captain Wyeth, in 1832. This is the same gentleman who headed the party across the mountains when the Messrs. J. and D. Lee and their associates came to the country as missionaries, under the patronage of the Missionary Society of the Methodist Episcopal Church, in 1834.

CHAPTER X.

Causes which induced the establishment of the Oregon Mission—Dr. Fisk enlists in its favour—Rev. Jason and Daniel Lee appointed missionaries—Missionary meetings, in furtherance of the enterprise, held—Mr. Jason Lee goes to Boston to consult with Captain Wyeth as to the propriety of establishing the mission—Messrs. Lee set out for the west, and arrive at St. Louis—Join a party, who start for the Rocky Mountains—Description of the party, and of their method of travelling—Kanzas Indians—The antelope—Buffalo—A company of emigrants attacked by Indians.

An event took place in the year 1832 which directed the attention of the American churches to Oregon, as a vast field of benevolent enterprise, ripe for the introduction of the Gospel among its benighted inhabitants. Four Indians, from beyond the Rocky Mountains, belonging to one of the tribes (for there are several) who flatten their heads, probably the "Nez percé" tribe, accompanied some of the white trappers from the buffalo country down to the city of St. Louis. The resident United States' Indian agent, General Clark, was known to them as the first great chief of the white men who visited their nation. He had been seen by their fathers, who had often told them of his greatness, and it was natural they should desire to see him. They also expected to return to their own land, and make known their interview, as among the most interesting occurrences of their toilsome journey. Having great confidence in him, they made inquiries about the book of which they had been informed by the hunters, which the Great Spirit had given to the white men to teach them his will. The answers they received were in accordance with what had been told them. The writer saw General Clark in 1834, two years after their visit, and learned from him these particulars in relation to it. Two of them became sick, and died in St. Louis, and the other two started to return to their own land. It has been reported that one of them died on the way, and the other reached his tribe. As to the truth of this report, some have doubts. That both perished in the wilderness, the victims of sickness, famine, or war, appears more probable. A high-wrought account of the visit of these Indians to St. Louis, by some writer in the vicinity, was published in the Christian Advocate and Journal, New-York city, in March, 1833. This is the most important periodical in the Methodist Episcopal Church. The sum was this: that these "red men" were from the Flat-head tribe, in the interior of Oregon, beyond the Rocky Mountains, from whom they had been sent by a council of their chiefs, as delegates to St. Louis, to inquire concerning the Word of the Great Spirit; that in prosecution of their great object they had travelled two thousand miles, through rugged mountains and barren plains and dangerous enemies, enduring cold and heat, thirst and hunger, and many hardships, and reached their destination in safety; and that having made known the object of their visit to General Clark, and gained the information they sought, two of them were snatched away by death, not being permitted to carry back the "glad tidings" to their anxious countrymen. These incorrect statements receiving the fullest confidence, many believed that the day had come, and that the call was imperative, to send the gospel to Oregon. First among these was that excellent man of God, "whose praise is in all the churches," Wilbur Fisk, D. D., at that time president of the Wesleyan University, Conn. Alive to everything favourable to the advancement of the kingdom of Christ, and seeing before the church "an open door" to the "red man" of the "far west," the "fields there white to harvest," he could not be silent. The Macedonian cry, as it seemed, reached him as a divine mandate. Immediately his voice was heard rousing the churches; especially did he urge on the Methodist Episcopal Church an immediate response. His appeal was heard: and the Missionary Society of the Methodist Episcopal Church determined to attempt the establishment of a mission among the Flat-head tribe of Indians, in Oregon; that tribe, for reasons before stated, appearing to demand their first missionary efforts in the country. The mission at first was designated by the name of that particular tribe; but since, the name has been changed for that of the territory. A call was soon made for men to engage in the projected mission. Two men, natives of Stanstead, Lower Canada, the Rev. Jason Lee, and some time after his nephew, Daniel Lee, the writer, offered themselves to the board to labour in the proposed mission, and they were accepted. The former became a member of the N. E. Conference at its session in 1833, when he was also ordained to the office of a deacon, and then to that of an elder, in the Methodist Episcopal Church. The writer had travelled more than two years in the New-Hampshire Conference, was in full connection, and was ordained a deacon in 1833. Subsequently, at the Baltimore Conference, in 1834, he received elder's orders. October 10th, 1833, the missionaries met at New-York, to make arrangements for as early a departure to their appropriate field as possible. On the 16th the missionary board held a special meeting, in view of the mission, and appropriated $3000 to be employed in its first outfit. They also directed the securing the assistance of two laymen, to add efficiency to the effort; and that the missionaries should travel and hold meetings, and raise funds for their missionary enterprise: first going south as far as the capital, and then west, to join a company of traders and trappers who might be going into the mountains the next spring. Previous to this, however, very deeply-interesting missionary meetings had been held in New-Haven and Middletown, Conn., at which the late departed Dr. Fisk, of sacred memory, lent his influence. November 20th, a farewell missionary meeting was held in the city of New-York, in the Forsyth-street church. Bp. Hedding presided. Dr. M'Auley, of the Presbyterian Church, and several others, addressed the meeting. We were now ready, and about to go south, pursuant to the directions of the board, when an event came to our knowledge which caused the postponement of our intended journey for more than two months. A gentleman, known as *Captain Wyeth*, had lately arrived in Boston, Mass., with two Indian boys, from beyond the Rocky Mountains. The board judged that he would be able to give some necessary information regarding Oregon as a field for missionary labour, and of the means of reaching it. This gentleman, Captain Nathaniel J. Wyeth, who resides now, as the writer has been informed, in Cambridge, near Boston, Mass., crossed the Rocky Mountains to Oregon the preceding year, to explore the country for the purpose of prospective trade, to be carried on by a business company formed in Boston, to trap and buy beaver in the mountains, and fish for salmon in the Columbia. Their plan was to send an annual ship with supplies to the Columbia River, and freight her with salmon and furs on her return voyage. Mr. Jason Lee being directed by the board to proceed to Boston, and seek an interview with Captain Wyeth, immediately left New-York for that purpose.

The information which was furnished by Captain Wyeth, of the state of the Indians in Oregon, deepened the impression of its importance as a field of missionary effort. The company with which he was connected was about to send a vessel to the Columbia River, and thus an opportunity was given us to forward the necessary outfit for the commencement of our mission. The vessel was a brig, the Maydacre, of Boston. Captain Wyeth was to recross the Rocky Mountains in command of a party of men in the employ of the company the following spring, and we could go with them in safety. Thus was the way prepared in a manner entirely unanticipated. January 29th, 1834, Mr. Jason Lee having returned from Boston, we went to the south, holding meetings for the benefit of the mission in Philadelphia, Wilmington, Baltimore, and several other places, with very encouraging results. The enterprise found many friends, not only in that branch of our Zion to which the missionaries were united, but many others also manifested a heartfelt interest, in various ways, to further the benevolent object.

Early in March Mr. Jason Lee left for the west. The writer, having attended the Baltimore Conference, followed him on the 19th. At Pittsburg he was joined by Mr. Cyrus Shepard, from Lynn, Mass., one of the laymen engaged in the mission. From this city they took passage to St. Louis, Mo., where the writer arrived in the early part of April, a few days later. The necessary mountain outfit had already been sent up the Missouri in a steamboat, in the charge of Mr. Shepard, near the place where the company for the mountains was to form, and make the necessary arrangements previous to the commencement of the journey. Mr. Jason Lee and myself proceeded to Independence on horseback. This is on the western border of the state, and the point of departure whence many a party of fur traders and mountain trappers have set off on their hazardous adventures. A layman, Mr. P. L. Edwards, of Richmond, near Independence, was added to the number, increasing the mission family to four; and Mr. C. M. Walker, of the same place, was hired a year, to cross the mountains, and assist in commencing the mission. After several days spent in rigging packs and pack-saddles, and making other provisions for our route, on the 27th of April everything was in readiness for our journey.

On the 28th we raised camp, and began our march toward the Rocky Mountains. The whole party numbered between fifty and sixty men, all mounted on horses or mules, and armed with rifles. Most of them had each a powder-horn or a flask, a large leathern pouch for bullets hung at his side, and buckled close to his body with a leathern belt, in which hung a scabbard of the same material, bearing a "scalping-knife," that savage weapon whose very name is a terror. The mules and horses altogether were over one hundred and fifty. Nearly one-third were for the men, and about two-thirds carried packs, each man leading two of them. Mr. J. Lee, besides the five horses to ride, one for each person with him, and four to pack, took some cows, and two of them made the journey to Oregon. Their milk was quite a luxury on the way.

Captain Wyeth, who headed the party, had a gentleman of Boston, Captain Thyng, for his assistant. Two naturalists were also in company, Mr. Townsend, of Philadelphia, and Mr. Nuttall, the gentleman mentioned in a preceding chapter, who accompanied Mr. Hunt some way up the Missouri in 1811. His characteristic ardour in his favourite pursuit had not been lessened by the lapse of three and twenty years. Our encampments were generally near some stream of water, where there was good grass for our animals; and our tents, eight in number, were pitched in a circular form, enclosing a space large enough to contain all our horses and mules, fastened to pickets. These are sticks more than a foot long and two inches wide, one for every horse or mule. They are driven into the ground, and are designed to prevent the escape of the animals in case of any sudden attempt of the Indians to frighten them away. A regular guard was kept up, and relieved every four hours during the night; and when the horses were without the camp feeding, morning and evening, a watch was set near them. One night, before we reached the Kanzas Indians, who are located seven days' journey from Independence, from some unknown cause our horses took fright, and many of them being loose within the camp, we not having yet come to the dangerous country, they rushed out and bounded off at full speed into the plain. Instantly some of the men mounted other horses and pursued the fugitives, whose tramping was heard in the distance. They soon overtook them, and one rode ahead as a leader, who gradually turned them in a long circuitous sweep, heading them toward the camp, where they soon arrived with them in safety, dissipating the busy fears of an anxious hour, and shedding a smile of satisfaction on every face. We generally travelled about twenty miles a day, halting near noon to bait and take dinner, and encamping early to give our animals time to fill themselves without the camp before dusk, when they were all brought within, where they remained till morning; then the cry, "Turn out!" was heard from Captain Wyeth. Soon the horses were seen without, and the breakfast fires before the tents. Each of the eight messes into which the company was divided, embraced from five to eight persons a-piece. Fried bacon and dough fried in the fat, with tea or coffee, made our meal; around which we sat on the ground in good Indian style, and braced up our craving stomachs for the toils of day. Each mess now prepared to move: tents were struck, packs and saddles put in order. "Catch up!" cried Captain Wyeth, and the whole camp was instantly in motion to gather the animals, pack up, mount, and away. Captain W. led the way, and Captain Thyng brought up the rear. The country over which we travelled to the Kanzas River, and thence to the Platte, is very beautiful, and most of it has a rich soil. It is a kind of rolling prairie, in some parts thinly wooded with oak, and, along its rivulets, fringed with the cotton-wood or balm of Gilead.

The Kanzas Indians are remarkable for shaving their heads: otherwise they have fine forms; their foreheads, in particular, are high and well developed. We encamped a night near one of their villages, where we were greatly annoyed by their ravenous dogs, which were attracted to our tents by the hope of a good meal at our expense. They were but too successful, for the next morning we found they had robbed us of a large share of our bacon, for which we could get no satisfaction.

Leaving the Kanzas we reached the Platte in thirteen days, past the middle of May, and pursued our course on the south side above the junction of the Forks. The Platte, as its name implies, is very shallow, and in some places more than a mile wide. The bottom is a quicksand, and in fording, it is necessary to keep in motion to prevent sinking. The water has a whitish appearance, and a thick sediment will deposite itself in a vessel in which it stands. The banks are low, and a level bottom, covered generally with grass, extends a mile, more or less, on either side, terminated by hills. The country is destitute of timber. The beautiful antelope inhabits this region, and its flesh made a considerable part of our supply of food to the Forks of the Platte, the *border* of the buffalo range. The buffaloes have a stately appearance. Their shaggy heads, necks, and high humps above their shoulders, declining back to their tails, with their great size, give them an awkward and terrific aspect, that might awe a stranger and prevent his approach. They will "show fight" in self-defence when wounded and hard pushed by the hunters. They are fleet on a race, and it is a good horse that can beat them on a long one. Their flesh is excellent, equal, if not superior, to the best beef, and has long supplied the surrounding Indians and the white trappers with the means of supporting life in a region otherwise uninhabitable. They are diminishing rapidly; but yet immense herds of many thousands range from the Forks of the Platte to the head waters of the Lewis River, over a tract extending far north and south of the general thoroughfare to Oregon. Crossing the south fork of the Platte, Captain Wyeth led his company in a north-west direction to the north fork, which he was to follow to the base of the Rocky Mountains. The Black Hills lifted their summits to the north-west on our right. Having crossed the north fork, we left the river, whose course had been our guide for sixteen days, and proceeding westward, we reached the Sweet Water, one of its small tributaries, at Rock Independence, June 8th. This is a vast block of granite, covering from one to three acres, and rising some twenty or thirty feet above the ground. A fourth of July being once observed here by a party of traders, they gave the rock the name it now bears. In the year 1842, as a party of emigrants were passing this rock, two gentlemen tarried behind the main body to cut their initials upon it. For this purpose they set by their rifles, and were busily engaged in making themselves immortal, by leaving their humble representatives on this grand portal of the Rocky Mountains—when, in the midst of their labour, they were suddenly surprised by a large party of Indians, who seized their rifles and horses, and then made them prisoners. Some of the party seemed determined to kill them on the spot, but were prevented by the authority of their chief. After learning that the party to which they belonged had gone on up the Sweet Water, they dashed forward on the trail, and soon overtook them; but before this, their approach had been discovered, and the party had thrown itself into as good a posture of defence as they possibly could. When the Indians had come within a short distance, they made a halt, and a few, leaving the main body, went forward into the space between, and held a parley with some of the whites, which resulted in the restoration of their prisoners, and a peaceable separation—the Indians to the chase, and the emigrants to their journey. From Rock Independence, Capt. W. pursued his way several days up the Sweet Water, crossing it many times, its steep banks compelling him to take sometimes one side and then the other of its zigzag course. This stream cuts the Rocky Mountains, and opens through them a highway to Oregon. Some of their snowy tops are seen to the south. Leaving the Sweet Water, we soon came to the Big Sandy, a branch of the Colorado which flows into the Gulf of California, to which we arrived soon after, and crossing it, proceeding still westward, we came to Hain Fork, one of the tributaries, *eleven* days from Rock Independence, June 19th, and here we rendezvoused.

CHAPTER XI.

Rendezvous—Description of country—Hunting and battle ground of the Indians—The party take up their line of march—Soda Spring—Erect a fort—Procure buffalo meat—Accident—Fort Hall sold to Hudson's Bay Company—Missionaries join another party—Description of country and of Indians—Blue Mountains—Travellers arrive at Fort Wallah-wallah—Summary of travel—Arrive at Vancouver—Location for mission selected.

This was the "rendezvous" of the trappers and traders this year. Here we rested twelve days to recruit our jaded animals. Here is the proper place to insert a brief description of the surrounding region.

The soil in the valley of the Colorado, or, as it is generally called at this place, Green River, is good; and grass is quite abundant; but the temperature is too low for the purposes of cultivation. Snow-capped peaks and naked hills rise in boundless masses around you on every side, the birth-place of the great rivers, that hold in their arms our continent. We are still within the great slaughter-house, where the white and red butchers of the buffalo have dealt death with the rifle and the bow, a thousand miles on every hand, whitening the valleys and the plains with the bones of myriads whose tread once made the desert earth groan beneath their ponderous weight. This region has not only been the hunting-ground of a hundred tribes of red men; but their great battle-field, on which they have wielded the tomahawk, and sped the arrow into the head and heart of many a foe, whose blood has reddened the parched earth, and whose scalps have been born away in diabolical triumph. Are they indeed the sons of Ishmael, that their hand must be against every man? When will their bloody strife end? When Christianity enters. Without that, contention will continue, and only end in extermination!

The Colorado, which runs south to its junction with Grand River, a tributary rising near the source of the south fork of the Platte, two hundred and eighty miles in length, flows thence south-west, seven hundred miles, to the Gulf of California, being navigable only thirty miles from its mouth. It is said that two Catholic missionaries once attempted to descend this river, and have never been heard of since; and that a party of trappers adventured so far down its deep dark chasm as to endanger their lives, and it was with the greatest difficulty that they extricated themselves from their almost hopeless dilemma. Early in the month of July, having been in camp twelve days, we left our retreat in the Valley of Green River, and took up our line of march again westward to the waters of Bear River, which empties into the Salt Lake, lying to the south-west. The country is hilly, soil poor, and timber scarce We followed the river several days, as far as the Soda Spring. This is the wonder of every visitor. This spring is on the north-west side of Bear River, twenty rods from the shore, and has some half a dozen openings, from *five* to *eight* feet over. The water is clear, and the escape of the gas through it keeps it boiling with a noise that can be heard several yards. Its taste resembles that of the soda-water in the shops. They have no visible outlet, but seem to have a subterraneous connection with the river. Some distance below is an intermitting spring, which throws out water violently from an opening in a rock in such a manner as to have received the appropriate name of Steamboat. Between these two springs, along the surface of the river, the water is continually agitated by the large quantities of gas escaping through it; and it ought to be also stated, that the water of the last spring described is also strongly impregnated with soda, and has a temperature of ninety degrees. The surrounding soil and grass are good. Here we left Bear River, and a few days' march brought us to one of the branches of Snake River, Ross's Fork. Some small trouts were caught here, and were a welcome exchange for dried buffalo meat, which had been our chief food many days. This is the western border of the present buffalo range, where we emerge from the mountains, and begin our descent to the Pacific. Nearly forty days had been consumed in the journey over them, and though the most dangerous part of the way, no enemy assailed our camp, and no evil was suffered to approach us. About the middle of July, Capt. Wyeth arrived at the Snake River, and after selecting a site for a fort, a part of his men were employed in its erection, and the rest went out on a buffalo hunt to procure the necessary supplies of meat for the rest of the journey. Messrs. Edwards and Walker made a part of this party. After being absent about two weeks, they returned with a good stock of dried meat, and diffused joy through the whole camp. Soon after our arrival at this place, Mr. Thomas M'Kay, having a trading party under his command, in the employ of the Hudson's Bay Company, came upon our trail, and soon reached the camp of Capt. W. It gave us great pleasure to meet a friend in a stranger, in such a place. Mr. Jason Lee preached once on the sabbath in a grove near his camp, and he very generously made a present of a sack of flour to the missionaries, which was a very seasonable and unexpected relief; and when they left Fort Hall, he was with them several days' journey. On the evening of the day that Mr. Lee preached, one of Mr. M'Kay's men, a Canadian, as he was riding very fast, was rode against by another man, and so badly injured as to die in a short time. He was buried near the fort. He left several children, two of whom are in the Oregon mission school in the Walamet, and one, Lizette Carponca, resides in Lansingville in the state of New-York. This gentleman is the son of Mr. M'Kay who fell in the Tonquin on the north-west coast in 1810. While at Fort Hall, one of the Kinse Indians in Mr. M'Kay's party made a present of a horse to Mr. Jason Lee, and from him received some present in turn. The horse was very serviceable in performing the rest of the journey, as some of the horses with which we set out were quite "used up." An extensive plain covered with grass, and intersected with creeks, and pure mountain rivulets, surrounds Fort Hall, stretching many miles along the river, and several miles back to the distant hills on the south. This establishment did not long remain in the possession of its original proprietors, but was sold to the Hudson's Bay Company, and the whole enterprise, to which Capt. Wyeth had devoted himself for four or five years, with great ardour and perseverance, and at an expensive outlay, from which very little profits were realized, was abandoned, and the whole fur trade reverted again to the Hudson's Bay Company.

Leaving Fort Hall about the 1st of August, and Captain Wyeth to complete the structure, and then to follow us with the two naturalists and part of his men, some of them being left in charge of the fort, we took up again our line of march, and proceeded down the south side of Snake River.

Our new party consisted of Mr. M'Kay, his Canadians, with their bows and arrows, wives, mounted in the fashionable native style, astride, and bearing muskets, and their children confined to a board, and hung on the horn of their saddles, or lashed on horseback alone, and some Indians with their squaws and children, in the same order: an English half-pay officer, Captain Stuart, with his servants, who had been some time roaming in the mountains, was also of the party. In this way we went on a few days through sandy plains, with scarcely sufficient grass for our horses, toiling through immense tracts of mountain sage, or, more properly, wormwood, an ugly shrub from two to six feet high. Mr. M'Kay remained in the Snake country to trap and trade beaver, where we parted from him; and with some of the Indians of his party, and Captain Stuart, pursued our way down the river, and on its banks we made frequent encampments. We saw occasionally a few Indians engaged in catching salmon. For some of these we gave them fish-hooks in exchange, on which they appeared to set a high value. They appeared very poor, almost naked. The Snake Indians are reputed friendly to the whites. The country is generally hilly, in some parts mountainous, with some rich intervening plains, and beautiful valleys. Considerable timber crowns the more elevated portions. Hot days, cold nights, and a remarkably dry atmosphere are characteristics here. Before reaching the Blue Mountains, we crossed a long, wide, rich plain, led by the Kinse Indian who presented the horse to Mr. Jason Lee at Fort Hall, to a village of his tribe situated on a small branch of the Snake River, which rises in the eastern part of those mountains. Their dwellings were lodges made of the skins of the buffalo deprived of the hair, and then made soft, and several of them sewed together. They are set up in the form of a cone, around a number of long smooth poles, used as a kind of frame. Their width on the ground, and their height, are about twelve feet, with an opening at the top to permit the smoke to escape, and to admit the light. These are taken with them in their migrations. Here we were content to pass the night, and the hospitality shown us was worthy their pretensions as a governing tribe, and their acknowledged superiority by the tribes around them. Presents of horses were made by some of the chiefs to Mr. Jason Lee, and one was presented to the writer by "Tee-lon-kike," one of the leading men in the tribe. In return for these, small presents of such goods as we had left of our mountain outfit were made to the donors, not as an equivalent, but as an acknowledgment of our confidence in their friendship, and a seal of our good-will to them. Passing on from this grass-clad plain, we soon reached the Blue Mountains, over whose high and rugged summits lay our trail to the valley of the Columbia. The new accession of fresh horses from the Indian camp was favourable to the remainder of our journey. Fires were crackling among the mountain evergreens, and smoke hid from our view the extended landscape, otherwise delightfully beheld around us, while we wound our zigzag way upward to the height, and down its dizzy sides, and crept along its dark rocky chasms, two toilsome days, till we came to the vale of the Um-a-til-a. Here we quenched our thirst, and the horses got a bite of grass. Leaving this stream we rose to the divide on the north side, which lies between it and the Wallah-wallah River, and pursued our way toward Fort Wallah-wallah, where we arrived in safety Monday afternoon, September 1st.

The summary of the distance, and the time occupied in the whole journey, may be stated as follows, which will be very near the truth:—

From Independence, Mo., to the Platte,	17 days,	340 miles.
On the Platte, - - - - -	14 "	280 "
From the Platte to rendezvous near Gun River, - - - - -	15 "	300 "
From the rendezvous to Fort Hall, -	12 "	240 "
From Fort Hall to Fort Wallah-wallah,	30 "	600 "
Independence to Fort Hall,	88 days,	1760 miles.

This estimate allows thirty-nine days' rest, and twenty miles for a day's journey.

Here we received a hearty welcome to the hospitalities of the fort by Mr. P. C. Pamburn, who was in charge of the establishment. Abundance of food was liberally supplied to his hungry visiters, who regaled themselves once more in the midst of plenty, and soon forgot their past privations, even their last day's march on an empty stomach. Scarcely had this capacious band finished their lengthened meal, when Captain Wyeth, Mr. Nuttall, and Mr. Townsend made their appearance at our camp, hungry as wolves. Part of a kettle of stewed rabit was standing by, which being given to the two naturalists, they showed off the way to get a living to perfection. Captain W. availed himself of the politeness of Mr. Pamburn at the fort.

Sept. 3d. Having left our horses and cattle here, we took our leave of Mr. Pamburn, and embarked in a boat of the Hudson's Bay Company for Vancouver, where, after a tedious voyage of twelve days, we arrived on the 15th. Meantime, we had heard of the safe arrival of the Maydacre, Captain Lambert, and that she was lying in the Columbia, near the lower mouth of the Walamet River. This intelligence was very gratifying to us all. At Fort Vancouver the missionaries were received with much politeness and kind attention by the chief factor, John M'Laughlin, Esq., and other gentlemen of the establishment. Leaving Messrs. Shepard, Edwards, and Walker, at Vancouver, for the time being, Mr. Jason Lee and myself started for the Walamet Valley to find a location for our mission, taking the Maydacre in our route. Dr. M'Laughlin kindly furnished two men to go with us, and horses to ride, and a good supply of provisions for the whole trip, which would employ us several days.

Arrangements being made, we embarked in a canoe and proceeded down the Columbia to the Maydacre, twenty miles; then up the west channel of the Walamet some way, and after that, up a small creek, arriving at a farm owned by Mr. Thomas M'Kay, our friend in the mountains. Here we obtained the requisite number of horses, and hastened on to the Walamet settlement, passing through what is now called the Tualatine Plain, a high, extended ridge, intervening between it and M'Kay's farm, where we took horses. This is a beautiful, rich, extensive, gently-rolling prairie, well watered, and in some parts well timbered. Beyond this we passed a delightful hilly tract several miles in extent, thinly wooded at intervals, and then open, and covered with grass. Descending from these by a gentle grade, we came to Che-ha-lim, a valley that stretches away east to the Walamet. Reaching the river at this place, we swam our horses and crossed to the east side, where the settlement had been commenced. Along the river we found about a dozen families, mostly French Canadians, who had been hunters in the service of the Hudson's Bay Company, or free trappers, and had very lately left that employment and begun to farm, that themselves and families might have a surer support and greater security than they could while following the hazardous life of hunters. They seemed prosperous and happy, and gave us a very polite and generous welcome to the best they could set before us. One night Mr. Gervais set up our tent in his garden, among melons and cucumbers. It reminded one of the scripture, "A lodge in a garden of cucumbers."

About two miles above Mr. Gervais's, on the east bank of the river, and sixty miles from its mouth, a location was chosen to commence our mission. Here was a broad, rich bottom, many miles in length, well watered, and supplied with timber, oak, fir, cotton-wood, white maple, and white ash, scattered along the borders of its grassy plains, where hundreds of acres were ready for the plough. We now hastened back to Vancouver, obtained horses of the company in exchange for those we had left at Wallah-wallah, and oxen and cows in loan ; men to drive the cattle to the place, and a boat and crew to transport our supplies. Taking in our cargo at the Maydacre, we ascended the west channel of the Walamet, opposite to Mr. M'Kay's farm, when Mr. Jason Lee and Mr. Walker went on with the boat, and Mr. Edwards and myself went to the farm to take charge of the horses which had been obtained from the company, and bring them through to the Walamet. We had left the river but a short distance when we came to a pond that lay across our way, which was connected with the river by deep slues. The water was shallow and the bottom muddy. We ventured in, and as we approached the middle, the mire deepened so much that we found it required a hard pull to get our feet off soundings. Having conquered these oppositions, we measured off a mile through the high wet grass to the farm, where we were received with a hearty French welcome by Monsieur Le Bonté. Next day we started with the horses to the Walamet, by the same route taken by Mr. Jason Lee and myself on our first visit, the son of Le Bonté, Louis, going with us. We struck the river at the lower part of the settlement called Campment du Sable, that is, " Sandy Encampment." The Indian name is Chumpoeg. Here we met the voyageurs in canoes, which they had taken at the Walamet Falls in place of their boat. Mr. Jason Lee now went on by land, while Mr. Edwards and myself embarked in the canoes. A few miles brought us to swift water, which continued at short intervals for many miles far above the mission. Forcing our way up the current about sixteen miles, we reached our destination and ended our voyage on the 6th of October. The cattle, eight oxen and ten cows, had also arrived in safety. Mr. Shepard remained at Fort Vancouver, the state of his health rendering it necessary for him to avoid the hardship and exposure attending the erection of a house at this season, the nights being damp and chilly, and the rains at hand. While here, however, he was not idle; but devoted himself to his favourite employment, teaching a small school in the fort that had been commenced under the patronage of Dr. M'Laughlin some time before. The three shipwrecked Japanese, mentioned in a preceding chapter, were among his pupils. In this service he continued till the next spring, and then came to the aid of his fellow-labourers in the Walamet.

CHAPTER XII.

Claims of the Flathead Indians not sufficient to induce the missionaries to establish a mission among them—Mission commenced on the Walamet—Description of the incipient labours of the missionaries—A party from California arrives—Indian youth left with the missionaries to be instructed—A party of whites, who had been attacked by the Indians, arrives at the mission—Intermittent fever—Mr. Nuttall, the naturalist—Death of a trapper, and addition to the mission family—Mr. D. Lee embarks for the Sandwich Islands for the improvement of his health.

In treating of the occasion in which the Oregon mission originated, it was shown that the supposed claim of the Flathead Indians on the first missionary efforts made in the country were unfounded; and subsequent inquiries had furnished reasons to the missionaries that could not justify even the attempt to commence their mission among them. 1. The means of subsistence in a region so remote and so difficult of access, were, to say the least, very doubtful. It was not a small matter to transport all necessary implements and tools to build houses and raise our provisions six hundred miles. 2. The smallness of their number. Their perpetual wars with the Blackfeet Indians had prevented their increase; and they were, for their safety, confederated with the Nez Percés. 3. Their vicinity to the Blackfeet, as well the white man's enemy as theirs, and who would fall upon the abettors of their foes with signal revenge. 4. A larger field of usefulness was contemplated as the object of the mission than the benefiting of a single tribe. The wants of the whole country, present and prospective, so far as they could be, were taken into the account, and the hope of meeting these wants, in the progress of their work, led to the choice of the Walamet location, as a starting point, a place to stand on, and the centre of a wide circle of benevolent action. Here any amount of supplies could be produced from the soil that might be required in the enlargement of the work; and here the first blow was struck by the pioneer missionaries in Oregon; and here they began their arduous and difficult toil to elevate and save the heathen from moral degradation and ruin.

The rainy season was fast approaching, and a house was wanted to shelter us when it arrived. But first we had to prepare our tools, and gear our oxen. We handled axes and augurs, hung a grind stone, split rails, made yokes and bows for the oxen, and made a yard to catch them in, for some of them were not half tamed, and then to yoke them—" ay, there's the rub"—our wits, and ropes, physical might, all took hold—no flinching, no backing out. When we had succeeded in this, then came the all-day business of driving them. Men never worked harder and performed less. Our house advanced but slowly, and we were caught in one violent storm of wind and rain, which was near drenching all we had, the tent which we occupied being but a poor protection. When it cleared away, the wet articles were taken out and carefully dried. Before the next storm came on we had a roof on a part of our house, and a piece of floor laid, on which we could lie thankfully secure from the pelting storm without. A few weeks, all the time hard at it, and the roof was completed; a good chimney made of sticks and clay, and a fire-place in one end; floors laid of plank split from the fir, and hewn on the upper side; doors procured in the same way, and hung on wooden hinges. Then a table, then stools, and finally the luxury of chairs added to our self-made comforts. Our good mansion was built of logs, twenty by thirty feet, divided into two apartments by a partition across the middle, and lighted by four small windows, the sashes partly made by Mr. Jason Lee with his jack-knife. As to a living, we had brought a supply of flour from Vancouver, and made unleavened cakes, baked before the fire, and from the settlers we bought some peas, which, with the pork we had sent along in our outfit from Boston, made good soup, to which was sometimes added a small quantity of barley. The cows also furnished a little milk, and from the Indians we sometimes obtained a bit of venison. Before our house was done, a party, headed by Mr. Ewing Young, an American from one of the western United States, arrived in the Walamet from California, embracing about a dozen persons, most of them from the United States. Some of them had been sailors, some hunters in the mountains and in the region bordering on California to the south, and one Mr. Kelly was a traveller, a New-England man, who entertained some very extravagant notions in regard to Oregon, which he published on his return. On their way they had encountered some hostile Indians, but nothing occurred to them of a very serious nature, and they all reached their destination in safety. To provide for our support in future, a farm was soon begun, rails made, and a field of thirty acres enclosed and ploughed, and the next spring planted and sowed. Potatoes, corn, wheat, oats, and garden seeds were put in. About this time Mr. Walker's time was out, and he left the service of the mission, and found employment as a clerk in one of the establishments of Captain Wyeth, at Fort William, on Multnomah Island. Mr. Shepard had now joined us from Vancouver. A man of the Californian party, an American, Ezekiel by name, built us a good pair of cart-wheels, the first that were made in the Walamet. A barn being needed to cover the returns of the farm, we set to work to erect one of logs, thirty by forty feet. Mr. J. Lee, Mr. Edwards, Rora, an old Islander from the Pacific, and John Calapooya, a boy of that tribe, with myself, shouldered our axes. The trees fell before us, and soon the timber appeared together on the spot.

After we had proceeded about half way in laying it up, we found it necessary to have more help, and called on our neighbours for assistance, who very kindly lent a hand to finish it. We then proceeded to the roof,—split shingles, four feet long, and confined them on the building by laying a heavy weight pole on each course, against which the butts of the next higher course were placed. This way of making a good roof without nails is common in the west and in Oregon. Having hired two of the men that came from California, to saw some plank and boards, doors and a floor were soon added, and thus the barn was finished.

While we were engaged in planting in the spring, a party of the Umbaqua Indians called on us, and one of them, named "Joe," known to the Canadian trappers, left a small lad with us, to be instructed in religion, and taught to labour; and a Killemook Indian, a friend of his, also left a boy of his tribe under our care, for the same purpose. This last one was very discontented, not inclined to work, or learn to read; and might often be seen on the bank of the river, gazing west with a tearful eye toward the sea-washed shore, where he was once free, and longed to regain it once more. It was not long till his people came to see him, and the sad tale of his exile which he told them, induced them to remove him, contrary to their engagement.

The Umbaqua boy was, on the other hand, docile and industrious; but our cherished hopes in him were soon cut off, for about midsummer he died of a consumption. But previously a messenger had been sent to notify his relations of his danger, that they might come and see him before his death, and that they might have no occasion for jealousy in case of his decease. However, some days before they came, he was dead. They gathered around his grave, and remained some time wailing aloud; but they appeared to be satisfied that everything had been done well on our part on his behalf; and, after a friendly parting, they returned again to their own country. John, the Kalapooya just mentioned, and his sister, named Lucy Hedding, orphans, had also been taken in the preceding winter. He did not remain long with us; but she, who was a subject of scrofulous disease, lingered along about two years, and then died. Another lad of the same tribe came to us in the winter, hungry and almost naked, and begged to be taken in, and we could not refuse to receive him; but as soon as the warm weather came, and there was some work called for, and a little submission required, he was off into the plains, free as a bird escaped from its cage. O self-control! how art thou loved; thy favours and thy votaries are found everywhere!

This summer, a small party of whites, who were coming through from California, were attacked by the Indians who inhabit south of the Umbaquas, and but narrowly escaped with their lives. Robbed and wounded, they made their way through to the settlement. Turner, an American, and his native wife, one of the daughters of the land, worn out by their long and hungry tramp, came to the river, where they resolved to adopt a new mode of transporting their famine-smitten personages. So, forming a rude raft, they committed themselves to the current, and at length landed at the mission. Here they were gladly received, and supplied with food; and Turner's story of their disastrous journey was heard with deep interest. The rest of the party, who had pursued their way by land, had not yet arrived, and what their fate had been remained for the future to reveal. After some days of painful anxiety, two others reached the mission, almost in a state of starvation. Their food had been little else than a few berries they chanced to meet in their way, as they dragged along their husky forms where miles seemed leagues, till they struck the trail, the Indian path which led them to the river. The welcome sight of cattle on the other side assured them that relief was not distant. One of them attempted to swim over, but was too weak to proceed far, and returned again to the shore, which he was only able to regain by the assistance of his companion. It was not long before they were discovered, and a canoe was sent to their rescue. Poor men! they had seen better days, and now they saw another: as the sun to the storm-tossed mariner, so joyous was this day to those remnants of men, snatched from the jaws of famine! One of them, Dr. Bailey, had been educated a surgeon. In the engagement with the Indians he received a deep cut with an axe in his lower jaw, which severed his lip. It was a bad wound, and having necessarily been mostly left to take its own course, was in a bad condition. On reaching the house they were liberally supplied with water and with food, and the writer had the honour to perform the office of a "barber" and a "surgeon" to the doctor's long-neglected face! Another of the poor stragglers kept more to the west, and went the whole length of the Walamet Valley, *sixty* miles below the mission, and reached Fort William.

In the month of August, in the time of harvest, the intermittent fever began to shake its burning, freezing subjects. One and then another was prostrated, till not one escaped in the whole household; but through the kindness of our heavenly Father, the disease soon yielded to the power of medicine. The missionaries had preached regularly on the sabbath ever since their arrival at the house of Mr. Gervais, a near neighbour, and those meetings were also continued some time after till 1837, when they were removed to the mission house. Besides this meeting, another was occasionally held at "Campment du Sable." A sabbath school was early begun where the meeting was held, and Mr. G.'s own children and some others attended. He had also a teacher employed who kept a day school for his own children. This was Mr. Solomon H. Smith, formerly of Boston, who came to Oregon with Capt. Wyeth in 1832. Mr. Nuttall, the *"grass man,"* as the Indians term a botanist, visited the settlement and spent some time at the mission about midsummer: we were much gratified with his visit. Seeing him gathering flowers and plants appeared to the Canadians no less idle and foolish, and a subject of merriment, now, than when he accompanied Mr. Hunt up the Missouri River in 1811.

About the 1st of September one of the settlers, Louis Shangaratte, formerly a trapper in the service of the Hudson's Bay Company, burst a blood vessel in the lungs, and died almost immediately. He left three orphan children, and four or five poor Indian slaves. Of this family, and the little property that fell to the heirs, Dr. M'Laughlin earnestly desired Mr. Jason Lee to take charge. To this proposal he assented; but in that moment the enslaved must be free, and in the mission equal with those they once served. This accession greatly increased the mission family, and the care and labour of the missionaries. Two of the number, youngsters, desiring yet more liberty, soon eloped, which was some relief, in a case where there was so little to hope. Some others, including one of the children of the deceased Louis, died in a short time, the victims of diseases of a date earlier than their reception at the mission. Only three were now left of this family, and one of these died in 1837 with the scrofula. Another child, taken into the mission not long after, was a little girl of the Calapooya tribe, named Lassee. Her father was a man far gone in years, and fast sinking in a decline. The lodge where the chieftain lay was distant more than a mile. A short time before his death, his little daughter was carried to see him: it was the last interview. A father's love appeared in his tears, and he caressed his "little one," endearingly exclaiming, "*Ni-kah ten-as! ni-kah ten-as!*" "My little one! my little one!" An eye witness of that scene saw demonstrations of the existence of ardent parental and filial love in untutored and unenlightened hearts, seldom surpassed in those on whom the light of science and religion had formed its influence. The thought that his orphan child was provided for in the care of those who by many attentions had proved themselves his friends, seemed to throw a cheerful light around him while he descended into his grave, as he did soon after. The daughter also died in a short time, before she could derive much benefit from being at the mission, except in the care she received in her sickness. Perhaps some may exclaim, "How discouraging, that so many taken in should die so soon!" In answer to this it may be asked, Who can affirm that the good done to these in relieving their sufferings the while was not a large compensation for all the sacrifice it cost?

This year a grist mill was built at Champoeg by Mr. Hanxhurst, which greatly added to the comfort of the inhabitants; who had previously, some of them, to pound their wheat in mortars. At the mission we had a small cast-iron corncracker, in which we ground wheat after a fashion, and a large wooden mortar, holding about a bushel, in which was pounded off the hull of the barley used in soup.

About the beginning of autumn an event quite unexpected took place, which removed the writer from the mission nearly a whole year. Having suffered some time from a diseased state of the upper portion of the windpipe, which affected the mucous membrane so much as to cause portions of it to slough off, which were evacuated by an irritating and frequent expectoration, attended with pain and soreness in the chest, particularly about the heart, it was thought advisable that he should go to Vancouver for medical counsel. Accordingly, in the early part of September he left the Walamet station for that purpose, and proceeded on horseback to Fort William, in company with Mr. Edwards, who was intending soon to leave the country, in a vessel going to the Sandwich Islands. On reaching Vancouver, the writer applied to Dr. M'Laughlin for the desired information in his case, and of the course to be pursued in order to ensure relief, or at least render recovery probable. The chill nights of autumn had already come, and the long rains of winter were near at hand, and the season unfavourable to his restoration. To avoid the dangers of the climate here, Dr. M'L. advised him to go to the Sandwich Islands, where the climate was better adapted to the improvement of pulmonary disease, as the most likely means to prove beneficial. One of the Hudson Bay Company's vessels was then in the river, about to sail to the Islands, and Dr. M'L. kindly offered him a passage, gratis, and to render every other assistance in his power, which his visit to the Islands might demand. In the way of accepting these very generous provisions there were some difficulties. He must leave the mission at a time when his help was much needed, without the direction, or counsel, or knowledge of his superintendent. It was a hard resolve. The vessel had unmoored, and was dropping down the river. To remain seemed to promise, in his state of health, very little good to the mission, while it was attended with great risk to health, if not life. He therefore determined to avail himself of the favourable opportunity now presented, and accordingly embarked for the Islands, having by letter informed his fellow-labourers at the Walamet of the step he had taken; and here we will leave them till his return.

CHAPTER XIII.

Voyage to the Sandwich Islands—Sea sickness—Arrival—Mr. Lee is cordially received by missionaries—Their mission—Arrival of a Quaker missionary from London—Return of Mr. Lee—Loss of a ship's crew—State of affairs at the mission during Mr. Lee's absence—Temperance Society formed—Mr. Lee engages in medical practice—Provision for mission family—First conversion of a white man in Oregon.

THE company's vessel in which he sailed was the bark Ganymede, Captain Eales. She dropped down the river, and in a few days was lying in Baker's Bay, waiting, as was also another of the company's vessels, bound to England, for a favourable opportunity to cross the bar. Mr. Nuttall was also passenger, going again to the Islands, where he had already made one voyage since our arrival here in 1834, to prosecute still further his scientific pursuits, particularly in the collection of shells and birds. Here we did not wait long, which was a particular favour, as sometimes vessels are detained here for weeks, the angry waters on the bar confining them in their safe retreat: but now they bore an inviting aspect, the seamen weighed anchor, made sail, and put to sea, the faithful helm directing our course mid-channel between the tremendous breakers on either hand. With what an awful power has the Creator armed these mighty waters—yet hath he set bounds that they cannot pass; yea, he holdeth the ocean in the hollow of his hand! To Capt. Eales the writer is much indebted for his obliging and gentlemanly regard during the whole voyage, which on account of a continued sea-sickness was otherwise sufficiently disagreeable. Perhaps there is nothing of disease from which so little real danger is in most cases to be apprehended that so unmans a man as this. It seems to prostrate as well the mental as physical powers, producing an inactivity and listlessness, yet when not too long continued it is often beneficial and improving to health.

On reaching Oahu, the particular island of the group to which the vessel was bound, we came to anchor in the harbour of Honolulu, the principal town not only of this isle, but of all the group, the resort of many of the whalers in the Pacific for the purpose of obtaining supplies of fresh provisions, which grow here in abundance; and also the residence of several merchants, who used formerly to obtain large quantities of sandal wood for the Chinese market, which article has now become scarce, and is of less value than formerly. Perhaps the votaries of the idols of the "Celestial Empire" have an extra supply to burn in incense to them. Here also is the frequent residence of the "royal family." The present king is the grandson of Ta-mahá-mahá I., the conqueror, who subdued the nation to his sway, and the son of Reho-roho, who, in 1820, when the first missionaries were on their way to evangelize his people, destroyed the idols throughout his dominion, unconsciously preparing the way for the servants of God. Some time subsequently he and his queen visited England, and died.

By Mr. Bingham and his associates, the missionaries, and Mr. Deill, the seamen's chaplain, the writer was received on his arrival with Christian salutations and a generous welcome, which made him feel himself to be among friends, where he soon forgot the disagreeables of the voyage in the enjoyment of the society which he loved. And he will not soon forget the repeated proofs of their kind and sympathizing regard, when, "sick and a stranger," his lot was thrown among them. May peace and success attend them still in their good work among the heathen, and may the writer meet them in a world of rest! At this time, November, 1835, the Bible was nearly translated, and a printing-press was multiplying copies of the Scriptures, which were circulated extensively, and read with great avidity by many, both old and young, who by the efforts of the missionaries had learned to read. There were at that time about twelve stations, and more than twenty-five labourers, besides the ladies employed in the various branches of their missionary work. A high-school, designed to qualify teachers and native preachers, was in progress, and an institution of considerable promise. Soon after my arrival a small vessel dropped anchor in the harbour, which was found to be the bearer of a Quaker missionary, sent out from London on a five years' exploring tour. He was a man advanced in life, his name was Daniel Wheeler, and he was attended by his son Charles. The writer has since learned that they returned in safety to England, where the father has since died. An account of this voyage has been published.—During my visit here my health was much benefited: some donations were also received from the native Christians and other friends, for the use of the Oregon Mission. And in August, 1836, taking leave of my friends at Honolulu, and bidding them farewell, the writer embarked in the bark Nereid, belonging to the Hudson's Bay Company, Capt. Royal, and sailed for the Columbia River. Here the writer was introduced to a clergyman of the Church of England, Mr. H. Beaver, who was going to reside at Fort Vancouver, as chaplain to the company. He was attended by his lady. After a safe but somewhat lengthened passage, we made Cape Disappointment; and the wind falling off, we let go anchor to the northward of the channel, without the north breakers, in ten fathoms water. Next day, the wind and bar favouring, we soon entered the river, and came to anchor, thankful for the care of that kind and watchful Providence which had brought us to our "desired haven." Little did any of our number think that at a time not far distant two of the crew then in our vessel would sleep the sleep of death, beneath the bosom of the smooth waters that spread out their unruffled surface between us and Fort George; that there they would lay their bones, by the side of a score of their comrades whom the deep had buried beneath us! But so it was: for some time after, the next year, it is believed, one of the Hudson Bay Company's ships was at anchor here, on the point of going to sea, and the captain (Holmes) took a boat and four seamen, and started for Fort George, distant seven miles. Next day the boat was discovered by the mast standing above the water, but of the hapless crew no trace was found. The boat was sunk in about twelve feet water. A mere circumstance prevented a passenger, Capt. Thyng, the gentleman before mentioned as being with Capt. Wyeth when we crossed the mountains, from being among the dead. Capt. Holmes had asked him to go, but when he embarked himself seemed to have entirely forgotten it, and left without noticing Capt. T. at all; and this kept him on board the vessel, and thus he escaped with his life.

Mr. and Mrs. Beaver took up their residence at Vancouver, where he officiated till the summer of 1838, when they returned to England. However, the English Church service is regularly performed here, except when a minister is present, in which event his services are generally invited. Since Mr. Beaver left, this has been the order, and it was the same before his arrival. Soon after reaching Vancouver, Mr. J. Lee arrived from the Walamet, which was an agreeable surprise to his friend, who was expecting to make a journey to that place before the pleasure of such an interview. To Captain

Royal the thanks of the writer were due for his obliging attentions on the voyage; and to Dr. M'Laughlin for the aid rendered to the writer in this voyage, without which he could not have availed himself of the benefit of a tropical climate for the restoration of his health.

After remaining a short time at Vancouver, to take care of the donations which had been received at the Islands, we embarked for the Walamet, where we found Mr. Shepard surrounded with the children in sabbath school,—glad to meet again, and desirous that we might once more labour together, and bear each other's burdens, and fulfil the law of Christ.

During my absence, the state of affairs at the station shall be here noticed, and the events of that period which may appear worthy of record. Forty-five acres of land were under cultivation, and produced about seven hundred bushels of wheat and three hundred of potatoes. They had made an addition to the house of sixteen by thirty feet, which, on account of the enlargement of the family, had become necessary; having taken in about twenty children, several of whom were orphans—a task indeed, to feed so many mouths, and clothe so many half-naked children, to say nothing of teaching and watching over them, or of attending on them in sickness. To these several were added from the families of our neighbours; so that on Sunday more than thirty met in sabbath school. Some of these also attended on week days, to whom Mr. Shepard devoted all the time his many duties would admit. At first, when the subject of teaching the children was proposed to the parents, the fathers, some of them, made slight objections; but these seemed soon to vanish away, and much interest, particularly by the mothers, was evinced in the efforts which were made to teach their children. In proof of this, they used to frequent the sabbath school themselves, and manifestly took pleasure in the exercises.

Mr. Edwards had also opened a small school near Champoeg, shortly after my going to the Islands, where he continued to teach for several months; and when he had finished, some of those he had been instructing were admitted into the mission school.

Another thing worthy of note is the formation of a temperance society. Previous to this, liquor had been obtained by some of the people in the settlements at Fort William, on the Multnomah, and had produced some of its usual effects, waste of property, neglect of business, drunkenness, quarrels, etc. Here is a man in harvest, living on pea-soup; but why does he not season it with a little pork? Walamet grows pork, I suppose? Yes, and it grew some for him; but, poor man! he was robbed of it all! Robbed? Yes; by one, too, who ought to have been his greatest friend. This fellow took his only pork and carried it away, and gave it for ardent spirits, which he barbarously compelled the owner to drink; and now, poor man, he has no pork to eat in harvest! But the temperance society was established, and a very large part of the residents joined. It is due to say that Dr. M'Laughlin seconded the efforts of the missionaries and the friends of temperance, and that the course he has taken in regard to spirituous liquors has done much to preserve the general order and harmony of the mixed community of which the settlement is composed. The good that has already been derived to the inhabitants of that valley from the absence of so dire a curse can never be told; nor is there a scourge so terrible this side perdition, that can be let loose upon them, that would do the devil's work and turn earth into hell so fully as the free distribution of that bane that changes men into demons. But with these as the certain fruits of using alcohol before their eyes, there were found men who determined to distil it! Yes, two men commenced the erection of a distillery, and expended considerable in preparation. With this movement almost the whole community were alarmed; not only those who had enrolled themselves on the list of temperance, but nearly all the rest, felt that if that *distillery* went on all was lost. At this crisis a general meeting was convened, which determined to approach the portentous evil with an aspect of mildness, by presenting them a petition setting forth the reasons which should lead to the abandonment of their attempt; and, as a further inducement, offering to remunerate them for all they had expended. This petition was signed by nearly every man in the settlement, and the voice of public opinion triumphed; for the persons concerned acceded to the voice of the people, but refused their proffered remuneration. Never was an evil of such magnitude arrested more timely, or in a manner more appropriate.

There were, however, still some who, for all this, indulged a private friendship for the " good creature," falsely so called, and longed to shake hands again with him as an old friend with whom they had passed many a merry hour. At length one of these set himself at work in as good earnest as ever man did to generate the alcoholic principle, that he and his familiars might regale and cheer their hearts in the tedium of sober and industrious life. Pursuant to his plan for a *spirited* entertainment, he addressed himself vigorously to the work—soaked, and sprouted, and dried his grain, converted some kitchen or camp utensil into a distillery, kindled his fires, condensed the vapour, and immortalized himself as the father of alcohol in the Walamet. The event was hailed with joy, and deemed worthy of particular note, and its celebration took place on the evening of the 25th of December. The party who availed themselves of the honours of that hour needed no introduction to young Alcohol, for in truth they found that he had been an old associate of theirs in days of yore. As usual, he appeared in a liquid condition, and weakly, in consequence of having, through some mistake, imbibed too much water, and so chilled his ardour as to render his constitution very delicate, or perhaps even endanger his life. They remembered, with some regret, that he was formerly more flush; but, strange to tell! though so many reasons appeared in favour of their pity and protection, they recklessly resolved to send him to destruction. This was to take place in their several stomachs, where it was hoped he might be so dissipated as to take refuge in the head, as on former occasions, and produce those pleasurable sensations for which the whole entertainment was especially designed. If report says true, after all their efforts, poor alcohol was unable to upset their sobriety; and, therefore, of sheer necessity, they were compelled to be sober, or at least nearly so. Till the writer left the country, no other like attempt had been made. Yet, as will appear in the sequel, it has been brought here from the United States since that time.

But, to return from this digression on evil spirits. The rainy season soon set in, and now all our hands were full of business. As for the writer, though no Esculapian, yet he was compelled to engage in medical practice on the first year of his apprenticeship on mission ground—very cautiously at first, but now, except in some new and difficult cases, he has acquired more confidence in his attempts to relieve suffering humanity. Besides frequent cases of the intermittent fever, and others of scrofula, there was an epidemic which attacked most of the children at once; so that our house was in fact an hospital, and in one small room sixteen children were down with it at the same time. Some of the symptoms were alarming, resembling the croup. Here were perplexities. Must do something—what? May do wrong! These were trying moments, reader! Mr. Shepard stood by, and, shoulder to shoulder, we weathered the storm. The dark clouds began to open, and finally, after a few days, they were dispersed; then the sun shone, and our plants grew again.

To get our wheat floured was a matter of some importance for a family of thirty souls, when the mill was more than twelve miles off, and the rains almost incessant, with very muddy roads. This was done on horses. A pair of large saddle-bags made of elk-skin are suspended over the saddle, and a sack of grain, holding a bushel and a half, is put into each side, over which a covering of some kind, a skin or a blanket, is laid, and then all is lashed close to the saddle with a strong skin rope. Having rigged the requisite number of horses or mules, two, three, or four, two of the larger boys mount upon other horses, and the embryo caravan begins to move. What disasters are to befall them cannot be imagined. With these difficulties we were sometimes a little short, and then boiled wheat was a substitute for bread. Thus did our heavenly Father provide for us, so that we were never destitute; but we saw abundant reason to praise Him who gave us strength as our day. The sabbath was a season of rest and refreshment to our souls. The family altar and the class meeting were owned of God, and oft did we prove his promise true, "Where two or three are gathered together in my name, there am I in the midst."

Here may be stated a case of conversion. On about the 1st of January, 1837, one of the American residents, Mr. Webley Hanxhurst, a native of Long Island, called at the mission house, and passed the night with us. It was the evening of our class meeting. His attention was at first arrested by the serious deportment of our children at evening prayers. Let me relate his exercises in his own words. In a letter he wrote, dated January 13th, he says: "I am thankful that my business led me week before last to your house. I learned more in that week than in thirty-one years before. When I saw the Indian children praying and worshipping God, I thought it was high time for me, who had lived thirty-one years in sin, without ever praying for my own soul; and being in your class meeting, and hearing you asking questions, and telling your feelings, I expected you would speak to me, and *what* could I say? I felt like a person lost for ever!" He was indeed truly alive to his danger. We pointed him to Jesus, to whom he looked, and ere long found peace to his troubled soul. This was the first conversion, the writer believes, of a white man in Oregon. Great was our joy at this event. "We thanked God, and took courage."

CHAPTER XIV.

Mission settlement receives a visit from Mr. Wm. A. Slocum—Petition to congress from people at the settlement, calling upon the American government to protect them by its laws—Mr. J. Lee procures cattle from California—Arrival of reinforcement to the mission, from the United States—An attempt to murder an Indian chief—Mission schools—Happy deaths—History of a sabbath in Oregon—Another reinforcement arrives—Attempt of missionaries to improve the condition of Calapooyas—Plans to extend the work formed.

JUST before this last cheering event, in December the settlement and mission received a visit from Mr. Wm. A. Slocum, a gentleman belonging to the U. S. Navy, then employed in a special service by the United States government, pursuant to which he had arrived in Oregon, and was to proceed to California. The vessel in which he came he had chartered at the Sandwich Islands, and it was commanded by an American, Capt. Bancroft. Mr. Slocum made calls at almost every house in the community, and took an account of the produce of their farms, and stock, and the number of inhabitants. A petition was now drawn up, and signed by the people, both French and Americans, praying the congress of the United States to recognise them in their helpless and defenceless state, and to extend to them the protection of its laws, as being, or as desiring to become its citizens. This was forwarded by Mr. Slocum, who seemed anxious to do all in his power to promote the prosperity of the residents, and to have their wishes, as imbodied in it, realized.

At this period, the cattle in the country nearly all belonged to the Hudson's Bay Company, and as it was then policy not to sell any, it became necessary for some measures to be adopted to obtain elsewhere what could not be bought of the company. In order to this, an expedition to California was in contemplation when

Mr. Slocum arrived. On becoming acquainted with the fact, and the reasons for it, he lent his aid to carry it into immediate effect; and tendered a passage to California to those who might compose the party. Of this very seasonable and unexpected means of reaching that country, they were happy to avail themselves. The better to effect their object a company was formed, and stock invested to a considerable amount, to which were to be added the avails of the labour which the party might perform during their detention in California, till the ensuing summer; when they were to return to Walamet, where the business was to be closed; and after deducting the expenses of the expedition, each owner was to receive his share of the cattle according to his investment.

It being desirable to stock the mission in view of securing a permanent provision for its future sustenance, in its anticipated enlargement and progress, Mr. J. Lee invested in the concern six hundred dollars, mission funds, for this purpose. The party was organized, and headed by Mr. Ewing Young, accompanied by Mr. P. L. Edwards, as purser of the company. After having enjoyed a very agreeable interview with Mr. Slocum for some days, he took his departure to re-embark and sail for California, and with the cattle party was soon on board his vessel in Baker's Bay. But here in this season of storms they lost two anchors, and but narrowly escaped shipwreck, and Capt. Bancroft was compelled to return to Vancouver and obtain an anchor, before he could venture to sea. By these disasters he was detained many days, but at length they all reached California in safety.

Here they went to work, and commanded high wages, till the next spring; and as soon as the arrangements could be made, with a party increased by the addition of several more men, they commenced their march toward the Walamet. Messrs. Young and Edwards, in securing the success of the enterprise, found it necessary to attempt the removal of a serious obstacle in their way. It was this: an old colonial law was in force, prohibiting the transportation of females out of the country. They therefore applied to the authorities for a special grant. They were favourably received, and obtained their request. The way being thus cleared up, they bought eight hundred cattle, at three dollars a head, and forty horses, at twelve dollars each, making the whole outlay $2480. Their journey was full of hardships, in a rough mountainous country. Numbers of the cattle were drowned in swimming a river, some strayed, and some were shot by the Indians; and one Indian was also killed by the party. They reached Walamet in October, with about six hundred head of the eight hundred, having parted with one-fourth of them on the way. Then followed a public sale of the horses, and the cattle were found to have cost the company about seven dollars and sixty-seven cents a-piece. Of these, more than eighty head belonged to the mission. Thus was the enterprise prospered, and answered the purpose for which it was undertaken; but it should be remembered that most of these cattle were partially wild, which made them less valuable.

About the close of the year 1836 the Board sent out a reinforcement to the Oregon Mission, consisting of the following individuals: Dr. Elijah White, wife, and two children; Mr. Alanson Beers, wife, and three children; Mr. Wm. H. Wilson; and Misses Anna Maria Pittman, Susan Downing, and Elvira Johnson. These all reached the Sandwich Islands in safety, where they, after some detention, embarked in an American vessel, Capt. Wm. S. Hinckley master, and sailed to the Columbia, where they all arrived in safety in May, 1837. We received them with great satisfaction and thankfulness for the care of a kind Providence which had brought them to us, to strengthen our hearts and hands in our too arduous labours, under which we were sometimes pressed as a cart beneath its sheaves. As soon as the news of their coming reached us, Mr. Jason Lee, leaving Mr. Shepard and myself at the station, hastened to Vancouver, to greet the newly arrived, and to assist them in their first attempts to navigate the Walamet in a mode of voyaging to which they were strangers, and to obtain storage at Vancouver for a part of the very large and liberal supplies which the Board had appropriated to carry on the objects of the mission; and to take measures to forward the rest up the Walamet, where they would immediately be required; which, in addition to the baggage to be transported, was a work of some magnitude, and it was found that some additional help was required to effect it. He therefore hired Mr. J. L. Whitcom, an American, who came with Captain Hinckley as second mate, but with the intention of remaining in the country. Some time after, he was employed in the farming department of the mission at Walamet, of which he had charge for several years after. This new accession of fifty souls filled our house. It was plain that more houses must be made. Mr. Beers set up his anvil, and erected a small shop. Mr. Wilson was carpenter and joiner; but the material for his axe and plane was in the forests. The subjects of the healing art were not so inaccessible, and Dr. White could employ his skill in his appropriate work at once; and my humble self, famous before, dropped into obscurity!

After an agreeable visit from Capt. Hinckley and his lady, in the height of strawberries and cream, they took their leave, with our best wishes and earnest prayers for their good. She is since dead, and he resides in California. To Mr. Whitcom he felt himself much indebted, having had a very badly-diseased leg cured by him perfectly, in the use of very simple remedies, which had been of many years' standing, and for which he had expended hundreds of dollars on various physicians, wholly in vain. Not long after the departure of Capt. H., Mr. Shepard was attacked with a fever, which reduced him very low; but by careful attention he gained his usual health, which we felt laid us under new obligations to our heavenly Father in sparing one to us whose services seemed almost indispensable. Thus were our eyes saved from tears, and we sung of the mercies of God.

About this period an atrocious attempt was made to murder an Indian chief, of the Calapooya tribe. Some enemy of his, as it was afterward found, had hired an Indian, who was formerly his slave, to go and assassinate his old master. So under cover of the night he approached the chieftain's lodge, as he lay wrapped in unconscious slumbers, and marking the place of his rest, to make sure of his victim, he aimed with deadly design at his head, fired his musket, and escaped. Next morning, which was sabbath, he was found alive, drenched in his blood; and though badly wounded, yet perhaps not mortally. He was taken and brought on a litter a mile and a half to the mission house, where he was laid on a table, and examined by Dr. White. One of the balls had cut away a portion of the upper part of the throat, opening a passage for the breath, and severed the lower jaw, carrying away some of the teeth, and then lodged in the right arm, above the elbow, fracturing the bone; and the other ball had passed through a portion of the breast, and then, entering the thumb on the left hand, at the large joint, passed through beneath the hollow of the hand, and lodged at the large joint of the little finger. His wounds were carefully dressed, and he was in the care of the mission till he recovered. But for all this care and attention he showed himself most undeserving—no gratitude was manifested; and he boasted that the "Bostons," as he termed us, "should never make him good."

The mission school was now in the charge of Miss Johnson, who laboured assiduously to promote the improvement of her pupils; but the amount of labour to be done took many of them away from their studies much of the time, which much retarded their progress; besides, there was much sickness among them, and this had an influence on the prosperity of the school, for which there was no remedy. In the settlement near us there were two happy deaths in those days, those of Mrs. Payethe and Mrs. Rondo, descended from French fathers and Indian mothers. They manifested a joyful hope in God, particularly the latter; but though with the former it was not so bright, yet there appeared good grounds to hope in her happy exchange. Another case was that of Joseph, their brother, who died before them—a boy who used to attend the sabbath school, and was always very attentive to his books and the instructions that were given him. During his sickness, which was a consumption, he was very serious and prayerful, and was baptized at his own request. We had good hope in his death. He was aged about seventeen years. They were all interred in the mission grave-yard. "These are the Lord's doings, and they are marvellous in our eyes."

Take now the history of a sabbath, July 16th. It was set apart for our communion service. At 11, A. M., we assembled near the mission house, in a grove of firs. The congregation embraced Frenchmen, Americans, Indians, half-breeds, the mission family and school, and some others, a mixed company strangely thrown together in this distant land. All were decently clad, and observed a becoming deportment. Mr. Jason Lee opened the meeting with the hymn, " When all thy mercies," &c. After the singing, the marriage ceremony was performed, and Mr. Jason Lee was married to Miss Anna Maria Pittman, and Mr. Cyrus Shepard to Miss Susan Downing. A third couple having been married, " Watchman, tell us of the night," was sung, and prayer was offered by Mr. Wilson. Mr. J. Lee then preached on Numbers x, 19 : " Come thou with us, and we will do thee good; for the Lord has spoken good concerning Israel." Many seemed much affected under the word, and the communion that followed was a season of refreshing to our souls. We now held a kind of love-feast, and all the brethren and sisters brought in their offerings, and the Spirit of grace rested upon us. Some others also spoke, who seemed alarmed on account of their sins, and we received two men into society. The number of communicants was fourteen. Thus did the God of missions meet with his servants in the wilderness, making " glad the desert and the solitary place," for his name's sake. To the Lord be all the praise for his faithfulness and truth. His word is steadfast for ever!

In September of the same year we received a second reinforcement to the Oregon mission, Mr. David Leslie and wife and three children, Miss Margaret J. Smith, and Mr. H. K. W. Perkins. Mr. Shepard and the writer met them on their arrival at Vancouver, and returned with them to the Walamet, where a small neighbouring house being purchased, Mr. Leslie was soon comfortably located with his family. Messrs. Leslie and Perkins were both preachers. This increased our numbers, and enlarged our circle of friends and fellow-helpers. But with these our responsibilities were also increased. To make provision for the sick, it was determined to build an hospital; and a building was commenced, but so slowly did the work advance, that it was not finished till 1840, and then it became necessary to occupy it for a dwelling-house, to accommodate the reinforcement of 1839. Our attention was now turned toward the Calapooyas, and efforts were made to give them instruction by holding meetings among them, and visiting them at their lodges; and for their special benefit a missionary society was formed, and a very liberal sum was devoted to that object, about four hundred dollars. The object of the society was to induce them to locate on a piece of ground, and till the soil, and to assist them in the building of comfortable houses. A man was hired to help them, and some efforts were made in order to induce them to work and help themselves. There was, however, so much apathy among them, that, after having used various means for a year quite in vain, they abandoned the attempt. Yet meetings have been held among them from time to time since, and at periods when their location admitted it, meetings have been regularly holden; and a house has been built near the mission mill which affords them a shelter, in worship, during the rains.

Since the coming of the first reinforcement in May, two dwelling houses had been built, one of logs, and the other of hewn timber and sawed plank, and the families of Dr. White and Mr. Beers were comfortably located. In November Mr. Perkins was married to Miss Johnson. The increase of our numbers made our seasons of public and social worship more interesting. At this time the question of occupying new stations came up, and it was the opinion of all the brethren that it should be done as soon as practicable. This was accordingly done the next year at the Dalls, as will be seen in the next chapter; and subsequently at Nesqually, on Pugil's Sound, where Mr. Wilson was labouring alone for several months, and built a house, which was afterward occupied by another missionary in 1840. The wants of the country as a mission field were brought forward and discussed, and the judgment prevailed, that much more help was needed to do the work, and that the time had come when Mr. Jason Lee should go to the States, and obtain the men and means wanted. After this he made a trip to Umbaqua; and then prepared for the journey to the States; leaving all for the cause of Christ, from whom may he receive a rich reward for ever, is the prayer of the writer!

CHAPTER XV.

Mission established at the Dalls—Visited by Mr. Jason Lee, on his way to the United States—Journeys of missionaries—Meetings among the Indians—Death of Mrs. J. Lee—Escape of Mr. Leslie and Mrs. White from imminent danger—Description of Mr. D. Lee's journey to and from Walamet—Carousals among the Dalls—Fire eater—Medicine men—Circumstances related, illustrative of the character of the Dalls.

The members of the Oregon Mission considering the Dalls on the Columbia River as a promising field for missionary effort, it was determined to begin a new station at that place, which is about eighty miles above Fort Vancouver, and accordingly, in 1838, Mr. Perkins and the writer were appointed to proceed to the Dalls for that purpose.

Leaving the Walamet station on the 14th of March, they embarked in two canoes with a small cargo of supplies, passed down the Walamet River, and then ascended the Columbia to the place of destination, where they arrived on Wednesday the 22d.

About three miles below the Dalls, and a half mile from the shore on the south side, was found a valuable spring of water, some rich land, and a good supply of timber, oak, and pine, and an elevated and pleasant location for a house, almost in their shade; with a fine extended view of the Columbia River, three miles on either hand. The back ground was broken, and hilly, and thinly wooded. Here, about the 1st of April, a house was begun. The Indians assisted in cutting the timber, and bringing it upon the spot. Meantime, Mr. Jason Lee arrived on his way to the United States, accompanied by Mr. Edwards, and another gentleman, Mr. Ewing of Missouri, and two Indian boys of the Chenook tribe, W. M. Brooks and Thomas Adams, who had been some time in the mission school at the Walamet station. The object of his visit was to obtain additional facilities to carry on, more efficiently and extensively, the missionary work in the Oregon Territory. April 9th, having hired horses of the Indians to convey himself to Wallah-wallah, where he was to purchase the horses needed to make the tour of the mountains, that being the usual place of outfit for parties going by land into the interior, he took an affectionate leave of his friends, Mr. Perkins and the writer, and set off on his arduous journey, accompanied by the afore-named gentlemen and the native boys. The same day Mr. Perkins embarked in a canoe for the Walamet station in order to bring his wife to the Dalls, and returned in safety on the 5th of May. The building of the house went on amidst many interruptions, and it was finished before winter. Mr. Perkins' family occupied it long before it was roofed; but as the climate was dry, and rain seldom fell in summer, it was quite safe. Several trips were made to Walamet and Vancouver by water during the year for supplies. One journey was made to Fort Wallah-wallah to get horses, and another over land to the Walamet station, to obtain cattle. These various journeys and voyages took us away from the station about five months each, during the year. Immediately on our arrival at the station we began to hold meetings with the Indians on the sabbath; speaking to them in the "jargon," through an interpreter. This imperfect medium of communication sprang from the traffic of the whites with the Indians, and it embraces some English, some French, and many Indian words, some Chenook, some Wallah-wallah, and some of other tribes, and is understood more or less by individuals in almost all the tribes beyond the mountains. Their behaviour at worship was very serious, and most of them would kneel in time of prayer. Our meetings were held without, among the oaks, or under a pine, whose cooling shade screened us from the burning sun. A few scattering stones afforded seats for some, and others sat quietly upon the ground; a manner of sitting to which they are well used, and which they prefer to any other. Often was the soul of the speaker refreshed while declaring to them "the love wherewith God hath loved us," and the hope that his labour would not be in vain "in the Lord," cheered his heart. In the month of June our joy was suddenly turned to heaviness by the occurrence, on the 26th, of that mournful event, the death of Mrs. Jason Lee, within a year from her marriage, and less than three months since her husband left her to go to the United States! An express, with the melancholy and heart-rending intelligence, was sent over the mountains to the bereaved husband, which overtook him in a little more than sixty days, at the Shawnee Mission. The bearer of the unwelcome message reached the place about midnight. Who can tell the anguish of that awful hour to him who was thus cleft in twain, by an inscrutable stroke of unerring providence. He needed the arm of God to support him, and on that arm he relied. His deceased wife was buried on the 28th, in one grave with her little son. Her funeral sermon was preached by Mr. Leslie. She was the first white woman who died in Oregon. A decent marble marks the place of her interment, near the spot where the missionaries commenced their labours in 1834, on the bank of the Walamet. There rests her crumbling dust in hope of a glorious resurrection. "The righteous hath hope in his death."

In the month of August, Mr. Leslie and Mrs. White came from the Walamet station to the Dalls on a visit, Mrs. W. having her babe with her. After remaining a short time, they embarked on their return to the Walamet. At the Cascades, as they were passing down the lower rapids, they ran among the breakers, filled, and upset their canoe, and were in imminent danger of being drowned. Mr. Leslie, though unable to swim, laid hold of Mrs. W., and throwing his arm over the canoe which was floating near him, an Indian on the other side, the same instant, seized him by the wrist, and in this way they were carried a mile, and escaped safe to land. On righting the canoe, Mrs. W.'s infant son was found entangled among the floating baggage; but its spirit had fled. Some Indians from the interior, on their way to Fort Vancouver, seeing their danger, came to their assistance, and kindly took Mrs. W. and Mr. Leslie into their own canoe, and paddled them to Fort Vancouver as quick as possible, where they were received by the gentlemen and ladies of the company with much sympathy and hospitality. Thus were mercy and judgment mingled together. Verily may we in judgment sing aloud of thy mercy, O Lord; for from the waves that threatened destruction thy servants have escaped. Praise the Lord, who hath saved us, for his name's sake.

September 3d. The writer left the Dalls to go to the Walamet over land after cattle, a journey of one hundred and twenty-five miles, taking ten horses, owned by the Oregon Mission, and ten others, some of them belonging to the Indians who were going to assist him, four in number, and a supply of provisions for six days. One of my Indians, the oldest, probably from forty to fifty, was blind of an eye, which had been destroyed by a violent inflammation, that nearly caused his death. But in his extremity he fancied some kind visiter from the invisible world, who assured him he should recover; upon which he soon revived, greatly to the surprise of his friends around him, who viewed his restoration as mysterious, since they had looked upon him as one dead, and on this account he received the name of Uk-woui-a-neete, that is, "heart," or "life." He was of Chenook descent, and a resident at the Dalls. Another was a Wallah-wallah, a stout young man of twenty-five years, good stature, with a fine forehead, and, what is rare, a Roman nose. His name, which signifies to "become dry," "empty," or "destitute," was Tah-lac-e-ou-it, and was given to him because once he had considerable property which he had lost by gambling, to which he was much addicted. One of the remaining two was a Chenook with the usual features, a flattened forehead and a wide mouth, about twenty years old. Proud of his skill in directing a canoe, and of his supposed horsemanship, he felt and boasted himself a man. My other, a Wallah-wallah, was a shrewd young rogue, a gamester, dishonest to the core; and, besides these, a poor cripple, with a short, shrivelled, crooked, cumbersome leg. To help his well one, he carried a strong cane or crutch, six to seven feet long, on which he poised himself as he sprang forward from one place to another, two yards or more at a leap. Thus he was active on a single leg, even to admiration. Our horses are now saddled; we mount, and away. Trotting is an unfashionable gait in Oregon. A cloud of dust marks our course westward. In sight of the mission we cross a beautiful plain of grass, half a mile wide by a mile and a half long, spotted here and there with small basaltic islands. On our right flows the Columbia; on our left are hills two hundred to three hundred feet in height, fringed at their base with a narrow, lengthened strip of oak and pine. Leaving this plain, we begin to ascend among hills, diverging south-westward from the river in our course. The country for twenty miles is broken, sparsely wooded with yellow pine and stinted oak. Some of the former are large, and may well be called the monarchs of the hills. A long kind of moss grows upon them, which the natives use as an article of food. The grass is as dry as if David's imprecation on the mountains of Gilboa had fallen upon the thirsty hills. Having passed this region, we reached the valley of the White Creek about noon, where we halted to bait our horses and take dinner; water from a cooling rill relieving our thirst. Having mounted fresh horses, we pursued our way along the elevated base of high hills on the left, and in about two hours came to the creek which, for many miles, lay far beneath on the right. It was three rods wide, and about three feet deep, of a milky whiteness, filled with large smooth stones. However, we crossed it without disaster. Here we entered the forest, at the base of that part of the President's range of mountains lying south of the Columbia, on whose summits stand four ancient volcanoes covered with perpetual snow. On we went, in a narrow, crooked path, among windfalls and under-brush, dodging right and left to avoid contact with the limbs that stretched across our way. At dusk came to a spot where the hazel and brake bore rule, permitting only a little grass to spring in their shade. Here we dismounted, hobbled our horses, and encamped for the night. A fire was struck, some dried salmon and lamprey-eels roasted; and we sat down and made a good hearty Indian supper. After a hymn and prayer, we wrapped ourselves in our blankets, lay down under the bushes to avoid the dampness of the night, and rested sweetly till the dawn of the next morning. A long day's march was before us, and we made an early start. My one-eyed man led the way, followed by the horses in bands, three or four to a man, one bringing up the rear. Going west a few miles, we came to a branch of White Creek, which empties into it below the ford before described. Up this, on the south side, we travelled several miles, and came to a rugged mountain barrier, where the water was confined in a deep ravine amid high precipitous banks. Here the trail crossed to the other side. Our route now lay several miles over a high hill, and then fell again upon the stream we had left, and descended along its tortuous course, one side and the other, and along its bed. Leaving this rugged path without regret, we rose gradually to the height of land lying to the south of the Cascades of the Columbia fifteen to twenty miles. The horses had become hungry, and the declining sun already chided our tardy progress. A long way to grass—stopping at such a time, turning out of the path to browse on the leaves—'tis too much! "Go along, Gray!" "Hup, hup!" The woods ring with continual shouts to our rebel quadrupeds. A long, hard drive brought us to the top of the hill, and we began to descend, with new courage and quickened pace, toward the valley of Sandy Creek, where a good encampment awaited our arrival. We passed on through a miry track, darkened by majestic evergreens. We were in the midst of these when night came on and compelled us to encamp. Some of the horses were tied to trees, and the rest were guarded during the night. Next morning we decamped early, and soon came to the Sandy. This rapid stream rises at the base of Mount Hood, whose silver summit appears to rest on the sky about fifteen miles off. The fires that once raged within its bowels, and blazed at its top, seem to have been long extinguished. Native tradition says that fire was anciently seen upon it, and that sounds were heard by the hunters, who approached near it, like the report of muskets, and that it is inhabited by a peculiar race of men who are destitute of the powers of vision. Travelling a few miles down the Sandy, we found a good encampment for our half-starved horses. This stream has a crooked, rocky channel, and rushes on in a continuous rapid through a good part of its course. At high water it overleaps its banks and rolls on in a sweeping torrent, filled with volcanic sand, and stones, and floating rubbish, causing perpetual changes in its bed. Its valley, in some parts one-fourth of a mile wide, exhibits piles of sand and rounded stones, and heaps of decaying drift-wood, scattered along its surface, with clumps of willows and dogwood, and a young growth of firs and white pines, and is carpeted here and there with grass. On both sides the high hills are thickly studded with heavy timber, chiefly fir, with some pine, hemlock, and cedar. This hilly and mountainous region abounds with a variety of berries, and is the September resort of many Indians, who pick and dry them, in large quantities, for food. The most valued is a large kind of whortleberry. Some, engaged in their berry harvest, were encamped near us. On coming here we found that my guide, an old chieftain by the name of Wamcuta, who had engaged to meet me at this place and conduct me through to the Walamet, was absent on an elk hunt, and when he would return none could tell. After waiting three days in vain, fears arose that our stock of provisions would not suffice for the journey if we tarried any longer. My old "one-eye," having some years before been through, in our necessity consented to act as guide.

Saturday, September 9th, raised camp, and travelled down the creek all day. Good grass for the animals. Put my company and myself on a small allowance of food—salmon, dried eels, bread. From this encampment the trail took the east side of the creek, and soon after ascended a hill that ran parallel to it, traversing its lengthened ridge several miles, and then descending to the creek, crossed it to the west side, and thence, running westward over rolling prairies and woodland, in two days reaches the Walamet at the falls. The trail that led to the ascent of this ridge being covered under several generations of leaves, was soon utterly lost; and after toiling most of the day among the dense windfalls on its side, we found it inaccessible. Turning back, we made our shortest way to the creek, and crossed to the other side on Monday afternoon.

September 11th, travelled a short distance, and encamped. No grass for the starving horses, and a dense wilderness around. Eight days out. Gloomy prospects ahead. Next morning gathered our scattered horses, and set forward to explore the dark unknown before us. Now descending into a deep defile, then flouncing through a miry creek at the bottom; then climbing a steep and rugged ascent, winding upward among fallen trees, jumping horses over high logs, axe in hand cutting our way through the thick underbrush. At great labour we have almost gained the top of a high hill in our course; but here we meet a pile of wind-falls, an impassable subject, back out, wheel the horses, a retrograde march, a turn to the right or left; a circuitous, rising and falling, zig-zag route along the hill side, the woods echoing our unheeded orders to our jaded horses. Toiling, pushing, driving, all day. Much haste, little speed, little progress.

Another woods encampment. Dark prospects for the poor famished horses; only leaves and brush. One of them, not liking the country, took French leave in the night, and we did not recover him. We went forward till noon, when all our provisions were spent, save one small loaf of bread. Being very hungry, this was divided equally among us, and we went on in the afternoon in the strength of it. As we were about to camp, just at dusk, one of the horses fell down exhausted, unable to go further. One of the Indians soon despatched him with a musket-ball, as he had been directed; and some of his flesh was soon roasting before a fire, on which we made a hearty supper! Yes, eat horse! and glad to get even that! Four crotches were set in the ground, and four poles were laid into them; and across these several other ones, both ways, a few inches apart, forming a kind of Indian gridiron. On this was soon spread a bountiful supply of horseflesh, and built under it a fire of dry bark, which soon dried, smoked, and roasted it "closh," good. Having thus secured a stock for ourselves, we only felt anxious for our poor horses, which were passing another night of famine.

Next morning rose early, and renewed our attack on horse meat. Packed what we had designed for the purpose, and continued our march. A few miles we came to open ground, and pushed our way through high brakes several miles; and at noon came to a creek where, to our joy, we saw grass again. On this stream we encamped.

Next day, September 14th, we passed on through timber and prairie, and encamped where our animals could get a good supply of grass. Here we rested about twenty-four hours. On the 15th, after going forward three or four miles, we were compelled to leave five of our animals on a small brook, at the foot of a very steep hill, which in their famished condition they had not strength to ascend. Went a short distance, and encamped in the woods. The horses had a plenty of good feed. Next day, sabbath, the 16th, had a short breakfast, and reserved a part of that for a time of greater need; but to our joy we came to the Clakamas River about noon, where we baited our horses, and ate the last of our dried horse meat, and then went on four miles to the Clakamas Indian village, where we obtained salmon, ate to satisfaction, and rested till Monday.

On Monday reached the mission just in time to prevent a party of the settlers from going in search of me, fearing some disaster had befallen me in the journey, as they knew we had left the Dalls, and looked for me eight or ten days earlier. My sun-burnt face, prominent cheek bones, and long beard, did not make me unwelcome among them. After nine days spent in Walamet, on the 27th we started for the Dalls, with fourteen head of cattle. Having a good guide, and two white men, in place of my young Chenook and Wallah-wallah, the return journey was made without much difficulty. On reaching the Clakamas, it was found that the Indian who had been engaged to bring in the tired horses had failed to fulfil his promise, so taking "One-eye" with me, we went to get them, leaving the cattle party to go on by themselves till we could return and overtake them. Friday evening we came to the place, but found one horse missing, which we were unable to find. Three of them, a mare and two colts, by slow stages, we got up the hill; but the horse could go but few steps, and the exertion caused his heart to beat with such violence as to shake his whole frame, and it could be heard several yards. His weakened limbs refusing longer to move, or bear up his wasted form, he fell upon his side, his head beneath his body, and died! Poor horse! The relator felt like weeping over his misfortunes; and had he been able would gladly have carried him to the top of the hill before he fell down, slain by famine. There was relief in the thought, "he will hunger no more." Night came on with heavy showers, from which we had no shelter to protect us, and we were soon drenched from head to foot. Next day evening came to the Clakamas River. Here "One-eye" remained in charge of the horses, and the writer rode on four miles to the village, where he arrived about midnight, wet, weary, and hungry. He went into a lodge, found fire and dried salmon, ate, and warmed, and then tried to sleep, but had little success, being much annoyed by small insects common among Indians. Fleas? Yes.

Monday we went on with the cattle party, and reached the Dalls safely on Friday, October 5th. The old man who was to have guided me through to the Walamet came to the place where he was to have met us a day or two after we had left, and went in pursuit of us; but could not follow our trail, and so returned. He probably supposed we should not be along so soon, and therefore went on a hunt, which eventuated in our want of his services as a guide, which would have prevented the disasters recorded in this chapter; yet, with grateful acknowledgments of the care of our heavenly Father in all these trials, the writer brings the story to a close, and it doubtless has interested the reader more agreeably in the perusal than it did the writer in being a witness and an actor in the scene described.

Mr. Perkins, who had waited long and with much solicitude for the writer's return, was at length surprised by the arrival of the young Chenook who went with him. " Now-it-ka," said he, " wake si-yah me-me-loosh !" " Certainly we were near dying !" " Tot-le-lum cu-tan me-me-loosh !" " Ten horses died !" " Moxt muc-a-muc !" " We ate two horses !" " Mr. Lee, yok-ah se-ah-hast cah-quah moxt stone cup-ah skin met-light !" " Mr. Lee's face is like two bones with the skin drawn over them !" " Ate two horses, and yet as poor as a rat !" thought the hearer; " incredible !" Shortly after this, Mr. Perkins and his wife left the Dalls station, and embarked in a canoe for the Walamet, where they were expecting to remain some months. When the writer returned they had been gone some days, and thus, as it proved, he was left comparatively alone through the next winter; for Mr. Perkins was prevented by the inclemency of the season, and could not reach the Dalls till about the middle of February. An American, named Anderson, who had been hired about the commencement of our labours at this station, for a year was employed in procuring lumber, overseeing three natives and one Owyhee, who were engaged in sawing boards. Besides, fencing timber and farming utensils were required for the ensuing spring; also bridles, collars, traces, a full equipment for the horses needed—all must be made ; and this demanded not a little of the writer's time. And one voyage to the Walamet occupied three weeks, leaving but a part of the time to be employed in the study of the Indian language. Morning and evening the Scriptures were read and expounded to the natives, who chose to be present at prayers. The usual services of the sabbath were continued, and the number attending greater than in the warm season. This was owing to the fact, that this was the winter retreat of many of the Dalls Indians, who pass the summer at the fishery, and the resort at this season of various bands from the Wallah-wallah, the Kinse, and the Nez Percé tribes, for the purpose of exchanging horses and buffalo robes for salmon; and to pass the cold season, which lasts about two months, where wood can be easily obtained, which is not the case between this and the Blue Mountains above Wallah-wallah, one hundred and fifty miles distant. From this station the forest extends to the ocean. The quantity of snow and rain that falls here is small. Horses and cattle subsist without hay. December is the snow month, and the season of festivity. The nights among the Dalls Indians were spent in singing and dancing, and their carousals could be heard a mile. One, and then another of the *medicine men*, would open his house for a dance, where it was generally kept up five nights in succession; men, women, and children, engaged in the chant, while a man, or a woman, or both, danced on a large elk-skin spread down on one side of the fire, that blazed in the centre of the group, keeping time to the loud-measured knocking of a long pole suspended horizontally, and struck endwise against a wide cedar board—the dancer jumping, and invoking his "tam-an-a-was" or familiar spirit; until, exhausted, he falls as one dead, by the overpowering influence of his "familiar."

To arouse him from this deep slumber requires the skill of a medicine man, or "*Mesmeriser*," who going around him peeps, and mutters, and hoots, at his toes, fingers, and ears, and wakes his tam-an-a-was; when he shudders, groans, opens his eyes, and lives again! With these dancers the feat of fire-eating is also connected. The writer going one night to witness a dance, was told that a medicine man present could eat fire; at first, he seemed not a little ashamed, and denied he could do it. "Let me see you eat fire," said the writer; "you dare not do it! You cannot do it!" This was calling his courage and power in question, before many who had seen him devour the blazing torch, as they believed, again and again. This was too much; his reputation was in danger, and his friends were urgent, confident that the doubter would be convinced. "Al-ta nan-ich!—Now see the doctor eat fire!" Having a bundle of small sticks of wood about two inches in diameter, and several inches long, he lighted one end, and when it blazed well thrust it into his mouth, instantly closing his lips and extinguishing the flame. At this a smile of triumph rested on every face. "Give me a bundle of sticks," said the writer. The sticks being given, were lighted and put into the hand of an Indian who was near. "Now see! all of you. He, only by keeping the wind away from it, makes it go out. He does not eat it. Putting my hands around this will do the same: there, it is out, you see: my hands did not eat it, only shut the air out. Fire cannot live without wind." All were mute. Speaking to the doctor he said, "You deceive the people:" "*Oh now-it-kah*—certainly," he replied. The people appeared to be convinced; but probably were thinking the writer was a very great *medicine man*, being more than a match for a fire-eater.

Formerly it was a prevailing custom for the "medicine men" at the dancing festivals to lacerate their flesh with sharp stones or knives, making deep cuts; and while the blood was gushing out, scoop it up in their hands, and drink it, to appease and gratify their blood-thirsty *tam-an-a-was* that raged within. Probably it was pretended by these deceivers that their "familiars" delighted in blood, in order to inspire the poor dupes of their black art with an abiding dread of their displeasure, who could command the service of such malicious agents. The limbs and bodies of many exhibit scars which originated in this diabolical practice.

During the winter a circumstance came under the

writer's notice, which may be related here, which is in keeping with the known character of the Dalls Indians since the whites first knew them. Several Indians from Wishham called one day at the mission, and being left alone in the room where they used to sit to converse or come to get medicine, one of them, when an opportunity served, went into an adjoining room and found a market under his blanket for two shirts and a vest, on which he and his party soon left, having lost their inclination to remain there any longer. The next sabbath he came to meeting, wearing the vest, which he carefully covered with his blanket, so that it was not seen till service closed, when he forgot to keep it hid, and thus the thief revealed himself, and showed that previous suspicions were well founded. The vest and one of the shirts only were recovered.

Difficulties often arise about property on the decease of relatives. A case of this kind took place at the Dalls station this winter. Tah-lac-eow-it, the Indian mentioned before, was living there, and at work for the mission. He occupied a small house, with his family, consisting of his wife and her mother, which belonged to the mission. After a time his wife, who had been long in a consumption, died. The writer was present at the time, and was engaged in prayer when her spirit took its flight. As he arose, the watchful mother caught with her eye the last gasp, and was instantly overwhelmed with loud and frantic grief. When the burial and the mourning had ended, the brother of the deceased began to annoy the bereft husband about the property, and made his visits so frequent, and urged his unreasonable claims so madly, that a quarrel ensued, and a battle of pulling hair, and after this a strife to wrench an axe from each other's grasp, that one might have it to fight the other to some purpose. At this state of the affray, the writer entered the little house where they were, seized the weapon, and wrested it from them; and then laying hold of the aggressor's long hair, showed him the way out into the yard in a hurry, and there the war ended! It is seldom the case that their engagements can be depended on. One was paid for ten deer-skins; and when he brought them, five were poor ones: and besides this cheat, he wanted to get other property worth at least half the skins. Agree to give one a shirt for his services, and when he has done he will often want a vest, or trousers, or half a dozen small presents.

CHAPTER XVI.

Mr. David Leslie has charge of Oregon Mission during the absence of Mr. J. Lee—His house burned—Glorious revival of religion at the Walamet station—One of the converts drowned—Happy deaths—Death of Mr. Cyrus Shepard, and extract from a letter written by him—Mr. and Mrs. Perkins return to the Dalls station—Farming operations—Statement by General Jackson—Description of Indian character and customs.

LEAVING the Dalls for a time, the writer will now proceed to notice some of the occurrences at the Walamet station. In the absence of Mr. Jason Lee, Mr. David Leslie was in charge of the affairs of the Oregon Mission. In the month of December he was called to sustain a heavy loss in the burning of his house. Very little was saved—not a change of apparel for his wife and three daughters. Mrs. Leslie's health was also very feeble. The loss which was caused by this disaster was made up to Mr. Leslie by the Board of Missions, under whose patronage he was sent forth. Since the departure of Mr. Jason Lee to the States, Mr. Leslie had administered the ordinance of baptism to five adults and nine children. In the mission school at the Walamet occurred one death, that of a little girl, ten years of age, a Calapooya. She had been in the mission family two years, and gave an evidence of a change of heart. The writer has now also to record to the praise of God the account of a glorious revival at the Walamet station, the first in Oregon. This work of God commenced at a protracted meeting held in connection with a watch-night, and began on Saturday evening, Dec. 29th. Mr. Shepard writing to me, Jan. 4th, says, " Our protracted meeting began last Saturday evening with a prayer meeting :" (I give the substance of his letter :) " there was nothing unusual. Sabbath morning a love-feast was held. The children, neighbours, and Indians present partook of the bread and water; then Mr. Leslie preached, and the word took effect in some hearts. James O'Neal, an American, who went to the country with Capt. Wyeth, in 1834, felt the arrows of conviction piercing his inmost soul. Two children were baptized—Mr. Beers's son, Joseph, and Mr. Shepard's daughter, Anna Maria Lee. The communion was a very precious season. At prayer meeting the awakening Spirit of God was present; and Chas. Roe, J. O'Neal, and Deportes M'Kay rose for prayers. Monday, 31st. Meeting continued through the day, followed by a watch-night. Those convicted above expressed desires and resolutions to 'flee from the wrath to come !' Meeting closed at half-past twelve o'clock. New-year's morning, J. O'Neal, being alone in prayer on the banks of the river, his burden of guilt was removed, and he found peace with God. At the close of the watch-night the mission children appeared unusually careless. On Tuesday I began to think Satan trembled. Some of the larger boys, particularly Ozro and Samson, were uncommonly rude ; and only Charles and Antoine were willing to attend prayers in the evening. The meeting commenced and continued with power. Campbell and Edmunds were deeply wrought upon, and cried aloud, almost in an agony of despair. The scene was awful. Poor C. felt as if he was just falling into hell, and with the greatest earnestness besought the prayers of all present. Prayer went up, and shouts of praise followed, for the soul of the prisoner was soon released. About nine o'clock several of the boys and girls came rushing into the room, fell upon their knees, and began crying aloud for mercy. There was united, audible, agonizing prayer, that could be heard, as Abbott says,' a great way off.' J. Edmunds found peace. He and Campbell were Americans. So did Samson Wilder. Here are the names of several who belonged to the school. This boy was of the Sasty Indians, who inhabit south of the Walamet Valley; and Elijah Hedding, son of the first chief of the Wallah-wallahs. Also Antoine Bingham, of the Calapooya nation; and Ozro Morrill, and his sister, Harriet Newell, Chenooks, brother and sister to Wm. Brooks, who was taken to the United States by Mr. Jason Lee, where he also embraced religion, and some time after died in the city of New-York. Mary Sergeant also found pardon. These continued happy in the divine favour." Such was the state of the work, that meetings continued to be held for some time, and the influence extended to many hearts. Several more of the mission children were justified, and some more of the whites. One of these was Mr. Smith, mentioned in chapter 12th. He was then living on the west side of the Walamet, near Chehalim. He had long felt his need of justifying grace, and had just heard of the work at the mission. At this time Mr. Perkins, who had witnessed the blessed work at that place, called on him, being on his way to Fort Vancouver. Finding him "not far from the kingdom," he urged him to an instant surrender of his whole heart to God, nothing doubting; and while they engaged in prayer, the blessing of God filled his believing heart! The joy of Mr. and Mrs. Leslie was crowned in the conversion of their three little daughters. Several others were also sharers in this merciful visitation. Of the fruits, twenty-seven were received into society; but several more it was believed had also tasted of the good word of life, and felt the saving grace of God. His name be praised! Henceforth it shall be said, "What hath God wrought!" since he thus visited his people, and the Gentiles in these ends of the earth, with his salvation!

The happy state introduced at the mission by this merciful visitation continued for many months; but, after a time, several turned away, and there came a season of trial, and the love of many waxed cold. But the flame of love that had been kindled continued to burn in some hearts, and was revived in others, and some who had wandered away had again returned at different times, and been reclaimed from their backslidings. One of the subjects of this revival was a youth named George Stotenburgh. He was from New-York state, and taken to Oregon by Dr. White, in whose family he lived mostly till his death, which took place on the 16th of August, 1839. He was crossing the river on horseback at a ford about a mile below the mission, when the current sweeping his horse into the deep water below the ford, he was suddenly drowned. His body was swept down several miles, where, after several weeks, it was found by some Indians, and, being brought up to the mission, was buried. The sabbath before he was at the sabbath school, and seemed to take an unusually deep interest in the exercises, as the writer learned from Mr. Shepard. We trust there was good reason for hope in his death. He was a lad in understanding in advance of his years, and had he lived would likely have been above the middle grade of men in good or in evil. But the Lord hath done as it pleased him, and he is too wise to err, and too good to do evil.

Another death was that of Thomas Pekah, about ten years old. He died August 22d. His father was a native of the Sandwich Islands, and his mother was of the Chenook tribe of Indians. He had been in the mission about two years, and most of the time was a subject of painful scrofulous disease. He shared in the revival, was remarkably patient in his sickness, and died in peace. One or two circumstances of his short and dying life I will mention. Being at the Walamet on the sabbath, some months before he died, the writer took him out to walk a little way along the bank of the river, when, in a point of wood-land near us, we overheard a larger boy engaged in earnest prayer. We knew his voice, and sitting down, waited in silence till we should know the result of his importunate wrestling at a throne of grace. He was acknowledging his backslidings, and crying unto God for pardon. He begged, and agonized, and, need I say, he also prevailed. His sorrow was changed to joy; and, rising up, he instantly began singing a hymn of praise to God. The heart of my little listener caught the "flying joy," when, smiling, he cried out, "There! Antoine is happy!" Yes, he knew that his cry had been heard, and the event filled his own heart with joy and gladness. In the latter part of his "suffering time" his reason was partially lost; but his mind would dwell on religion, and he would go often to Mr. Shepard and desire to kneel at his knees and pray. About two of the larger boys he would say, "They are cast down, and are not happy;" and then talk a great deal about praying for them. But of himself he would generally say, he was very happy. Thank God! he has gone where "sickness, sorrow, pain, and death, are felt and feared no more!"

One more happy death, that took place this year, was that of Rora, an old domestic servant, a native of Otaheite. He had lived with us from the commencement of our mission. He was converted at the beginning of the year, and exhibited the fruits of this change to the end of his life. His disease, which was a consumption, confined him to his bed for several months. He was very patient, resigned, and happy—his sky always clear. In his last wishes, expressed in a letter from Mr. Shepard, he says to me, "I am very sick and weak; I cough a great deal; but it is good for me to be sick, because it is God's will. I do not expect to live long; but I am happy here, and when I die, I expect to go and see God and Jesus Christ, and shall be sick no more. You must pray much, and when you die, you will come and meet me in heaven:" and "Good-by!" Mr. Jason Lee was now absent in the United States, and to see him return again was all, he said, that he desired to live for; but many months before his return, the happy spirit of his ardent old friend had entered into rest. Jesse Lee was a youth of the Clickatat tribe of Indians, whose country lies to the north of the Dalls. He had been with us from two to three years, and was among the subjects of the revival. He endured with much patience the protracted sickness which terminated his life. May we not exclaim, in view of these things, " Verily, God hath chosen the poor of this world, rich in faith, and heirs of the kingdom." God hideth from the " wise and prudent," but is made manifest " unto babes." But the time has come when we must part with a beloved brother and distinguished fellow-labourer, Mr. Cyrus Shepard. He had " fought the good fight, finished his course, kept the faith." Since his first engagement in the mission, he had employed himself in labours beyond his strength, and that, too, under a load of bodily infirmities which knew no permanent relief, but increased more and more till they ended in death. Our brother loved society, but he was happier in doing good. In labours he was abundant, endeavouring to do good in every way in his power to all around him, both to their souls and bodies. Often did he visit the Indian lodge with food for the hungry and medicine for the sick. For the children in the mission under his care he felt a deep and abiding interest. To teach, to clothe, to feed, and to save them, soul and body, was his utmost desire; and this, with the blessed hope of his own salvation, made him constantly " trample on pleasure and pain." By many of the early inhabitants he will long be held in grateful remembrance; but those only who knew him from the first can place a just estimate upon his character. His disease was the scrofula, and in the spring of 1838 it attacked his right knee. By recourse to medical treatment, however, the danger was averted, and for eighteen months some hopes were indulged that he would recover. But on the commencement of the rainy season, in the fall of 1839, the disease forced him to take his bed, where, after suffering greatly for about twenty days, it became necessary, as the only hope of saving his life, to resort to the painful process of amputation. This was done December 11th, by Dr. White, assisted by Dr. Bailey and Mr. Wilson. He endured all with remarkable patience and resignation. "Through all his sufferings," said his sympathizing and excellent wife, in a letter of the 22d of December, "I have not heard a murmur to escape his lips; but in his most trying hours, he could rejoice and sing praises to God!" An opportunity to forward the letter of which this is an extract not occurring till the 27th, he wrote me a few lines in the margin, the last his hand ever penned, which breathe the same spirit with that quoted above. Including all at the Dalls station, he says, December 27th: "Dear Brethren and Sisters,—Feeling a desire to say a few words to you this morning, Susan has kindly unsealed her letter to favour my purpose. I am very feeble in body, and obliged to lie on my back from morning till night; excepting of late I have been permitted to turn on my side, or to lie raised on my bed for a short season, to relieve the pain caused by lying in one position so long. But the doctor begins to think that even this, on the whole, is injurious, and discourages it. I have lain from midnight till ten o'clock, A. M., in the same position, and bear it very well. Dr. White has been very attentive indeed since my sickness, and has done all fully to satisfaction. All the brethren and sisters seem to take delight in exerting themselves to manifest their sympathy and kindness in every manner possible. I think no person under heaven ever was more kindly and faithfully attended to than I have been during my sickness. Expressions of deep sympathy are pouring in from every quarter. French, English, Americans, nor must I exclude the poor Indians, have given unequivocal proof of their sympathizing love. I cannot say I think I shall get up from this bed whereon I have gone down. God has dealt with me in a manner which it is impossible to describe to you. Such support, such a removal of every care, the mind constantly far from every anxious thought, I could never have conceived to be possible. Under the most excruciating pain, when at every breath it seemed impossible to refrain from screeching as loud as my strength would bear, these cries were mingled with shouts of praise! I would say to you, such has been the abundance of peace given, that not a rising of impatience or fretfulness, nor a murmur or a complaint has ever been felt by me during my sickness. Farewell! The God of all peace, grace, and consolation be with you continually." Signed, "A part of Cyrus." The stump of the amputated limb healed gradually, and strong hopes were entertained that he would recover; but they proved delusive, for an abscess formed in his hip which baffled medicine, and so rapidly wasted the powers of life, that on the ushering in of the new year, 1840, his happy spirit, "disburthened of its load," mounted upward to the abode of bliss! Many who called to see him he warned and exhorted to repentance. Happy they if they lay these warnings to heart. His voice is now hushed in the grave. Though dead he yet speaks to all who knew his holy life and godly conversation.

Mr. Shepard was born in Philipstown, Mass., August 16, 1799. He obtained the blessing of justifying grace in Marlboro', Mass., January 1st, 1826—joined the Oregon Mission at its commencement in 1834—was married to Miss Susan Downing, of Lynn, Mass., in Oregon, July 16, 1837, and died January 1st, 1840. He left a widow and two little daughters; but he left them a legacy, the divine favour, God, the widow's husband and the orphan's father.

Thus did the Lord remove his servant from the ranks of his fellow-labourers; but their loss was only temporary, his gain eternal. Thus does the Lord bury his workmen, "and take them home to rest," while he still provides for and carries on his work. Jan. 2d the funeral rites were performed, a sermon being preached by Mr. Leslie. Most of the Americans in the settlement attended to pay the last tribute of respect in death to him who in life was to many of them a friend and brother. One wish filled every heart, " Let me die the death of the righteous, and let my last end be like his." He rests now from his labours. Yes, we may add:

> " His languishing head is at rest,
> Its thinking and aching are o'er,
> His quiet, immovable breast
> Is heaved by affliction no more."

In the sickness and death of Mr. Shepard the mission school was deprived of his valuable services as a teacher; but a watchful Providence supplied another guardian, in the person of Mr. Wm. Geiger, a Presbyterian, who passed the winter there, on his way to California. The school prospered while under his management, till the return of Mr. Jason Lee, May, 1840.

Leaving other accounts of the Walamet for the present, we will now return to the Dalls, and after noticing Mr. Perkins in his return to that station, lay before the reader the doings there, and some account of the Indians, their history, location, character, superstition, medical practice, and means of subsistence.

Early in December of the then present year, 1838, Mr. Perkins left the Walamet station to return with his family to the Dalls, Mrs. Perkins having the care of her babe, only a few weeks old. They descended the Walamet, and reached Fort Vancouver in safety. Hence they proceeded up the Columbia about twenty miles. Here a strong head wind met them, and obliged them to encamp. The cold was so great as to freeze the river and interrupt navigation—the wind also blew a perfect gale for many days; at length, after much exposure, which threatened serious consequences to Mrs. Perkins, who was in delicate health, they turned back to Vancouver, where they found welcome and comfort in the kind hospitalities of Mr. James Douglas, the chief factor, and the other gentlemen and ladies of the establishment. Mrs. Perkins being thus provided for, soon regained her vigour, so as to permit Mr. Perkins to attend the protracted meeting described in the preceding pages at the Walamet. After his return, he was detained at Vancouver, the season and the ice in the river not admitting the trip to be made to the Dalls till February. While here, he spent his time in preaching and in other efforts for the spiritual good of the gentlemen of the company, and their hired servants. Meantime it will be recollected that the writer was at the Dalls station. December 25th he had the pleasure of the company of Mr. Pambem, the gentleman in charge of Fort Wallah-wallah. He had been to Vancouver, and was ascending the river with several boats freighted with merchandise, when the head wind described above compelled them to land. Here they waited twelve days, and then the goods and boats returned to Vancouver, one excepted—this was taken up by the wind and borne a considerable distance, and broken to pieces in its fall. He then pursued his way by land, with a few men, along the snowy, icy shores of the rock-bound river, about sixty miles in five days, to this station. The news of the good work at the Walamet cheered the lone winter about this time. And the arrival of Mr. P. and family, to which a first-born, a son, had been added in their absence, was another source of renewed enjoyment, welcome as a stream in the desert to thirsty travellers. They returned Feb. 13th.

We now took hold of our farming business, making fences, ploughing, sowing, and planting about twenty acres. One field of several acres we held in shares with some of the Indians, who helped to fence and plough it. The ground being new, the returns were small; and even these were partly stolen. These discouragements, with the abundance of salmon, and roots and berries, easily obtained, prevented them from ever again, while the writer dwelt among them, degrading themselves by an attempt to till the soil! Besides some grain, some garden vegetables, and a fine crop of potatoes were produced this year; the ground was irrigated from the spring. The Indians, some of them, showed a disposition to avail themselves of the fruits of our industry, by harvesting some of the potatoes without our consent. Of this propensity we had frequent proofs, in one form or another. So that we were often reminded of a statement which the writer heard General Andrew Jackson make, when Indian honesty was mentioned as existing in a particular tribe, "You need not tell me," said he; "Indians will steal!" Besides attending to the farm, another house was also begun, and so far finished as to admit the holding of meetings in it, in the winter, which was some improvement on the preceding year; when we had to meet without and worship in the wind, while the natives sat down in the snow.

Before the revival among the Indians at the Dalls, and in its vicinity, which took place in the fall and winter of 1839 and 1840, and which, in order of time, has its place here, is treated of, let me introduce the reader to a more particular acquaintance with the Indians in these parts, and with their character. Ten miles above the station at the Shoots are two villages, *Tekin* and *Wiam*. These are Wallah-wallahs. At the Long Narrows on the north side is *Wishham*, here we first meet with the Chenooks. Next three miles below is *Ka-clas-ko*, near which the mission houses stand, (improperly called Was-co-pam.) Ten miles, you come to Clat-a-cut on the north side. Fifteen miles further down is Kle-miak-sac and Kow-il-a-mow-an. Three miles more, Ne-nooth-tect, then Scal-talpe, and Wah-he at the head of the Cascades. Besides, on the north side of the river, a short distance inland, were the Chick-atat Indians, and to the south twenty-five miles the village of Til-han-ne, inhabited by the Wallah-wallahs. The villages named along the river from the Dalls down to the Cascades are the winter residence of many who pass their summer at one or the other of these fisheries. All these number less than two thousand of all ages. From the Dalls Indians the Kinse used formerly to take an annual tribute of salmon, allèging that the fishery belonged to them. Whether or not their claims were well founded, their superior power in war kept their tributaries in abject submission. These exactions were formerly more rigorous than now; at present they are concealed under the show of traffic. They buy at their own price, compelling them to sell even their own stock of provisions, so as to have little left to subsist on themselves. Another cause, nearly as oppressive, which occurs almost every year, and makes a draft on their salmon stores, is the aggression of some of their poorer neighbours of the nearer inland tribes. These come to the fisheries after the end of the salmon season, while the fishermen are gone into the mountains to gather their yearly stock of berries, and rob their salmon caches. These are cellars which they dig in the sand, where they deposite with much care and secrecy the fruits of their summer's toil, and their winter's hope. Thus pillaged, every returning spring finds many of them in abject want. Formerly they had wars with the Clam-aths and the Zwan-hi-ooks, who inhabit the country far to the south and southeast. Some of the former tribe they hold in slavery. Many years ago the rich hunting ground of the Walamet Valley attracted the Kinse thither in chase of the deer. On their return they were waylaid in the wilderness, when within about twenty-five miles of the Dalls, by a party of the Chenook race residing between this and the Cascades, and nearly, if not entirely, cut off. This bloody conduct soon brought a war-party of the Kinse upon the aggressors, when a battle ensued, and the revengers of their brothers' blood were conquerors. A disposition to take every advantage of white men in their power, by force or fraud, has been more manifest in the Indians here than in any other part of the territory, from the first introduction of the traders among them. Such was their determination to plunder, that for many years the Hudson's Bay Company were compelled to pass them with a large force, and restrain them by the dread of their arms. So late as the year 1826, as Mr. M'Leod, a gentleman of the company, and Mr. Douglas, the naturalist, were passing there, they manifested hostile intentions. Mr. M'Leod, being apprized of his danger, ordered his men to put their boats into the water, on which the Indians interfered, and as Mr. M'Leod was pushing one of them away from the boat, another drew a bow to shoot him. Mr. Douglas seeing this, uncovered his piece, and aimed it at the Indian. At this moment a Kinse chief and three of his young men arrived, and set the matter at rest. When one of these Indians is detected in stealing, or with stolen property, and it is restored, or taken from him, it is often the case among themselves that the thief receives some article of less value, for which he has the boldness to stipulate with the owner of the stolen property. For instance : one wants a shirt,—he goes and steals a horse ; and when he is found tells the owner, "Give me a shirt, and you shall have the horse ;" and he, preferring to do this to having any further trouble, gives the thief a shirt, and feels gratified with his good fortune. One of these gentry who dread to get an honest living, having stolen a horse from the mission here in 1838, which he sold, and which was afterward recovered, when in the course of justice he had to give up the musket for which he had sold the horse, was much afflicted that the whole affair was not likely to benefit him at all ! But being determined not to steal for nothing, he demanded a shirt of the writer, "to make his heart good." The idea of paying a man for stealing ! Never ! Not succeeding, the next day he renewed his demand, bringing with him some of his relations, having knives and a war-stone to intimidate me to a compliance, but he met with no success ; and the determined reply he received, though it did not reform his heart, yet it improved his conduct toward the mission ever after. The war-stone mentioned above is a smooth stone, nearly round, and about two inches in diameter, strongly enclosed in a piece of elk-skin, which covers a handle about fifteen inches long, having the stone at one end. A blow with this would fracture a man's skull.

Let the reader now be introduced to the most influential persons among this people. These are the "medicine men," or conjurors, who can, it is believed, set the evil spirit of disease at defiance, cast it out where it has dared to enter, and make it seize with an unyielding, deadly grasp the objects of their displeasure. The people believe that they hold intercourse with spirits, that they can see the disease, which is some extraneous thing, as a small shell, or a pipe, or a piece of tobacco, or some other material substance, which they (the doctors) describe. It is firmly believed that they can send a bad "tam-an-a-was" into a person, and make him die, unless it be cast out by some other "medicine man." If a threat is made, or it is intimated, by one of them, that a certain person will not live long, no sooner does he hear of it than he is alarmed, and feels himself a dead man. For their services they are paid in advance, and often their demands are high, and their practice is lucrative. When their patients die, they restore the fees. This is necessary for their own security, for otherwise they might be charged with having caused his death, which would render them the mark of revenge. If one of the order is his rival or enemy, and he wishes this obstacle to his own advancement removed, the affirmation that he caused the death of some person will probably be followed with his death by the relatives of the deceased. Several deaths from this cause took place at the Dalls the first year after the station was occupied, and this is a common occurrence among many of the surrounding tribes. Sometimes it happens that the doctor takes all his patient has, not leaving a dying man his last, perhaps his only, garment or covering. A case of this kind occurred at the Dalls. A young man was in a consumption, and was in the writer's care,—he was frightened away to the doctor by some one who saw he had a shirt and trousers, and shoes, and a light blanket, which he had received in part from me; and it was not long before he had stripped him of the whole, and then left him to die, or hastened his death. The poor man had no friends, and the doctor was safe.

As we shall have occasion to notice instances of these practices in the progress of our work, the writer will only mention briefly the manner in which it is sometimes performed, which will give the reader some idea of its degrading nature. Several poles are tied together at the ends, and from six to ten men are arranged along them in a sitting posture, each having a stick with which he beats on the poles; and thus a loud jarring noise is produced, which may be heard a long distance. This is accompanied with a kind of singing, in which the "medicine man" leads, while he kneels near his patient on the other side of the polls, making horrid contortions and grimaces, as if some demoniac was raging within. The chant is not long, and then, after a few minutes, is renewed again, and thus repeated several times. The way being now prepared, he approaches his patient, and, after a painful and persevering effort, with his mouth applied as a cupping-glass, he transfers the "sko-kom," or "tam-an-a-was," or disease, wholly or in part from the patient to himself! In this stage of the treatment two men approach him, and taking hold of ropes about his waist and beneath his arms, free him from the patient, when he appears as one dead. Very soon he begins to show signs of life— a limb moves, he mutters, turns, gets on his hands and knees, rises slowly up, can hardly stand, grows stronger, summons a mighty effort!—music lifts, labours! makes an unearthly scream, and violently throwing out his arms at full length, ejects the evil principle, and he is now ready for a new onset!

Leaving their medical faculty, we will now look into their habitations. They are covered with bark, and the walls are made of boards split out of the cedar. The boards are set on end, and support the plates, rafters, and ribs. The floor is about three feet below the ground, and the fire-place in the middle, sometimes a little lower, and the smoke escapes through an opening at the top. Several families often unite together and occupy one house. Twenty or thirty are sometimes seen living thus together. What a group! Stop, reader, and dwell a moment on their condition, and contrast it with your own; and thank your Maker that he has given you a lot more suitable to your improvement and happiness.

As to their means of subsistence, these consist of salmon, roots, berries, and game. Besides the dried salmon, which we have already mentioned, they also store large quantities in sacks. This is first dried in the sun, then pounded fine in stone mortars; and then the sacks, being first lined with the skins of the salmon, are filled with it, so compact that twenty salmon only require one about one foot in diameter and two feet long. Their roots, which are a substitute for bread, they dig in the spring. This is done by the women. These are pounded into a pulp, and then formed into thin cakes of an oblong form, measuring about six by ten inches, and being well dried in the sun, are stored for future use, and will keep a long time. In autumn they lay in large stores of berries dried. Acorns, also, which are abundant some years, are used as an article of food. These are gathered and baked with heated stones—a method of preparing food common both to the Indians and Pacific Islanders. Heated stones are put into an excavation in the ground three feet across, and covered with leaves or grass so as to prevent the articles to be cooked from burning. Then these are laid on, and carefully covered in the same manner. Last of all, earth is spread over the whole to keep in the heat, and the process of baking is done up in real native style. After the acorns are thus prepared, deep pits are dug near the water, in which they are buried in mud, where they remain through the winter; when they are taken up and eaten, much improved, it is supposed, by the soaking process.

CHAPTER XVII.

Account of the "work of God" at the Dalls in 1839, '40—Specimen of an Indian prayer—Dancing-hall used as a meeting-house—Preaching of the missionaries, and formation of classes—Baptism of converts—Camp-meeting—Communion administered to several hundred Indians—Affairs at the Walamet station—Trip to Walamet and Chenook—Arrival of the Lausanne with a reinforcement to the mission, accompanied by Mr. J. Lee.

IN the preceding chapter mention was made of the "*work of God*," as it has been rightfully designated, at the Dalls in 1839 and '40; some account of which the writer will now proceed to give.

While Mr. Shepard, as has been related, was confined to his dying bed, and not long before his decease, his heart was cheered by hearing that the Lord was visiting the Dalls station in the awakening and conversion of souls. That this was the work of God at its beginning and in its progress, the writer fully believes. What if some, or even most of the anticipated results failed? Does this prove that it was not God's doing? By no means; for instances are frequent in which he revives his work in portions of his vineyard, and most of the anticipated fruits never appear. See this illustrated by an unerring Teacher in the parable of the sower, Matt. xiii. The writer, when this good work commenced, was absent, having gone some time previously to the Walamet, and did not return till past the 15th of November. When he arrived, Mr. Perkins met him at the shore, and told him that a gracious work was begun among the natives. Of this he had strong doubts, and could not assent till the proof appeared; for before he went to the Walamet, they had become so lawless and daring that our safety was endangered, and he had just brought several muskets and a supply of powder and balls from Vancouver for defence, intending to garrison the dwelling-house and resist any hostility they might attempt. But now these munitions of war were not needed, for it appeared truly that the God of peace had come to the help of his servants, and the salvation of his people. Mr. Perkins was found labouring zealously night and day, going from lodge to lodge, praying and exhorting, holding prayer meetings and preaching. His own soul had been recently blest with a signal salvation, and walking in the "comfort of the Holy Ghost," he had the cause of God greatly at heart. Large numbers of the natives attended meetings as earnest hearers, and several had begun to pray. One had already been converted. After several weeks of deep repentance, in which he met with much opposition, and devoted many hours to prayer, his soul was set at liberty in a prayer meeting; and although his joy was not great, yet the change was soon manifest. He began at once to "declare what God had done for his soul," exhorted all he met to come to Jesus, and prayed with deep and fervent longings for the souls of his relations and others. This event awakened a deeper and wider interest among the people; in so much that the number of inquirers obliged Mr. Perkins to give himself entirely up to the work, as mentioned above. As to Mr. Perkins and the writer, their hearts were knit together in love, and long will those seasons of "refreshing from the presence of the Lord," which we enjoyed in those happy days, be remembered, when the language of our hearts was, "Jesus is mine and I am his." Our object and aim were now one—the salvation of the souls around us; and we desired no higher employment than to serve them as the heirs of eternal life. We felt that they belonged to Christ, and he could and would save them.

With these views our united strength was now consecrated to this work, which the Lord of the vineyard had evidently assigned us. Our meetings were held in the house mentioned in the last chapter, which was thirty by twenty feet; but on the sabbath it would not hold the people, so that sometimes it was necessary to hold a meeting in the other house at the same time. Every morning and evening they were assembled for public prayers, when a portion of New Testament history was expounded by one of us. Such was their interest in the meetings, that the want of clothing sufficient to protect them from the cold, or of shoes to keep their feet from the frost and snow—for even many of the women had none—could not keep them away, though they had to walk a mile in going and returning. Who, let me ask, in this Christian land, would do more than this in order to hear the blessed gospel? Some time after my return from the Walamet, there being about twenty souls, men and women, in deep distress on account of their sins, and apparently near the " kingdom," we met in a special prayer meeting, where few except those were present. Here was earnest, united praying, and the " kingdom of heaven was taken by violence." More than half the number gave evidence of a happy change. Their agitated hearts felt an unknown peace, a joyful smile sat on their faces, and their lips praised the name of Jesus. " Mi-cah Jesus Christ e-toke-te!—Thou, Jesus Christ, art good!" " Cupet mi-cah mi-mah e-toke-te!—Thou alone art good!"—" Can-nu-it e-toke-te!—Certainly thou art good!" " Jesus good!" " Jesus good!"

The " Spirit of adoption" was now as manifest as had been a little before the " spirit of bondage." One of these, a leading man, who is sometimes called " Boston" by his people, because his head is not flattened, was some time before asked by Mr. Perkins why he rose so much earlier than formerly. "Why," said he, " I cannot sleep. When I go home and lie down, I think of your teaching, and I cannot sleep. I sleep a little, and then dream I am in meeting, and my heart is all the time talking over what you say. My heart was formerly asleep, I see, but now it is awake." As soon as his own proud spirit was humbled, and his troubled conscience had found peace, he sought his wife and daughter, knelt by them, and told them to pray.

Here may be given a specimen of their praying.

O thou great God on high, we now pray to thee. Our fathers knew thee not, they died in darkness, but we have heard of thee,—now we see a little. Truly we are wretched! Our hearts were blind,—dark as night, —always foolish,—our ears closed! Our hearts bad, —all bad,—always bad,—full of evil,—nothing good, *not one!* Thou knowest! Truly we pray now to thee. O make us good! Put away our bad hearts. Give us thy Holy Spirit to make our hearts soft! Our hearts are hard like a stone. Give us light. O make our hearts new,—good,—all good,—always good! Formerly we stole,—told lies,—were full of anger; now done! "*Nash-ke alka ka-dow!*—Never again so!" Now we desire thee, O come into our hearts,—now come! Jesus Christ thy Son died for us; O Jesus, wash our hearts! " Minch't-cah-meet cow-o-lute quich-cah!— Behold and bless!"

Several others were soon after added to this number. Mrs. Perkins now devoted a part of every day in prayer meetings with the females, and the work continued to prosper. The voice of prayer was now heard in the lodge, and wood, and glen; the early morning and the evening were vocal with the suppliant's voice, and the place where the "church-going bell" was "never heard," was honoured with the presence of the "Head of the church" in many a hallowed spot where he met the contrite " sinner returning from his ways."

There was an old man, who for some time stood aloof from the work, because others of a lower class took the lead in it; and this made him of less consequence than he desired, and he had opposed the little band for several weeks. During this time he was in a very unhappy state of mind. One day as the writer was speaking with him closely about God, whom he was bound to obey and love, he seemed deeply affected, and wept, and while we prayed together his tears flowed freely; he did not, however, yield his heart to God till the 1st of May, several weeks after. " How do you feel?" said Mr. Perkins to another old man as they were going out to pray in the wood. "O," said he, "my heart is very small and sorrowful. Yesterday I prayed most all day out behind that hill," pointing to a distant hill; "but my heart is still bad!" "Jesus can change it," said Mr. P.; "Jesus has died for you!" So kneeling down they prayed. The poor old man believed in Jesus, and light, love, and joy filled his heart—another proof of the love of God to the poor, whom he makes "heirs of his kingdom!"

These pages relate to the work at the station, chiefly among the Indians of the Caclasco Village near it, and this continued to spread till but a small number were left, and also extended to two small villages a few miles below, embracing also a little village of Wallah-wallahs, living near Caclasco; most of them were formed into classes by Mr. Perkins before the 10th of January, 1840. The writer had been labouring among the Indians on the river below, down to the Cascades, of which he will speak hereafter, and first notice this work at its introduction among the Indians at Wishham.

Mr. Perkins visited this village on the 10th of Jan., 1840. The *round-head* man, "Boston," was with him, as an interpreter: this man had assisted him from the day of his conversion, and was found an efficient helper: the season was cold, and the first night they took little notice of him: encamped in a lodge of sticks and mats. There, next day, he found a large cellar, which was formerly used as a dancing hall, and clearing it out, used it for a meeting house. It was large enough to hold all the village, three hundred souls. A few men and boys, and about twenty-five women, came in the forenoon. Their number increased at every meeting, till on the fourth day almost the whole village were present. Such subjects never met your eyes! Naked, squalid, deformed, blind, halt, lame: Mr. P. truly adds, "*destruction* and *misery* are in their ways," as saith the Scriptures. After he had preached two days, they seemed to awake as from a dream; many began to pray, and the cry became general as the meeting progressed. The barren rocks behind Wishham echoed their earnest prayers, and many afterward testified that they became happy while thus engaged, and many spoke feelingly of their past wretchedness and darkness, and seemed to feel a deep abhorrence of their sins, and expressed a determination to serve God henceforth. One old man, on hearing Mr. Perkins' interpreter tell the history of Jesus, exclaimed, "This is the talk I want to hear!" Then addressing Mr. Perkins, he with a poker drew some coals from the fire, saying, "There, you have come just so to pull me out of the fire!" At his subsequent visits, during the winter, the work appeared to be continually advancing, and several were found to be useful as exhorters. Here he formed several classes, including a very large part of the village.

A similar work was witnessed by the writer in the villages down the river as far as the Cascades. They numbered about four hundred and seventy-five souls. To them the word was communicated through an interpreter, who was the first fruits of this work of God. The preaching was the simple story of the gospel, the history of Him who died to take away our sin. The interpreter and another convert who was with us laboured in exhortation and prayer; and the people in most of the villages, it was believed, repented, like the Ninevites, "from the least to the greatest;" and, like the people of Samaria, "gave heed with one consent to the things they heard." The aged and the young all seemed to rejoice in the glad tidings which were now first brought to their ears. Classes were formed in all the villages, six in number, and leaders appointed; and after this, while the writer was labouring the rest of the winter at Fort Vancouver and among the Indians in the vicinity, Mr. P. made them frequent visits, and found them holding fast the truths they had received. At the station, too, the good work had continued to advance. Besides, Mr. Perkins spent some time among the neighbouring Wallah-wallahs, at the Shoots, with good effect. He had acquired the previous summer a sufficient knowledge of their language to enable him to speak it with fluency. The writer's labours among the Indians at Vancouver were not attended with as much success as above the Cascades; yet he has no reason to regret his attempt to do them good, but rather is happy in the thought that he was permitted the honour to unfold to them the love wherewith Christ hath loved them. Night and day, from house to house, he preached unto them Jesus. They then heard, and never before, the simple, pure truths of the gospel; and that, as a people, they will ever again hear them, is not probable, for there are influences thrown around them which cut off the approach of truth. But he that goeth forth, and with tears sows the precious seed, has no cause to be ashamed— the seed may appear after many days; but if not, if the tares spring up, he knows their origin and his Master's direction, " Let them grow until harvest." While here the writer preached frequently to the hired servants of the Hudson's Bay Company, and they appeared to hear with some interest. Often while he was speaking to them was his own spirit refreshed. Was the word mixed with faith in them who heard? O that the " fruit may be found after many days!" In the fort he usually preached twice on the sabbath. The attention of all was serious, and the Lord stood by his servant, that he might " open " his " mouth boldly, and speak as he ought to speak." In the various efforts which he made here to benefit the different classes, he believes that he was actuated with a pure desire, embracing his own salvation, the glory of God, and the good of souls. The Lord be praised who strengthened my hands, and cheered my heart, in the toils, and trials, and temptations of that period. To the gentlemen of the company he will ever feel under great obligations for their many " kind attentions toward him," during his residence there at that time.

On the 13th of February Mr. Perkins met me there,

having just come from the Dalls. He found much snow at the Cascades, and suffered considerably from exposure on the trip. We were glad to meet, and to speak of the work of God, and to pray together once more for its advancement.

In March the writer left Vancouver on his return to the Dalls, visited all the villages above the Cascades, where he had laboured, on his way down, and found them in a prosperous state, "walking in the truth." Having been previously instructed in the nature and design of the ordinance of baptism, they were most of them now baptized, both adults and children. Who could "forbid water" that they should be baptized? Especially when, according to Scripture example, they might have been admitted to that ordinance on the day in which they first believed. The season was one of great joy to the writer; and the happiness of these poor yet simple believers was another proof of the power of the gospel to triumph over the deepest degradation and the most abject destitution. This *only* did, and this only could, produce the change that was seen among them. Their former enmities and quarrels among neighbours and in families, which were frequent, were subdued, and peace now prevailed among them. Arrangements were now made for a camp meeting, to be held early in the month of April, about six miles below the Dalls, and three miles from the mission house, at a place called Cow-e-laps.

Arriving at the station, one more interview with Mr. and Mrs. Perkins was my joyful privilege; and here a large number of the Caclasco Indians, and others near them, were, on the few following days, including a sabbath, baptized. Here my spirit was greatly refreshed by seeing the extended influence of the gospel among them.

Taking Mr. Perkins, we went to Wishham. Here we found the people engaged in the duties of their profession; and held several meetings in public, in the open air, the hearers sitting on the ground; visited and prayed from lodge to lodge, and administered baptism to about two hundred and fifty souls.

After this Mr. Perkins, accompanied by his wife, went down the river, labouring at the villages both going and returning, till the time appointed to hold the camp meeting; and the writer, meantime, taking two of the converts from Wascopam, and one from Wishham, went to preach to two villages of the Clickatats residing inland to the northward, and numbering more than two hundred souls. Here he saw such a readiness to hear and to follow the teachings of the gospel as had not been surpassed in any other place. The old, and the middle-aged, and the young, even little children, received it as the most joyous tidings that ever saluted their ears; and their earnest prayers and confessions told how fully they believed it was the word of the Great Spirit, given both to govern them and to save them. Never did the writer enjoy his work more than while engaged among these poor red men in preaching, and exhorting, and praying for their salvation. That numbers of them were converted there was no room for him to doubt. Subsequently they attended the camp meeting, to which the reader's attention is now called. At this meeting about twelve hundred were present from the villages along the river, from the Cascades, from Wishham and Caclasco, and from the neighbouring Wallah-wallahs, and the Clickatats, as named above. The spot was chosen in the open plain, bounded on one side by a ridge of rocks, at the foot of which the writer pitched his tent, while on either hand were ranged the wigwams of the natives, gradually rounding in a circle, meeting in front, and enclosing an area of half an acre. The wigwams were made of willow poles set in the ground in a circular or oblong form, inclining toward the centre at an angle of fifty degrees, and enclosed with mats of grass, having a large opening at the top, and a door at each end, with a fire in the middle, and sometimes two fires, when the tenement was long, and then it was occupied by a large number, perhaps thirty. When it was completed, the tops of the poles were the most prominent elevation of our city, which had grown up in a day. The good order observed throughout the whole meeting was never surpassed in an assembly of such numbers, and which continued so long together. At daylight they were awakened by the sound of a trumpet, and soon after engaged, first in singing, and then in prayer, in their houses. Then followed the washing of hands and faces, after which they took breakfast. For public exercises they were called together three or four times during the day, the women and the men apart, with a space of four or five yards intervening, sitting on the ground, sometimes with a mat or a bear-skin spread beneath them, and a blanket or skin or mat over their shoulders; presenting a dense mass of black heads and sunburnt faces, alternating between adults, and babes, and little children, withered old age, and gray heads, remnants of other days! and—— The pencil drops. The company beggars description! To know, the reader must see. But they were met to hear words by which they might be saved—to hear those truths repeated which had so much interested them for several months—truths which they delighted to hear. The great and most important facts of revelation were spread out before them in a connected chain, beginning with accounts of the creation, then of the formation of man, the institution of the sabbath, and marriage; the fall of man; his punishment; the promise of Christ; the first murderer; the wickedness of man causing a flood; Noah saved; man's wicked attempt to build Babel; its consequences; the history of Abraham, Isaac, and Jacob and his sons, particularly Joseph; the Jews in bondage; Moses in Egypt; the Jews led by him through the desert; brought into Canaan; the wicked Canaanites destroyed; disobedience of the Jews; its punishment; the coming of Christ according to the prophecies; baptism, temptation, miracles, instructions, persecutions, death, resurrection, ascension, and second coming to judge, to reward; commission to his disciples; Pentecost; labours, and sufferings, and success, and death of the apostles; their own duty to obey the word of Christ, never turning again to their former wicked ways; the Holy Spirit; the new heart, without which nothing would avail; that this was necessary in order to *be* good, or *do* good, or *ensure* good; this through Jesus Christ only; he *died* for them. To these truths they listened with the most earnest attention and apparent devotion. Such deep and general solemnity the writer has seldom witnessed. In the intervals of public worship they withdrew some distance from the ground and engaged in prayer alone. Prayers in their houses in the evening closed the day. Thus the time was employed till the ensuing sabbath, our meeting having continued from Monday, when the communion was administered to several hundreds. To the administrator it was a day of labour, but one of "refreshing from the presence of the Lord." The solemn presence of God seemed to pervade almost every heart, and a deep conviction that great was the love of Christ in dying for us, whose death we now recognised in the bread and wine which we ate and drank as emblems of "his broken body and his shed blood."

Thus ended a day that the writer will long remember with thankfulness to the God of love that he was ever permitted to see it; and he expects to meet precious souls, with whom he enjoyed that communion, in the kingdom of heaven, and will ever pray in hope of that event. The next day our meeting closed in great peace; and all the Indians scattered to their various quarters to engage in removing to their fishing-grounds against the arrival of the salmon: and thus the writer will leave them for the present, and notice the movement of affairs at the Walamet station down to the present period.

The mission school, under the care of Mr. Geiger, **numbered** thirty-six children, and their improvement was encouraging. After the decease of Mr. Shepard there followed a revival of the work of God, and the result was a higher state of enjoyment in the hearts of his people. The Lord also made bare his arm in the conversion of several white men : to his name be all the praise. The sabbath school also numbered forty-six scholars, and was in a prosperous state—a good state of religious feeling prevailed.

Mrs. Leslie was in bad health most of the time, and this with other cases of sickness in Mr. Leslie's family demanded much of his time for watching and nursing, and almost all the etceteras of the household affairs often devolved in a great measure upon him; besides, he had frequent attacks of the intermittent fever, which left one only half a man, and with all this, how much missionary labour could he perform? Let the friends of missions but remember that sickness disables for efficient labour, and that the missionaries in Oregon have suffered a large amount, and they will be convinced that their efforts must have been feeble, and therefore inefficient, and that the good done equals the work actually performed, at its lowest estimate. Returning from this digression to the Dalls, the reader will please to embark with the writer for a trip to Walamet, and thence to Chenook. Immediately after the camp meeting he started down the river, preaching to the Indians wherever he found them, they having broken up their winter residences, and pitched along here and there on the river, in stations convenient for obtaining a good supply of roots. Pursuing our way we came to the Walamet station: this was my first visit there since the death of my ever dear brother Mr. Shepard, and now he who used to meet me at the gate and embrace me in his arms, on former visits, met me not—no, his place was empty; but at the door the writer was met by his once smiling companion bathed in tears; words could not tell her sorrows nor reveal my sympathies! How changed! The husband, the father, the brother, absent, gone! Will return no more! But the widow's heart was found trusting in God, and she felt that his consolations were neither few nor small. In communion with his Christian friends here the writer enjoyed a season of rest and delight for a few short days, and bidding them farewell glided down the Walamet, and calling on Mr. Smith was with his crew hospitably entertained over night. His wife had lately professed to meet with a change of heart, and appeared zealously affected for the welfare of the Indians in the lower country near the mouth of the Columbia; and soon as arrangements could be made, Mr. Smith determined to accompany me, taking her with him, on my trip to Chenook. Having got all ready for the voyage, Saturday, May 16th, we stepped into our canoes, and in the evening encamped at the falls. Here we passed the sabbath and held meetings with the Indians. Monday we left the falls and proceeded on our voyage, and on Wednesday, P. M., reached a small village, near Oak Point, called Ne-co-ni-ac. Here we put ashore, and held a meeting, Mr. and Mrs. Smith using their endeavours to persuade the poor inhabitants to believe the instructions they received. Thence we proceeded to Chenook, where we arrived on Thursday about noon. We had but just arranged our camp, when, casting my eye toward the mouth of the river, a vessel was seen sailing up the channel close under Cape Disappointment, and in a few minutes more she dropped anchor in Baker's Bay.

The vessel, as the writer anticipated, was the Lausanne, Capt. Spalding, with the reinforcement to the Oregon Mission which sailed from New-York, as we had been previously informed, in Nov., 1839, and whose arrival had been anxiously expected for some time. Mr. Smith and myself now went to Chenamas, the Chenook chief, and let him know that we wanted to go on board, as probably our people had come in the ship. The water being rough, he launched a large canoe with a crew of fifteen to twenty men, in which he and his wife also embarked, and we were all soon bounding delightfully over the proud waves, and in a short time we found ourselves alongside the good ship Lausanne, which we boarded, and were kindly received by the captain, and soon became acquainted with the welcome passengers, through the aid of repeated introductions, as they thronged around us. Here an acquaintance, Mr. David Carter of Missouri, met me: we were glad of the unexpected interview. Mr. J. Lee had gone on shore, but soon returned: a hearty greeting followed. The names of the gentlemen and ladies of this reinforcement will appear in the next chapter, giving an account of their embarkation and voyage. We had an agreeable interview, very gratifying, but associated with some very tender and painful remembrances; we had since we last met been subjected to some sore bereavements! But the next day we left with Chenamas, and Mr. J. Lee proceded in a canoe directly to Walamet, leaving the new recruits to ascend to Vancouver in their well-tried sea-boat, and myself and Mr. Smith to go on with the mission among the Chenooks. Here we remained some days, giving the people instruction, held meetings, visited, exhorted, and prayed, from lodge to lodge, in which Mr. Smith and his wife laboured zealously, as did also the converts who came with me from the Dalls. Leaving the Chenooks, we went to the Clatsops, and then to Fort George.

Having obtained another canoe, for Mr. J. Lee had taken the one we came in, we started up the river, and on Monday, June 1st, reached Vancouver. The occurrences of the next two months, during which time my associate writer and myself were together, will be found in a succeeding chapter. Before resuming the story of the Dalls station, it is due to the reader to have a fuller account of that part of the Columbia called the Dalls. This shall be done in the next chapter, which shall also include some account of the Shoots, and of the Cascades.

CHAPTER XVIII.

Description of the Columbia River, dike, rapids, rocky islands, &c.—Whirlpool, in which a party belonging to the Hudson's Bay Company were engulfed, and most of them perished—Indian mode of fishing—More than one thousand Indians employ a portion of their time in the salmon fishery—The Cascades—Indian hymn and translation.

ASCENDING this majestic river two hundred and eighty miles, amidst basaltic columns and overhanging mountains, we arrive at the Dalls, where the whole volume of the river, half a mile wide, rushes through a deep narrow channel, which the action of the water has formed in the course of ages, through an extended tract of the hardest basalt. Two miles below the Large Dalls, or, as named by some, the Long Narrows, is a dike extending from the south shore three-fourths across, which is bare in low water, turning the current into a deep bay on the north side; but the high water pours over it, and forms a dangerous rapid. Reaching the foot of the Dalls, our attention is arrested by several rocky islands that for ages have borne unmoved the shock of the mighty billows which, at an earlier period, severed them from their neighbouring rocks. One of these is a depot for the bodies of the dead. Those square wooden huts, ten feet every way, are their tombs. Some of them are very ancient; but the climate is dry, and decay slow. How many generations of red men here mingle their dust? Who can tell? That long, black rock, mid-channel, some distance below, is covered in high water, and there is near it a fearful whirlpool. Many years ago a boat of the Hudson's Bay Company was drawn into it, and most of the crew perished. A mile brings us to the head of the chasm, which, diminishing in breadth to this point, is here only from thirty to fifty yards broad. Along this the fishers swing their nets, standing on a scaffolding fastened to the rocks, and extended a few feet over the foaming waters. See there, the net will hold from two to three bushels, and the handle is fifteen to twenty feet long. He has caught a fine salmon, and struck his head with a club. That is the way they kill them. More than one thousand Indians, of all ages, pass from May to September on these rocks, catching and curing salmon, laying in large supplies for themselves, and for trade with some of the other tribes.

One writer supposes that the water here rises sixty feet; but that this has been recently the case appears to me improbable, the present bed of the river having been formed evidently at a very remote period; since which the cuts at the Short Narrows, and below the Shoots, have been made; the latter having opened a passage half a mile in length through a compact basaltic bed, the work, no doubt, of several centuries. The agency by which these changes were produced had previously, by slow and certain progress, destroyed the adamantine barrier which for hundreds of years had obstructed the course of this grand river here at the Long Dalls. Before this it must have flowed at a greater height, and precipitated itself down a fall of forty or fifty feet, or more probably, over a succession of smaller falls, whose dread roar, for ages before even the red man's foot assumed this wide domain, echoed, in vale and mount, monotonous minstrelsy, that cheered the desert solitude around. Indian tradition says that there were falls at this place formerly, and that they prevented the salmon from ascending the river above. Long, however, antecedent to this period, the mighty and resistless waters of this great artery of Oregon must have been widening and deepening their bed, till it now lies several hundred feet below its early elevation. This opinion, which is not a solitary one, derives support from certain appearances at such heights:—
1. Many of the stones exhibit traces of the action of the water. 2. The dry rocky islands are lengthened in the probable direction of the current. 3. The frequent deep cuts in the basalt like those along the present bed. But the immense piles of sand which the winds have

been heaping up here for hundreds of years, conceal, doubtless, far more than is now apparent of the mighty deeds of these ancient waters. Sometimes the shifting sands discover the polished rocks in perfect preservation; and also caldron-like excavations are met with above the bed where the river now flows. The rocks on both sides of the river have much the same appearance, as having belonged to the same continuous bed from which a portion, half a mile wide, has been removed, apparently not by the violent agency of an earthquake, but by the unceasing action of water alone.

Leaving these conjectures, the next object to be noticed is the Small Dalls, two miles further up. Here the river passes through a very deep and narrow cut in the basaltic rock, which rises some twenty or thirty feet above its surface. The water pours through this channel with great velocity, except at high water, when it spreads out over the sands to the eastward. In low water they run these narrows in boats. Standing on the verge of the rocky bank, you would be almost petrified with fear for their safety as they career midst the angry whirlpools and breakers. In September, 1834, the writer thus witnessed the passage of a boat through this place, and the performance appeared to him as one of great risk and imminent danger.

Three miles further we arrive at the Shoots, (French, Les Chutes.) They are on the south side, close to the shore, and less than fifty yards over, to a point of rocks widening into an extensive bed, and extending thence across the river to the bank on the north side. This rocky bed, in low water, is mostly dry, but cut here and there with small streams which have opened for themselves a way on its surface. The shoot is nearly perpendicular, and from fifteen to twenty feet fall. During the great annual rise which occurs in May and June they are flooded, and then boats pass them without making a portage. Here is an excellent salmon fishery, and from two hundred to three hundred Indians spend one-third of the year at these Shoots. Two miles further on we come to the Shoots River, which has its name from the falls just described, or from a fall near its mouth, a short distance from the Columbia, into which it empties on the south side. It rises toward the south-west, and is about one hundred and fifty miles long, flowing through a very broken country, generally void of timber. The current is very rapid, and broken with frequent falls. Its chief tributaries rise near the base of Mount M'Laughlin, which lies to the south of Mount Hood. Twenty-five miles from its mouth there is a fine salmon fishery, where from three hundred to four hundred Indians assemble during the season of salmon, and catch immense quantities of that excellent fish, which is their principal support. John Day's River, ten miles higher up, rises in the Blue Mountains, and runs north-east one hundred and twenty-five miles, through a country destitute of timber. The man whose name it bears was a Rocky Mountain hunter, a Kentuckian, who was robbed here and stripped naked by the Indians, as before stated.

Of the Cascades.

This great obstruction to the navigation of this noble river needs a further description than has ever yet been given by any one of the various authors on Oregon. We find them about 140 miles from the mouth of the river, in a deep gorge through a chain of mountains, which are forty miles in breadth, and, at this point, rising in grandeur 4000 to 5000 feet on either hand. From these tremendous elevations, the massive and overwhelming avalanche has rushed impetuously down, at successive periods, into the gulf below, till now the distant mountain tops across are separated several miles. Has all this been done by the water? Perhaps not wholly, but only chiefly. This region has been the theatre of extensive and dreadful convulsions. That these have done much to level the river in its present channel is highly probable. The Cascades appear to be of a comparatively recent date, perhaps formed within the last three or four centuries. Above them, for more than twenty miles, the river appears to be twenty feet and upward above its former bed. The Indians say these falls are not ancient, and that their fathers voyaged without obstruction in their canoes as far as the Dalls. They also assert that the river was dammed up at this place, which caused the waters to rise to a great height far above, and that after cutting a passage through the impeding mass down to its present bed, these rapids first made their appearance. The extensive sands in this part of the river, and the trunks of trees standing *erect* where they grew, twenty feet below high water, make it probable that the Cascades are of modern date, and that the channel was formerly much lower than at present. Some of these trunks are from twenty to thirty feet high, and two to three feet through. The wood within is hard and sound; no part appears petrified. The supposition that a subsidence has occurred here appears groundless. Admit a dam at the Cascades, and these appearances perplex no more, their origin seems natural. At the Cascades there are indications that the stream has left its former bed, in which its course was westward, and abruptly turning to the south, rushes on and plunges down in that direction nearly a mile. Then gradually turning to the west one-fourth of a mile, we find the *first rapid;* thence a mile, the *middle rapid;* and a mile and a half further, the *lower rapid.* This appears to be a new channel.

Above the Cascades, at the point where the river begins to turn toward the south, and where probably it used to flow, is found a very low shore, which extends back, forming a deep bay among the hills, in the direction of Strawberry Island. Further on in this course are several small ponds, separated by intervening ridges of land; and then crossing a level half a mile we come to the slue, which at the time of high water runs east of the island. The land on both sides of this route is much broken, the deep glens and precipitous piles being covered with trees and shrubs. The banks near the river present a mixed formation of various kinds of earths, of different colours, and stones in equal variety. Basaltic and granitic rock abounds, and immense masses of the conglomerate are frequent. Petrifactions are very common. Blocks of it may be seen two to three feet long, and more than a foot in thickness. One very large has been noticed, one-fourth of a mile from the river, at an elevation of one hundred feet.

The stream, forced into a new channel, now washes the base of the mountains that bound its southern shore, whose ragged sides retain the recent avalanche in pause or rest, the voracious element beneath having long been satiated with the massive contributions of remoter periods. Often from these fearful heights the severed rock,

"—— exulting, with a bound,
Whirls, leaps, and thunders down impetuous to the ground."

To make this vast excavation between the opposite mountains has taken many centuries, and the river has doubtless been the "chief workman;" but other agents have been employed, and among these the earthquake has been the most powerful and effective, rending the adamantine barrier, and shaking down the overwhelming slides. The Cascades are not probably formed of any portion of the supposed immense slide, nor by the upheaving of the rocks beneath by an earthquake; but it seems reasonable to suppose that this stern barrier occupied anciently the same position, and that the river had to climb over it in order to follow its new channel. But, leaving these thoughts to the scientific, what say you to a visit to this little world? To see the "works of God, what desolation he hath made in the earth."

Embarked on the placid waters, we emerge from between two almost naked mountains, six miles above the Cascades. "I-ak! wake Sci-yah," (turn water,) cries the man at the stern, "quick, the falls are near." Away we fly, might and main. "These men are expert with a paddle." Turn now your eye to the right, on the mount we have just past. It has something of the sugar-loaf form. It is called the "Old Man," and that opposite the "Old Woman." There they have stood for ages, witnesses of the power and wrath of "Tal-i-paz," an imaginary god of various tribes in this country. By him, for some misconduct, they were changed into these mountains, and received the names they now bear. That island on our left is a mile above the rapids. We must keep near the north side to avoid the draft toward the falls. "How they roar!" Here are several small islands—we shoot past them like an arrow. The channel between the shore and this nether islet is dry, and we must pass inside of it. "Keep near the land." "Close nan-ich—Look out." A little below we disembark, and the Indians run down to the head of the portage. "See them!" There is no danger, they will strike into the back current, and land in that small bay. "Wake me-si-kah quos?—Were you not afraid?" "No, we are *men*." We now carry baggage and canoe more than half a mile. The Indians back heavy loads, confined by a strap over their foreheads. From two to ten men will manage the canoe, according to its size. They turn it over, and take it bottom up, on their shoulders. While this is going on, we do well to keep in mind that the company around will bear considerable watching; for what General Jackson says is true, "Indians will steal;" and this statement has often been proved correct in this very place, by many witnesses, and to the writer's certain knowledge, annoyance, and injury.

Passing along the portage, we find a rough, sidling, narrow, rocky path, sometimes undermined by the rising waters, and at others blocked up with the broken fragments of the contiguous bluff. Midway we halt, amidst the deafening roar of the Cascades, as they dash their yielding billows on the steadfast rocks. It is over one hundred yards across, and presents a rapidly-declining, irregular sheet of snow-white water, beautiful, grand, sublime.

At flood, the view is very different; the current from the two opposite sides then meet at an angle here, heaping up the water mid-channel, in a turnpike form, where it is less broken than toward the shores, and runs with great rapidity. Leaving this scene of grandeur, one-fourth of a mile brings us to the lower end of the portage, where we re-embark. But first, the canoe carriers must be paid,—" Powder and ball," four charges each. Now buy a salmon for supper. " Close o-koke— That is good." It will weigh fifteen pounds. In descending, we shall find the current strong, and sometimes rapid, about five miles. At the first rapid, during flood the boisterous breakers present a fearful aspect, and with the greedy whirlpools threaten destruction to every daring adventurer among them. Yet in their wildest mood, the light canoe rushes through them and shuns each crest and whirl in safety. But in low water, as now, there is no danger. The crew know their business. "Sit still, sir; you need not be alarmed. Those whirlers, and white caps ahead, have between them smooth water, you see." " Close nan-ich a-lip!—Look out well ahead! Paddle hard!" Now we move gently down to the middle rapid, and at this stage we find the water quite smooth. But it is a place of great danger when the river is high, and then a portage is made on the north side back of that hill which thrusts its rocky point down to the edge of the water. Generally in descending, however, both boats and canoes run the rapid; but at great risk, as they are sometimes overwhelmed with the raging billows, and the lives of their crews greatly endangered. We now proceed down to the lower rapid, which lies below the large island we are passing on our left; we must keep near this, to avoid being swept away into the dangerous water on the other side of the rapid. It was there that Mr. David Leslie, of the Oregon Mission, with Mrs. White, so narrowly escaped a watery grave. However, we must not run too near the island, but keep toward the middle and thus avoid the dangers on either hand. East of us is

Strawberry Island; where in June we might regale ourselves on its welcome dainties. Suppose we land there, take supper, and encamp for the night. Reaching the shore, we take out lading, and haul up our canoe and make all secure in a snug pile; for you know what Jackson says, and in case of rain, cover it with an oilcloth. Now one of the crew strikes fire, others dress and wash the salmon and potatoes, and some scatter, and collect fuel. Soon we encircle a blazing fire, with a large camp kettle full of potatoes and salmon suspended over it from three sticks lashed together at the top and set astride the fire. As the smoke disagrees with our eyes standing, we will sit down. Here are some stones handy. Now being seated, take a survey of the crew; dressed in substantial striped cotton shirts, one has a pair of good cotton corduroy pants in addition, and another has an old capean, which he wears wrong side out. See how cheerful they all are—over the breakers in safety, well warmed before a blazing fire, and close to a good supper. Now they boast of their courage and skill. "Now-it-kah mah-sach-e chuk—The water was very bad." "Weke quos en-si-kah—We were not afraid." "Hi-as en-si-kah tum-tune—Our hearts are large. We are men!" Let me spread a cloth. This chest contains povisions, to which we will add a little more out of the camp kettle—soon on our table you observe knives, forks, and spoons, tin basins and tin plates. Here comes the salmon. The crew have turned out their part, you see, on a few clean branches and leaves of the willow, which they have spread down, and which answer the purpose of a table and its outfit. It is our practice to say grace at meals, and it is for this that they are waiting.

"O Soh-ole Ish-tam-ah, e-toke-te mi-kah; tow-e-ah e-toke-te-itl-hul-am mi-hah minch-e-lute co-pah en-sai-kah. Ka-dow quon-sim mincht-cah-meet en-sai-kah. Um-in-sheet-ah con-a-wa e-toke-ta co-pah mi-kah e-me-han, Jesus Christ, amen!"

"O God, thou art good, this good food thou hast given to us. In like manner always kindly look upon us, and give us all good things, for the sake of thy Son, Jesus Christ, amen!"

Now we will use knives and forks, while they employ their fingers. They will soon take care of the solid part of their supper, and then attack the broth, with clam shells for spoons. Supper ended, we will pitch our tent. It covers a space of eight feet every way. The ridge is a pole six feet long, having a support under each end of the same length. For our bed we will break some willows and get some grass, and laying these down, smoothly cover them with mats, and then our blankets will keep us warm, and we shall rest without feathers very well. We will now have prayers. The Lord has brought us safely through the dangers of the day. Let us not forget his benefits, let us praise him, and pray unto him. Read the nineteenth Psalm. "The heavens declare thy glory, and the firmament showeth thy handy-work; day unto day uttereth speech, and night unto night showeth knowledge," and the rest.

> "In reason's ear they all rejoice,
> And utter forth a glorious voice,
> For ever singing as they shine,
> The hand that made us is divine."

"A-ka eglah-lam en-si-kah—Now let us sing."

HYMN.	TRANSLATED.
1. Ak-ah eg-lah-lam en-si-kah Mi-kah ish-tam-ah em-e-hol-ew Kup-et mi-kam toke-ta mi-mah Mi-kah quon-e-sim ka-dow Mi-kah ek-ah-tlah gum-ohah Mi-kah dow-ah gum-e oh Kon-a-wa e-toke-ta ten-mah Mi-kah an-kut-e gum-toh	1. Here we now unite in singing Glory, Lord, unto thy name, Only good and worthy praising, Thou art always, Lord, the same. Of the sun thou art Creator, And the light was made by thee, All things good, yea, every creature, At the first thou mad'st to be.
2. Mi-kah minch-ah-koke en-si-kah An-kut-e yuk-um-a-lah Kon-a-wa e-dinch-ah-gu-it quah Quon-sim po-nan-a-kow Mi-kah gum-inch-e-lute e-me-han Yok-ah waw-wot gach-ow-eet Uk-ah en-si-kah quot-lanch-ke-hah Mi-kam toke-ta can-neo-eeb.	2. We, O Lord, are all thy children, In the past we wicked were, We were all most deeply wretched, Always blind and in despair; Thou didst give thy Son our Saviour, He to us instruction gave, Knowing this, we now are happy, Thou art good and thou wilt save.

After a season of prayer, in which some of the crew join in their native tongue, we repair to our tent; and they wrap themselves in their blankets, and lying down near the fire, soon fall asleep. How welcome now is "nature's sweet restorer."

CHAPTER XIX.

Missions of the American Board and others—A monomaniac burned to death—Introduction of a printing press, and the publication of books in the native tongues—Children drowned—Indians form a civil compact—Hudson Bay Company's express—Catholics establish a mission—Two Scotch naturalists drowned—Mr. Pambeam thrown from his horse and killed—A body of emigrants settle in the country.

THE missions of the American Board and others, with some miscellanies, may be properly introduced here, and then we may resume the narrative.

The arrival of the first missionaries in Oregon in 1834 was a new era in its history; and from that time it became a topic of much interest to many in the United States, as a promising field for additional Christian effort, and others were found ready to follow in the work. Among these was the Rev. Samuel Parker, of the American Board of Commissioners for Foreign Missions, who was sent out to explore the country for missionary purposes, and who has published an account of his tour, which contains much valuable information, while it greatly overrates the number of the Indians, and sets too high an estimate on their character. Prospective temporal gain will make them ardent professional friends and serious hearers in the absence of all higher motives, as every man will affirm who has had a long acquaintance with them. Mr. P. saw many of the tribes who inhabit on the Columbia, and was everywhere agreeably received, and surprised by the apparent anxiety which many manifested to have the gospel brought among them. In November, 1835, he visited the mission begun the preceding year at the Walamet, at the time the writer was at the Sandwich Islands. His call was more than welcome to Messrs. Jason Lee and Cyrus Shepard, in their early and arduous toil, exiled as they were from the society of other Christian friends. Having completed his tour of observation in Oregon, Mr. P. sailed to the Sandwich Islands on his way to the United States. Another gentleman, devoted to the interests of this country, was Dr. Marcus Whitman, associate of Mr. Parker, and who accompanied him on his way as far as the American traders' and trappers' rendezvous in the mountains, and then returned to the States to obtain men and means to establish a mission among the Nez Percé Indians, residing on the Snake River from one hundred to two hundred miles above its junction with the Columbia. To this, perhaps the most important tribe in Oregon, he came in 1836, having crossed the mountains with his wife, Mr. and Mrs. Spalding, and Mr. Gray. These two ladies are the first white females who came to Oregon, and the first who adventured across the American desert, the pioneers of many who have since gone with their husbands to the far, far west. These labourers commenced two stations, one among the Kinse Indians, at Wai-let-pu, on that small tributary of the Columbia, the Wallah-wallah, twenty-five miles from its mouth, where the Hudson Bay Company's fort of that name is located; and the other on the Clear Water, a branch of the Snake River, one hundred and twenty-five miles eastward of Wai-let-pu, among the Nez Percés. Mr. Spalding, who is a minister, had charge of the latter, and Dr. Whitman of the former station.

They first erected dwelling houses, chiefly with their own hands, and, as it was necessary to their support, they commenced as early as possible to till the ground, in order to raise their own supplies of provisions. Till they were able to do this, they obtained them from the Hudson's Bay Company, chiefly from Fort Colville, one of the company's trading posts situated on the Columbia River, more than two hundred and fifty miles distant, in a direction nearly north-east of Fort Wallah-wallah, and about twenty miles below the mouth of Clarke's River. It was a long distance to transport wheat and flour and potatoes on horseback to eat and plant. Besides these various labours, they devoted themselves to the acquirement of the Indian language, and embraced every means in their power to give instruction to the dark hearts around them. Such was the apparent encouragement they met, and so extensive the field of usefulness before them, and the demand for increased missionary efforts so urgent, that in 1837 Mr. Gray returned to the United States to get additional help. He took some of the Nez Percé Indians with him, and some horses designed to transport the new reinforcement over the mountains, and to save the expense of buying them on the confines of Missouri. He went part of the way in company with Mr. Ermetinger, a gentleman of the Hudson's Bay Company, who led a party that year to the American traders' and trappers' rendezvous in the mountains. From the rendezvous he proceeded quite alone as far as the forks of the Platte, where, being attacked by a party of the Sioux, he was wounded, made a prisoner, and his Indians were slain. After suffering various abuses and insults, and being robbed of most of his effects, he was permitted to proceed on his journey, glad to escape with his life; and at length, after suffering many additional privations and hardships, he got through in safety. In 1838 Mr. Gray with his lady recrossed the mountains again to Oregon, accompanied by three new labourers and their consorts, Rev. Messrs. Eales, Walker, and Smith. A new station was now commenced among the Nez Percés above Clear Water, by Mr. Smith, assisted by Mr. Cornelius Rogers, who had been some time with the Indians, migrating with them from place to place, to acquire a knowledge of their customs and language, with the sole object of benefiting them by facilitating the labours of the missionaries in their evangelization. No one in the country was so well qualified as Mr. Rogers for this department, as his success sufficiently proved. Messrs. Eales and Walker located themselves to the northward, among the Spokan Indians, where they have laboured under many privations, but with much perseverance, and with some success.

In 1837, or '38, Rev. Mr. Clark, Mr. Littlejohn, and Mr. Smith, Presbyterian self-supporting missionaries, and their ladies, came over the mountains, designing to sustain themselves in some part of the mission field, independently of the patronage of any organized board. In 1839 Mr. Griffin and Mr. Munger, and their wives, came over with similar intentions. After various trials to carry out their plans of benevolent action, all which proved abortive, they abandoned the undertaking as hopeless.

In the spring of 1840, Mr. Griffin, with his wife, and an Indian for a guide, and several horses, packed with an outfit to begin an independent mission among the Snake Indians, where he intended to plant, and sow, and live by the sweat of his brow, and to Christianize and civilize the natives, left the Clear Water station, where he had passed the winter, and set off on his perilous journey of several hundred miles. His way lay across high mountains north of the Snake River, from which the snow had not yet dissolved. After several days of toiling forward in their rugged way, they were forsaken by their guide, who, not relishing the prospect ahead, returned back.

They, however, pushed on, forcing their path through mountains covered with snow, sometimes several feet deep; leading and driving their heavy-laden beasts, worn with toil, and pinched with hunger. Arrived in the valleys, torrents, like themselves from the Oregon Alps, dashed along to impede and prevent their progress. Some of these they had to trace far toward their source to find a ford, or make bridges to pass them. After running innumerable hazards and hair-breadth escapes, they arrived at Fort Boisais, on the Snake River, where they were received with every kind attention by Mr. Payeth, the gentleman in charge of that post. The length of time which had been occupied in their journey, the sufferings they had endured, the uncertainty of finding a suitable location for the purpose they had proposed, and perhaps the fear that they should not, after all, be able to sustain themselves, unpatronized and alone, led them to abandon any further attempts, and they returned again to Dr. Whitman's station at Wailetpu.

Fort Boisais is a trading post of the Hudson's Bay Company, situated about half way between Fort Hall and Fort Wallah-wallah. It was built soon after the operations of Captain Wyeth were begun, in 1834, and designed to command the fur trade in that section, as a rival of Fort Hall. It is a parallelogram one hundred feet on a side, with adobic walls, enclosing a store and some dwelling houses.

Leaving Wailet, Mr. Griffin proceeded to Vancouver; and after spending there a considerable part of the winter of 1840, went to the Walamet Valley, where he was still living in 1843. While at Vancouver, in Jan., 1840, leaving Mrs. Griffin, he accompanied one of the settlers on a visit to the Walamet. Some way above the falls he left the canoe, it being unusually cold, to walk a little along the shore, designing to embark again after going a short distance. The path he took, however, did not return back to the river; but gradually diverged more and more from it. At the same time the snow was falling very fast, (an uncommon occurrence here,) so that his way and course were entirely lost. Still he went on over many miles of prairie, till, tired and hungry, he stopped under a large fir tree to rest, perhaps to die with the cold and hunger, without a fire, without a blanket. If he could make a fire, there was still hope. In his pocket he found a stone that he had picked up in his journey, before described, in the

Snake country, among the mountains,—succeeded in kindling a fire from a spark smitten from that stone, and thus averted an inevitable death. Next day he continued his tramp across the dreary plain, till at length he became entirely exhausted, thought he could proceed no further, gave up all hope, and lay down, as he expected, to rise no more! to die *alone!* to leave his wife a *lonely widow,* in utter ignorance of his tragical end. While his thoughts were thus absorbing his spirits, the sound of human voices fell on his ear. Suddenly hope revived; and strengthened anew, he hasted to the spot. It was a lone wigwam, hidden by the bushes around it. Here was relief! The poor inmates had fire and food. They shared it with the lost stranger. The next day they conducted him to the mission at the Walamet, about ten miles, where he was gladly welcomed, fears having been entertained that he had perished. His feet had been injured so much by the cold that he could scarcely walk, and several days passed before he could do so without great pain.

Mr. Munger, who was associated with Mr. Griffin in coming to Oregon, spent some time with Dr. Whitman at Warlotgos, and in 1841 went to the Walamet. He was an ingenious mechanic, but was destroyed by *monomania.* Under the influence of this disease, or *error,* if the term seems more applicable, he appeared to think that Christ would work a miracle to convince the people that certain peculiar religious notions he entertained were from God. So going into his shop, he fastened one hand with a nail to the side of, or above the fire-place, and hung himself into the fire. It was in the evening; and he was so badly burnt before he was discovered that he died within three days. But before this he seemed deeply sensible of his error, and deeply to repent of it. His widowed wife and orphan child were thus left as aliens in a strange land.

Messrs. Clarke, Smith, and Littlejohn, went to reside in the Walamet in the autumn of 1841. They left most of their little effects at Fort Wallah-wallah, to be forwarded down to Fort Vancouver in a boat, while they made the overland journey with horses to the Walamet. But the fort accidentally taking fire before the goods were moved, nearly all they had deposited there was an entire loss, and to them a heavy and irreparable one. They however found many sympathizing friends, who were happy to afford them some relief.

To return to the interior missions. In 1839 Mr. E. O. Hall arrived in the Columbia River, from the Sandwich Islands, with a printing press. He was accompanied by his lady, with the hope that the voyage and climate might have a favourable influence on her enfeebled health. Mr. H. is a printer, and a member of the Sandwich Islands mission. He set up the press at the Clear Water station; and some elementary books have been published in the Nez Percé tongue; and recently also in the Spokan, by Mr. Eales and Mr. Walker.

The station which was occupied by Mr. Smith, above Clear Water, was left in 1841; and Mr. S. sailed to the Islands, where he is now employed in labouring for the salvation of the natives of Hawaii. At Clear Water a saw-mill and a grist-mill have been erected; and the Indians have engaged in the cultivation of the soil with much success. Mr. and Mrs. Littlejohn came from Walamet to this station in 1842; and soon after were called to the painful trial of parting with their little son, an only child, who was drowned near the mill. He was soon taken out of the water, and every means used to restore him, but the vital spark no more returned. A similar painful providence had also previously occurred in the family of Dr. Whitman, in the year 1838. Their only child, a daughter, two years old, going to the river a few yards from the house, fell in, and was drowned. It has been the lot of few persons so circumstanced to be thus painfully bereft. She was a child of peculiar promise, and could speak both the English and Indian tongues considerably.

At Hailetpoo a saw-mill and a grist-mill were in operation in 1842; but they were soon after accidentally set on fire, as was supposed, and destroyed, with a large amount of grain which was stored in them at the time. The Indians here, as well as at Clear Water station, have made considerable progress in tillage, some of them raising corn and other supplies nearly in sufficient quantities to support them. They possess large herds of horses; and have some hogs, sheep, and cattle, which they have recently obtained from the whites. This is also the case with the Nez Percés, at Clear Water station. They are more numerous than the Kinse; and the women have succeeded in the manufacture of some coarse woollen cloths. The efforts of the missionaries in schools have been very encouraging, a great desire to learn being general, and progress rapid.

In 1842 Dr. Whitman visited the United States, to obtain further assistance, in order to strengthen the efforts that had already been made. About the same time Mr. Gray went to reside in the Walamet; and Mr. Gerger, mentioned in a former chapter, supplied in the absence of Dr. Whitman his place at Waietpu. Mrs. Whitman, whose health had suffered much for some time before the doctor left, spent the following winter at the Dalls, with the resident missionary families at that station. In 1843 Dr. W. returned again to Oregon, and resumed his labours. During his absence the Nez Percés and also the Kinses had instituted laws, and appointed a head chief over each of the tribes; thus forming a kind of civil compact to regulate their intercourse among themselves, and also toward their white neighbours and the surrounding tribes. Some of these have taken on them the profession of Christianity; and the truths inculcated by the missionaries are exerting a wide influence on the whole mass, and in some a deep and regenerating power. Truly, their " work of faith and labour of love " have not been in vain. Though several things have transpired to put their faith into the furnace, and they have endured much personal abuse from those whose good they have sought, and from whom they deserved good and not evil,—yet still have they hoped in God, and he has strengthened them to go on and faint not, and to see some fruit of their toil for his "name's sake." Should not anything occur to drive them from their work, lasting good must result to the tribes for whose evangelization they have devoted their lives. There are grounds, however, to fear that hostilities between them and the whites may yet commence, and this would break up the mission. From no other quarter is any danger to be justly apprehended. And may the God of missions (will every Christian pray) avert this threatened curse, to the end that his word may accomplish all " his good pleasure" in the salvation of these tribes, and may his servants there prosper!

This brief outline of the missions of the American Board must suffice for this work; and the writer will close this chapter with some items of miscellaneous matter. We will begin with the Hudson Bay Company's Express. This is a communication by which despatches are sent annually from Vancouver to Canada. It leaves on the 20th of March, and proceeds by water up the Columbia to Fort Colville, and then to the head waters of that river, where they leave their boats, make a portage of the mountains, proceed to the Saskatchawan River, embark in boats, and follow it to Lake Winnipeg, and then proceed to Fort York, on Hudson's Bay; where it intersects a counter express from Lachine, near Montreal, in Lower Canada, and which leaves every April for the Columbia, where it generally arrives about the 25th of October. By this express we were favoured with an opportunity to forward letters to our friends, and to receive letters from them, and seldom did the express arrive without some such messenger with tidings of home. In the express of 1838, arrived Messrs. Dimars and Blanchette, French Canadian Catholic priests. Mr. B. took up his residence in the Walamet settlement, in charge of the Catholic portion of the residents; where a church had been commenced some time before, and was nearly ready for service. Here he has passed most of his time; but occasionally visited Vancouver in the performance of his official duties among the Catholic servants in the employment of the company. His associate, Mr. Dimars, has been chiefly engaged in visiting the different trading posts for the same purpose. The wives and families of these servants also demand much of their attention, and are a very numerous and influential class. The women are from almost every tribe in Oregon. In 1841 they were reinforced, and a mission was begun among the Indians on Clarke's River. Two others arrived in 1842. Their worship is established constantly at Vancouver. Schools and missions were in contemplation. With the same conveyance which brought them to the country were two Scotch gentlemen, Messrs. Wallace and Banks, naturalists; but, sad to tell, they were both drowned in one of the interior rapids of the Columbia, between Fort Wallahwallah and Fort Colville. The boat was upset, and from eight to ten others, crew and passengers, perished with them. How often did like painful events remind us of the uncertainty of life! We may always say, "In the midst of life we are in death!"

In the year 1840 Mr. P. C. Pambeam, at Wallahwallah, died very suddenly, leaving a widow and a large family of children to mourn his loss. To his kindness the missionaries near him, not excluding the writer, were much indebted. He was a gentleman of very generous and friendly feelings. He was riding, and the rope by which he guided his horse, according to Indian custom, slipped from the horse's mouth, when he ran with him, bruised him very badly on the saddle, and threw him with great violence upon the ground. He was so badly injured that he had to be carried to his house. Dr. Whitman, from Waíletpu, was called to see him; but all his efforts to save him proved abortive, and a rapid mortification soon closed the painful scene.

This year, 1840, a large emigration of one hundred

and twenty-five persons, adults and children, came from Red River, which empties into Lake Winnipeg, to settle in Oregon. They went to Nesqually, on Pugit's Sound; but, after spending a year, it was found that the land was of a very inferior quality, and that they could not subsist upon it. Thus, after having subjected themselves to many hardships, and privations, and losses, for almost two years, they had yet to remove to the Walamet Valley, as promising to remunerate them for their future toil, and make them forget the past. Accordingly most of them removed and settled in the Walamet in 1841-42.

In the next chapter we will resume the account of the Oregon Mission.

CHAPTER XX.

A reinforcement to the mission set out from New-York—Incidents of the voyage—Arrive at the Sandwich Islands—Occurrences there—Reach Astoria—Disappointed on finding that it consisted of but three or four houses—Voyage to Vancouver—Missionaries appointed to their various fields of labour—Marriage of Rev. D. Lee—A company of missionaries arrive at the Dalls—Trip to Vancouver—Dr. Richmond's journey—Two of the missionaries set out for Astoria—Return to Vancouver—Incidents of the journey.

In 1838 the Rev. Jason Lee arrived in the United States from Oregon, for the purpose of obtaining a reinforcement to that mission, as has been already stated. After meeting with the Board of Managers of the Missionary Society of the M. E. Church, and stating the wants of that country, as it was supposed, and the prospects of civilizing and Christianizing the aborigines of that land, the authorities of the church published a call in the Christian Advocate and Journal for five missionaries and a number of laymen, such as mechanics, farmers, and physicians, and young ladies for teachers. This call was promptly responded to, and the Rev. J. P. Richmond, Gustavus Hines, W.

W. Kone, A. F. Waller, and J. H. Frost and families, and Mr. J. L. Babcock, physician, George Abernethy, W. W. Raymond, H. B. Brewer, L. H. Judson, Josiah L. Parrish, James Olley, H. Campbell, and families, and Miss M. T. Ware, C. A. Clark, E. Philips, A. Phelps, and O. Lankton, stewardess, were appointed to return with Mr. Lee, and labour, in connection with those already in the field, for the benefit of the souls and bodies of the Indians of that territory. This reinforcement, including Mr. Lee and wife, consisted of fifty-one souls, adults and children. These all met in the city of New-York on the 1st of September, 1839, but were detained until the 9th of October, before they could take their departure, as the ship employed for the purpose of conveying them to their destined field of labour and suffering was not in readiness; and it is but just to state, that during their sojourn in the city of New-York, they received every needed attention from their kind friends residing in that city. At length the time of their departure arrived, and after the usual preliminaries, which render such scenes at all times interesting, but particularly so on this occasion, as this was the largest company of missionaries that ever took their departure from the United States, they entered on board of the ship Lausanne, commanded by Capt. T. Spaulding, and were towed out of the harbour by a steamer. Many a tear found its way from the eyes of the multitude upon the wharf, and many a fervent prayer reached the ear of the Father of all mercies in behalf of that mission family, as the vessel was being borne toward the mighty troubled ocean, and the handkerchief of the passenger was waving a last adieu to friends on shore.

O the pain of separating from parents, and brothers, and friends, with no hope of meeting again until " the trumpet shall sound, and the dead shall be raised!" It was under such circumstances that these missionaries separated with their friends; and yet there is a pleasure accompanying such a pain—a pleasure such as the Christian only can enjoy. It originates in the hope of meeting their friends again, when the storms of life shall have subsided, upon those blissful elevations where it shall be said unto them by the King in his glory, " Well done, thou good and faithful servant; thou hast been faithful over a few things, I will make thee ruler over many things;" and then, at his bidding, they shall, hand in hand, enter into the joy of their Lord, never, never more to part. In the possession of this hope, we trust, the missionaries looked for the last time upon their friends, when the steamer cast off her hawsers, and the Lausanne filled away for Sandy Hook ; but as the wind was unfavourable, she came to anchor, and on the following morning, all things being in our favour, excepting the symptoms of sea-sickness, we weighed anchor, dismissed our pilot, and put out to sea.

On this voyage we were accompanied by the Rev. Mr. Dibble, a missionary to the Sandwich Islands, who, after having laboured in that interesting field during eight years, and having been called upon to bury his companion, which left him with two small children and a broken constitution, had returned to the States, to recruit his health, and visit the churches, for the purpose of advancing the cause of missions, and to prepare himself for another season of labour in the land he had left, where were the lambs which he had been instrumental in gathering into the fold of Christ, and where were also the graves of his friends.

While in the States he had another visitation of Divine Providence, and his youngest child was taken away by death. But previous to his joining the Lausanne, he was united, in matrimonial bands, with a very excellent and intelligent young lady of Brooklyn, who with himself and little daughter constituted a very pleasant and interesting addition to our very extensive family.

After we got fairly under way, it must have been very amusing, and at the same time annoying to the seamen, to behold such a motley group, lying on deck, in every direction, and hanging over the rail; heaving with all the energy, and to a much more discordant tune, than so many lusty sailors when weighing anchor; and they were all so much engaged that when the dinner bell rang, there were but two or three out of over fifty to grace the table. This strange state of things continued for such a length of time that we decided that "Old Neptune" was not to be satisfied with anything short of all the good provisions which had been furnished us by our kind friends during our sojourn in the city of New-York.

Seeing that the journal of that voyage was published in the Christian Advocate and Journal, it may be considered superfluous for us to give a history of it in this work; and as incidents of sea voyaging have become so common, that those who have not read that journal, even, might not find such a history interesting. In view of these considerations we will pass this subject over with simply observing, that after experiencing some rough weather, we arrived at Rio Janeiro on the 9th of December, where we put in for recruits. Here we had an interview with our missionaries who were labouring for the salvation of the Brazilians. These were the Rev. Mr. Spaulding and Mr. Kidder, and families. And we must here mention that Mrs. Kidder was called from this scene of toil and privation to, as we trust, a better inheritance, even a heavenly, and left her husband and little children to feel and mourn her departure. As this mission did not prove successful, probably in consequence of the deep-rooted prejudice against Protestantism, the missionaries have since been recalled from that field.

Having obtained our supplies, we weighed anchor on the 15th, and bore away for Cape Horn in company with the French fleet, who were bound to Buenos Ayres for the purpose of blockading that port. We soon lost sight of the men of war, and pursued our course without any serious obstruction until we reached the Cape on the 10th of January. Here we were met with the westerly winds from the South Pacific which prevail in this region, and generally prove a serious hinderance to vessels on an outward-bound voyage: this obliged us to shorten sail and "lie to:" the wind being accompanied with rain and some sleet, continued to blow until we drifted down to the 61st degree of south latitude, and we did not succeed in doubling the Cape until after the 28th. During this time we amused ourselves with catching the albatross, that splendid sea fowl that inhabits the region of the Cape. They are often found to measure from twelve to fifteen feet from the tip of one wing to that of the other. They are taken with hook and line in the following manner: the hook being baited with a piece of fat pork and permitted to drift astern of the vessel, attached to a long line, is seized by the bird, and fastens in the crooked upper part of the beak, and is thus hauled on board.

We have now passed the troubles and dangers of Cape Horn, and on the 19th of February arrived at Valparaiso. Here we expected to behold a pleasant place, but were very much disappointed. The town was not large, and quite shabby in appearance, having narrow dirty streets; and a stranger admixture of human beings we had not met with. They were nearly of all sizes and of every colour. The Europeans appear to be as distinct and peculiar a people here, as the Jews do everywhere else in the world. They inhabit an elevated section of the town, which they have dressed up, and appear to have entirely to themselves, under certain restrictions; for although they have a church, they are not allowed to put a steeple upon it, nor cause a bell to be rung, lest, as we supposed, it might not give a true *Catholic* sound. Or, perhaps, "his Holiness" might have imposed this silence upon them, as a penance for the crime of leaving their Protestant homes for the *love of money*, which is the root of all evil.

On the afternoon of the day of our arrival several of us went on shore, and wandered along the coast to the southward; and soon after we passed the light-house, which is situated on a gentle elevation, we found ourselves at the mouth of a cave or den, which, by the human bones that were scattered around it, discovered itself to be a general depository of the city dead. And as the small-pox had just concluded a visit to that devoted place, no doubt many a score of Chilians had recently passed through its greedy jaws to the land of forgetfulness.

Having finished our walk by a circuitous route over the thirsty hills we returned to the vessel; and on the 22d, having recruited our sea stores as well as we could, weighed anchor, hoisted sail, and bent our course for the Sandwich Islands, where we arrived on the 10th of April.

Here we were met by Mr. Brinsmade, the United States consul, Captain Stetson, and the missionaries and foreign residents, who welcomed us to their homes, and entertained us most hospitably during our stay. Here, at Honolulu and Oahu, we found two native churches and a seaman's chapel. The Rev. Mr. Bingham and the Rev. Lowell Smith were pastors of the native churches, in which they preached two sermons every sabbath in the Hawaian language, to immense congregations of natives. Rev. Mr. Deal was the seaman's chaplain, but was on a tour to the United States in consequence of ill health. During his absence his desk was supplied by the missionaries, and strangers, such as ourselves. While here, the writer, in company with others of the mission family, visited Waialua, another missionary post on the opposite side of Oahu. The Rev. Mr. Emerson had charge of the native churches at that place, and as we spent the sabbath with that gentleman, we had the happiness to see his congregation, and assist in administering the "Lord's supper" to his church, which consisted of twelve hundred members, all natives.

We continued to enjoy the friendship and hospitality of the above-named gentlemen and their excellent companions until the 27th, when we received "sailing orders." Having been much refreshed during our visit here, both in body and mind, we prepared for our departure; and on the following day bade adieu to our dear friends, and also to Honolulu, and after a favourable passage arrived at the mouth of the Columbia on the 21st of May. The religious exercises of the voyage consisted of preaching, class meetings, and prayer meetings; besides which we had prayers morning and night. And notwithstanding several of the mission family had suffered considerably in consequence of sickness, we were all spared, and permitted to behold the land upon which we were to labour and suffer, and some of us to die. But we were prepared to give unto God sincere and hearty thanks for mercies past, and to trust in him alone for time to come.

Soon after we cast anchor in Baker's Bay we were visited by Captain Duncan, who had charge of one of the Hudson Bay Company's vessels, which was also at anchor in the bay, waiting a favourable opportunity to cross the bar on an outward-bound voyage. This gentleman furnished us with some excellent salt salmon, which made a very acceptable change of food for all on board. Some of us went on shore in the afternoon, and took a ramble through the wood in the vicinity of Cape Disappointment, and on our return found Rev. Daniel Lee on board. He had just arrived from his station at the Dalls, which, as has been observed, was commenced about the time that the Rev. J. Lee left for the United States. He brought us intelligence from that station which had a tendency to encourage our hearts, and cause us to look forward with hope of becoming instrumental in turning some of the benighted savages to the ways of virtue and religion. The Chenook chief and a number of his clan had come on board, in company with brother Lee, so that we had a specimen before us of the people among whom we were to live and labour; and as Sally, the wife of the old chief, who could speak a very few words of English, inquired for "*lum,*" i. e. rum, very soon after she reached the cabin, we had an early exhibition of one by no means encouraging trait in their character. On being informed that we had *no* rum, the old woman, with a look of surprise, nodded her head, and exclaimed, "Oh!"

On the morning of the 22d it was stormy, and the ocean presented a frightful appearance; but having sailed over twenty-two thousand miles upon the bosom of that and the Atlantic since we left New-York, we were happy at this time to be beyond its reach. The clouds passed away in the after part of the day, when the Messrs D. and J. Lee left in a canoe, with the Indians, for Vancouver. On the 23d, the wind being favourable, orders were given to "man the windlass;" and before night we dropped anchor at Astoria. As we had heard and read much of this place, we expected to see something like a village, or at least a large trading establishment; but our astonishment may be imagined, when, instead of what we had been expecting, was a house, built after the custom of the country, but one story high, sixty feet long by twenty feet wide, the posts having been set up, and then filled in with hewn blocks, and covered with boards. In addition to the above, there was a store-house and two small out-houses, all of the same height, and built of the same material. This constituted the whole establishment at the far-famed Astoria. Here a number of our company went on shore, and were very kindly received by Mr. Birnie and his interesting family. Mr. B. himself having met us at the bay, acted as our pilot thus far up the river; and now very kindly furnished us with a plenty of good milk for our tea and coffee, the like of which we had not had since leaving the Sandwich Islands.

On the 26th we met the bark Columbia and the schooner Cadborough coming down from Vancouver, on their outward-bound voyage. The Columbia was bound to the Sandwich Islands. Mr. Hall and lady, who were returning from a visit to the Presbyterian Mission, in the Nez Percé country, were on board, thus far on their way to the mission at the islands to which they were attached. The first printing-press, and the only one in the Oregon Territory up to the time we left, was taken up by Mr. Hall at this time, for the use of the above-named mission in the interior.

We now obtained an abundant supply of fresh salmon, which was a grateful change of food, as our sea fare had been principally salt. And we were now daily visited by the Indians, who brought salmon and other articles for the purpose of traffic, and manifested no want of intellect by the manner in which they conducted their bargains. Many of us had already commenced getting the Indian language, and had succeeded so well by this time as to be able to count ten. Tht, mauxt, clone, lacket, qunum, tuhum, sunamauxt, stochtakane, quiust, tat-le-lam!!

On the 28th Mr. Latty, mate of the Cadborough, came on board, and piloted our ship up as far as Pillar Rock, which rock is as well described by its name as it can otherwise be. The channel lies between this and the shore. This rock stands up out of the water about twenty feet, and is about twenty feet in diameter. After this, George, one of the Chenook Indians, was to be our guide up the river. George could speak a very few words of English, and felt quite important in the discharge of his duty. He was dressed in a very comfortable style; and had it not been for the loss of one eye, which he said a hair seal had scratched out, he would have been quite a respectable looking Flathead.

The next day we were joined by a coloured man from Vancouver, bringing, as a foretaste of the kind reception which awaited us at that post, some excellent fresh bread and butter, from the larder of John M'Laughlin, Esq. The name of the coloured man was George Washington, who reported himself to be a good pilot, and that one part of his errand was to see the Lausanne safely up to Vancouver. Thus Chenook George (who called himself, at times, *King* George) was superseded in the pilot's office, which bid fair to blast his prospects of obtaining a respectable fee from

Captain Spaulding. However, determined to enjoy the privileges, he remained, sat down upon a spar, filled his pipe, and soon sank down into a state of unconsciousness, while George Washington took charge of the ship.

We had not proceeded far when the vessel brought up upon the sands, giving evidence that our pilot's knowledge was altogether inadequate. Upon this the old Indian awoke from his revery and stepped forward, with a smile of satisfaction beaming in his weather-beaten countenance. and said, "Me know George Washington one very good *cook*, but he no *pilot*." After the vessel was got off again into deep water, the charge was given to the old Chenook, who pointed out the channel in a very accurate manner. On the 30th we reached the lower mouth of the Walamet River, and on the following day, being the sabbath, we arrived at a place where we heard a number of voices engaged in singing, but could not discover any person; but it was not long before the Rev. D. Lee, another white man, and some Indians came from behind the willows which skirted the bank of the river, having been engaged, in this temple of nature, in worshipping the great God of nature, with a band of Clickatat Indians who were camped here. Our vessel soon came to anchor, when Mr. Lee came on board, and the white man in company with him proved to be Mr. Solomon Smith. During the afternoon we enjoyed a season of prayer with these brethren, who had long been isolated from the civilized world; and it is worthy of remark, that we had ocular demonstration of the fact that the spirit of Christianity is one in whatever region of the earth it is met with. And is not this an evidence in favour of its genuine and heaven-born character?

On the afternoon of the 1st of June we arrived at Vancouver. After the ship was anchored, Dr. M'Laughlin came on board, and was introduced to the mission family, and gave them a very kind invitation to partake of the hospitalities of the fort, which is situated on the north side of the river, about one quarter of a mile, or perhaps less than that, from the water. On the following day all were comfortably roomed in the fort, and nothing was lacking on the part of the ladies and gentlemen of the establishment to render our sojourn comfortable and pleasant.

On the Thursday evening following our arrival, Mr. J. Lee having returned from the Walamet in company with Dr. White and others, we all met in one of the halls to receive our several appointments from the superintendent.

Here we learned that the Rev. J. P. Richmond and family were to repair to Nesqually, where there was a house prepared in part for the use of his family—Rev. W. W. Kone and G. Hines were to commence a new post at the Umbaqua—Rev. A. F. Waller at the Walamet Falls—and J. H. Frost, the writer, at the mouth of the Columbia. The remaining part of the reinforcement was to go to the Walamet, except Miss Clark, who was to accompany Dr. Richmond as teacher, and Mr. Brewer and Dr. Babcock and families, who were to reinforce the Dalls station, and Miss Maria T. Ware, who was, on the 11th of June, united in holy matrimony with the Rev. D. Lee.

Nearly all were now fully employed in receiving baggage and goods from the ship, and in preparing for their several appointments; so that, on the afternoon of the 11th, they were nearly all on their way to their several fields of labour, except Dr. Richmond and the writer, it having been previously determined that the writer should accompany Mr. D. Lee and his reinforcement to the Dalls. Accordingly, leaving my family at Vancouver, we also departed in peace for the last-named station. Our company consisted of Mr. Brewer, Dr. Babcock, and Mr. D. Lee, and families, and Mr. Rogers, a young man in connection with the mission among the Nez Percés, and myself.

We set off with two Indian canoes and one of the Hudson Bay Company's boats well laden. We had proceeded but a short distance up the Columbia, when we found our boat to be in a leaky condition; so we determined to camp for the purpose of repairing. On the following morning we calked the boat and set out again on our voyage. Our sails were so small, and the current so swift, that we made but little headway through the day; but on the following morning, having rigged a larger sail, and given the management of the boat entirely into the hands of our Indian crew, we made much better progress through the day, and camped that night on Prairie du Terre. The next day being the sabbath, I preached to the brethren from 1 Peter iii, 18; in addition to which we had a prayer meeting morning and evening, and Mr. Lee preached to the Indians. It was a profitable day to our souls, and we were much interested with the apparent fervency with which many of the Indians called upon God.

On the following afternoon we arrived at the Cascades, where we had a portage to make at that stage of water of three miles. The families proceeded to the head of the portage, and the Indians carried up some of the goods; after which I was left to take charge of the remainder. When night came on I prepared my bed in the bottom of the boat as well as circumstances would allow, and lay down to sleep under the protection of that Being to whom the darkness is the same as the light. On the following morning all hands set to work, and on the evening of the 19th all our goods were not yet at the head of the falls. Such are some of the obstructions to be overcome by missionaries in a wild heathen country.

Here we met brother and sister Perkins, from the Dalls, who had been so anxious to hail us as fellow-labourers in this dark region that they could not await our arrival. And, as the next day was the sabbath, both parties were rejoiced at being permitted to lay by the toils and anxieties of the present life, and unite their voices at a throne of grace to give praise unto

God for mercies past, and to implore his aid for time to come. Mr. Lee preached in the morning; after which we crossed to the Indian village on the opposite side of the river, where the same gentleman preached to the natives in their language; and after our return Mr. Perkins preached from Eph. v, 15, 16.

We now had a voyage of two days before us before we could reach the Dalls; and as we were obliged to dimiss our boat below the Cascades, we must needs make the rest of the trip in Indian canoes. Canoes were accordingly procured from the Indians, and crews to manage them; and when our cargoes were all stowed, we stepped, or rather crawled on board, for an Indian canoe, when deeply loaded, is a very ticklish affair, and ours were loaded down within a hand's breadth of the water; so that a slight cant would fill them with water, and to strangers, as we were, it seemed impossible to manage them without turning them over. Previous to this the writer had boasted of never being afraid when on the water, but now his boasting was at an end; for no one could have suffered much more with fear for such a length of time than he did during the conclusion of that voyage; and on the afternoon of the second day, as the Dalls mission house hove in sight, he prayed the Indians to put him on shore, feeling thankful for the privilege of going the remainder of the way on foot. And when near the house he met with another disaster, for there he was obliged to witness a scene which is sufficiently disgusting to an old mountain trapper, namely, two young Indians squatting on the ground and regaling themselves with vermin which they had picked from each other's heads!

This was too much for his nervous system to endure at the termination of such a voyage; but this was found to be a matter of every-day occurrence with his new neighbours. A missionary, on another occasion, reproved an old Indian for being caught in the same filthy practice, upon which the old man, very honestly, answered, in his own speech, " Cultus, cultus shicks, cahqua salmon claska—Nothing, nothing, friend; they are all the same as salmon."

In the course of an hour we all met at the house and took tea together under a roof, with thankful hearts; and on the next day set about stowing four families into a house, which had, heretofore, been none too large for the accommodation of one family and a bachelor. This work, with the necessary interruptions from the Indians, occupied our time until the 2d of July, when Mr. Lee, Dr. Babcock, and the writer, bid our families and friends farewell, and set off for Vancouver. The canoe in which we were to perform the trip as far as the Cascades, we found to be very leaky, and so crank that it was very much inclined to go upon one side: this awakened all my former fears, and after proceeding about a mile, being swept down by a stiff current, and realizing, perhaps, all the fears, solicitudes, and anxieties, of a poor shipwrecked mariner upon a hen-coop on the broad ocean, I cried out for quarter, and declared my determination to go no further as passenger in that vessel, unless they would consent to go on shore, calk ship, and take in ballast. This Mr. Lee, who had by this time become almost amphibious, and cared but little which side of the canoe was uppermost, so long as she went ahead, thought to be a needless waste of time; but finding the doctor to be in favour of my proposition we carried the point, put to shore, calked the largest cracks in the canoe with cedar bark and some bits of cloth, took in some stone for ballast, and then cast adrift again; the Indians now hoping, as they said, that I would be a woman no longer, (for whenever any one expresses, in their estimation, needless fear, they say he is no better than a woman,) struck up the tune " ho ha ho, ho-ho ha ho," at the same time plying their paddles with admirable dexterity: we glided down the stream at the rate of eight or ten knots an hour, with but little further difficulty, save the occasional shipping of a wave, which would wet us nicely, in addition to that of bailing out the accumulated waters about every twenty minutes; this last work, however, the doctor and myself performed to admiration, as we were the only passengers that felt in the least incommoded, and as our good friend Lee did not, generally, trouble himself with such trifling affairs.

On the next day, in the afternoon, we arrived at the Cascades, ran our old canoe into the mouth of a small creek, made it fast; and sent word to its owner, who lived at the foot of the falls, to come and get it. Took another canoe, and crossed the river and held meeting with the Indians at their village; returned and camped for the night. On the following morning we left Dr. B. to load a canoe with goods which had been left on our passage up, with which he was to return to the Dalls, and Mr. L. and myself made further arrangements for our downward passage to Vancouver.

Just before we were ready to depart, the Indian to whom the old canoe belonged, in which we had floated from the Dalls, which was not worth a dollar, came to Mr. Lee, and said in a very expressive tone, " Friend, my canoe, which you left at the head of the falls, got loose somehow last night, went over the falls, and is entirely destroyed, and as I am very poor now, what will you give me ?" We were satisfied that the canoe could not have gone away without help, and that the rascal had taken this course to obtain a good price for his worthless property; but as we had no proof that he had sent the old canoe adrift, and as it was important to retain the good-will of this fellow, especially as he was a head man in his clan, in order to prevent further impositions, and to secure their assistance when making the frequent portages at this place, Mr. L. promised to make him satisfaction, and redeemed his pledge on his return by giving him a musket: this made his heart good, and when in conversation with the writer afterward at Vancouver, he said they all did as Mr. Lee told them; that his heart "*full of pray!*"

We arrived at Vancouver, without any further difficulties, on the afternoon of the 4th, and were happy to meet our friends there in comfortable health. Rev. Dr. J. P. Richmond and family had left on the 2d for Nesqually, his route to that place being by the way of the Columbia and Cawalitz Rivers in boats until they reach the settlement on the latter stream. There they were furnished with horses to ride, and others upon which to pack their baggage, their furniture and supplies having been left to go around in one of the company's vessels by the first opportunity. And now the reader may witness, in imagination, the doctor's preparations for this new and novel mode of travelling by land. In the first place, several horses are packed, some with trunks, boxes, and valises, others with sacks of flour, pork and bread, pots, kettles, and pans, etc., etc.; and the last with tents, beds and bedding. This done, other horses are saddled, then Mrs. Richmond is assisted in mounting, and takes the youngest child, a fine little boy of about nine months in her arms. The doctor mounts next with one daughter in his arms, and another up behind; then Miss Clark is assisted in seating herself in the saddle; after which Mr. Wilson, who was by this time an old hand at the business, springs upon his horse, and all are ready for a two days' march; upon which a Canadian or two, who are to act as guides and escorts, sing out to the horses, "*Marche-dan*," that is, Go there, and off they move in single file along an Indian trail. With nothing but a smooth path ahead there would have been but little to apprehend; but instead of that, they must cross rugged mountains, deep defiles, and rapid streams, besides wading dangerous mud-holes. But as my good friend, the doctor, was not prone to borrow trouble from the future, I doubt not, when the dangers and toils of the day were over, they enjoyed their humble repast, which was served up upon as clean a mat as could be found, with thankfulness to the Author of all mercies. After which followed the reading of the Holy Scriptures and family prayers; the ladies then prepare their beds upon the ground, stow away the already sleeping children, and all hands lie down to rest their weary limbs, and recover strength for the remainder of their journey. And despite of the hooting of owls, and the howling of wolves in the surrounding forest, their sleep is sweet and refreshing, and on the following day they reach their place of destination in safety, and take possession of their new, half-finished house, which was located within about half a mile of the Hudson Bay Company's fort on Puget Sound. Here we leave them, to finish their dwelling, and commence their labours as missionaries among the Indians of that vicinity, while we return to Vancouver.

The day after we arrived at Vancouver. Being the sabbath, Mr. Lee and myself each preached one sermon in the public hall, our hearers consisting of most of the gentlemen of the fort, the scholars from the school in the establishment, and the few of the mission family still remaining. Here we continued transacting business until the 10th, when Mr. Lee and myself set out for Astoria, for the purpose of examining the country and ascertaining the most favourable location for a missionary post near the mouth of the river. Our means of conveyance down the river was a small canoe, manned by a crew of two Indians; and after travelling most of the time, day and night, we arrived at Astoria on the morning of the 12th; and this being the sabbath, we spent the day with Mr. Birnie, the gentleman of whom mention has already been made, and partook with him of most excellent fresh salmon, and strawberries and cream. During the day Mr. Lee and the writer retired to the adjoining grove, where we enjoyed a most refreshing season of prayer, and besought the God of missions to direct us in selecting a spot where to erect the standard of the cross. On the following day we crossed the river, and visited the Chenook and Checalish Indians, and spoke to them on the subject of establishing a mission in their vicinity, at which they appeared to be very well pleased; but manifested a degree of disappointment when I informed them through Mr. Lee, who acted as interpreter, that my principal design was to teach them how to worship the Great Chief above, and not to trade for beaver or salmon, only so much as we might need for food. For it should not be forgotten that they never act from any higher motives, in their transactions with the whites, than the prospect of temporal gain; and it is perfectly reasonable that they should not, since they possess no correct knowledge of the relation they sustain to God, as rational and accountable beings, nor of the future state as a place of retribution. It is true, they have some strange and indistinct notions of the continued existence of friends departed; but, as nearly as we could ascertain, the employments of that state were considered to be similar to those of the present; consequently the oldest woman among the Chenooks, a descendant of Comcomly, when she buried a daughter, a number of years ago, it is reported that she caused two slaves to be killed and deposited in the same canoe with the dead body of the deceased, for the purpose of attending her in the future state. And in addition to the above, we ask, does any man, while in an unconverted state, of any nation or climate, act from any higher motive in anything that he may do than from a principle of supreme selfishness? If not, and the writer fully believes that the person cannot be produced in the wide world, even from Adam, after his fall, down to his youngest son that now treads the earth, that ever acted, under the above circumstances, from any other motive— this being the fact, those who have found the Indians of Oregon to be very anxious, as they have stated, to have missionaries sent among them that they might be taught " how to worship the Great Spirit aright," have been led into error, not being sufficiently acquainted with the beings with whom they had to do to understand the secret drift of their pretensions. And, no doubt, this is one, if not the greatest reason, why the church has been led to put an improper estimate upon the prospects of Christianizing and civilizing the natives of that region, and must now realize the consequences, namely, disappointment and regret—disappointment because the work which she expected her missionaries to be instrumental in accomplishing has not been accomplished by them; and regret that so many thousands, which ought to have been employed in the cultivation of a more promising field, have been spent in Oregon for the purpose of effecting that which, in all sober reason, ought never to have been expected. It should not be inferred from this statement, however, that no good has resulted to the inhabitants of Oregon through the exertions of the church and of her missionaries, who have spent, and are still spending, "their sweat, and blood, and pains, to cultivate Immanuel's land," in that dark portion of our earth. But, on the contrary, we feel ourselves fully justified in asserting that great good has crowned their labours; and doubt not that a host will come up in the end from that region to unite in celebrating the praises of Him "who hath loved us, and washed us from our sins in his own blood."

We camped at Chenook for the night, and on the following morning crossed the mouth of the river, and visited the Clatsops on the south side; after which we returned to Mr. Birnie's. Here we purchased a large canoe, and after spending this and the following night with the above gentleman, we engaged three Checalish Indians to man our canoes, and prepared for our departure for Vancouver. But when we were ready to embark, our faithless crew was entirely missing. We were now in a dilemma—two canoes to navigate up the river, and not a man to help us, and as for myself, having never had any experience in canoeing, except the dread created in consequence of the probability of upsetting every moment, I was no better than so much ballast, no, not half so good, for ballast would lie still, but that I could not be persuaded to do, so that, by my continual endeavours to balance the canoe, I caused it to rock ten times more.

We were measurably relieved, however, from our present embarrassments by the proffer of a servant of the company, who was going up to Pillar Rock to the salmon fishing, with a boat, to take one of our canoes in tow. This done, we rigged a sail in the other; and, as the wind was fair, we bid adieu to our kind host at Astoria, and set sail, Mr. Lee acting as captain and helmsman, and myself going before the mast on the broad of my back, lest by my movements the canoe might be upset. In this strange plight, being favoured with a fine breeze, we soon found ourselves at the salmon fishery. Here we found old Skumaquea and his wife. This was a head man of a small band of Indians a few miles above. They took charge of one of our canoes; and encouraged us to hope that when we arrived at their place we would obtain a crew. So after replenishing our empty stomachs, we hoisted sail again, and with considerable difficulty reached the old man's lodge; but, unfortunately, all the men had just gone about four miles up the river, to one of the Cathlamat Islands, to witness a great medical operation. What now could we do? We must either camp here for the night, or devise some means to get along as far as the above-named island, which was the only place at which we might expect to find a crew. And as there was no other means within our reach of effecting the latter, we proposed that four of their women should become our seamen and guides to the island, for which services we would give them a handkerchief each. To this proposal, after some talking and laughter among themselves, they assented; and in a very short time we were all on board, and on our way; and the women soon gave evidence that they were by no means inferior to their men in point of managing a canoe, for no sooner had we cleared the land sufficiently to get the strong sea breeze, which had increased to nearly half a gale, than they set up sail, one of which consisted of a rush mat, and away we darted with incredible speed, and were soon safely landed at the place of appointment. Here we discharged our fair crew, and soon engaged four young Indians to assist us in getting up to Vancouver.

But perhaps we ought not to take our departure from this place without noticing the great medical operation which was being performed here. The patients consisted of a young woman, who, upon examination, was found to have a slight fever; and a child, in much the same state, neither of them being dangerously ill. But the doctors affirmed that they had been filled with skokoms; and as proof of the truth of their statement of the cases, they produced a small snail shell, with a small string attached to it, and a small bunch of hair, wound up with a thread, and several other articles of the same nature, which they professed to have taken from the stomachs of the sick, and there were still several to be dislodged before a cathartic would take any effect; but after these were removed, they said it would be good for Mr. Lee to give his medicine. They now made preparations for a trial of their skill in endeavouring to rout another of these evil genii or skokoms. One of the doctors out of the six or eight who constituted the grand council, all of whom appeared as wise as serpents, it would seem had been the most successful in his attacks upon the strong-hold of this combination of skokoms, so it was decided he should be the leader in another general onset. Upon which he crawled near the young woman, (who was stretched upon a mat, with a female attendant at her head,) for the purpose of ascertaining the precise position of the enemy. Having determined this point, and made known all the particulars to his brethren of the faculty, he prepared himself for the tug of war. This he did by drawing his right arm through the hole in his blanket around the neck, so that his arm was now entirely disencumbered. He then threw his long hair up over his head, which entirely covered his face. Being now ready, he kneeled down, while all the other doctors, and men, women, and children, were arranged on either side, equipped with sticks and long poles which reached to the board roof. The kneeling doctor now commenced a wild and frightful song or chorus, in which all joined, keeping time with their sticks. He now commenced moving with well-dissembled caution toward the patient, extending his hands toward her stomach, as an eagle would his talons, ready to seize his affrighted prey; and the nearer he approached the lodgment of the skokom, the more furious became the singers and thumpers, and when he reached the stomach, at which he had been aiming, his distorted form and strained muscles evinced the appearance of perfect agony. The choir now bore down with might and main, and the practitioner now plunged his two fists into the patient's stomach most unmercifully; and seizing one of the enemy by the neck or heels, or somewhere else, he appeared to find it very hot; but drawing back quickly, plunged his hands into a trough of cold water, which was standing hard by, and then seized the unyielding foe again; but as it had then assumed something of the nature of the eel, and slipped out of his hands, he quickly caught up some ashes, rubbed it on his fingers, then laid hold upon it for the third time, screaming and yelling in the most terrific manner, while the company plied their sticks, and singing, or rather screaming, pipes with redoubled energy. The battle now became doubtful; but after many manly efforts victory turned upon the doctor's side, who, by one mighty effort, broke the hold of the skokom upon the patient, which now turned wholly upon the doctor, causing him to cry out for help. The company was now in perfect ecstasies, pounding as though life and death depended upon every stroke; and bellowing at the very top of their voices, "Ha ha yeh, ha ha yeh." Two of the faculty now caught the almost overpowered doctor around the waist, and bore him, screeching and writhing, away from the patient, amidst the thundering noise of the transported spectators and attendant physicians; but all of a sudden the victorious doctor cried, "*Ho ho ho*," and making an effort, as though he was catching after something toward the top of the lodge, exclaimed, "*There*, he has gone through the roof!" The music now ceased, every Indian and squaw appeared astonished, while the doctor explained the whole process in an elaborate speech. After witnessing several such feats, Mr. Lee commenced reproving them for their folly; but a venerable old doctor informed him that it would be best for him to depart before he found himself in trouble. So taking the old man's advice, we laid in a stock of fresh dried salmon, got our crew on board, and left the doctors to manage the remainder of the skokoms according to their ancient mode of practice.

It was now night, but the pale moon had taken up the tale of creating goodness, and was pouring her silver rays upon the expansive bosom of the virgin waters, while the owl upon the opposite mountain, more rational than his unfledged neighbours of the island, was pouring forth the praises of his creator God in solemn notes. A few moments' calm reflection upon the exalted privileges of the Christian, who has abundant proof of an all-surrounding Deity in the works of his hand, in connection with the assurance that all things shall work together for good to them that love him, had a tendency to dispel the excitement created by the inhuman and most ludicrous scene which we had just witnessed; and now wrapping myself in my blanket, I stretched out in the bottom of the canoe, and fell asleep. But this sweet slumber, like all our endearments here, was but momentary in its duration; for the expiring breeze from the Pacific, like frail man after his last convulsive effort to cling to life, fell off at once, which produced such a reaction upon our sail that it was well nigh upsetting the canoe, and caused all the fears hitherto experienced by the sleeper to rush on his mind like a mighty flood, and of course there was no more sleep. My worthy associate was now awakened, having dreamed of no disasters; and after a kind lecture upon the unprofitableness of being disturbed with needless fears, consented to go ashore. We soon reached the north shore of the river; and hauling our canoe partly upon land, under the brow of a frowning precipice, we placed our blanket in the bottom of our frail bark, and after committing ourselves to the protection of the God of missions, lay down side by side, spread the other blanket over us, and slept until morning as sweetly as many hundreds in the civilized world upon their beds of down. In the morning we found our two Indians curled up in the bow of the canoe, enjoying that sweet slumber peculiar to such as are not pressed with the cares of the world and the deceitfulness of riches: a most convincing proof of the truth of the poet's lines,

> " Man wants but little here below,
> Nor wants that little long."

All hands were now called; but only called to contend with new difficulties, for in hauling our canoe ashore it had come in contact with a stick or stone, which had loosened a large knot, which caused it to leak alarmingly. It was now hauled on shore again, and with some difficulty repaired. This exercise excited a morning appetite, which determined all hands to take a munch before commencing the journey of the day; but to our surprise and grief, the ample store of fresh dried salmon which we had taken the precaution to lay in the previous night had been stowed in the other canoe, and how far our fellow-voyageurs were ahead or astern of us was impossible for us to decide. Here we were, with a heavy day's work on hand for our crew, and no more provision than one hungry Indian required for a day's allowance. We however took a bite of what remained to us, and pushed ahead as soon as possible, in hopes of overtaking the other canoe, with the prophetic announcement from the Indians, that if we did not succeed in coming up with the dried salmon their hearts would be very poor before night. And, as it turned out in the sequel, our other crew were pulling ahead with all their strength, hoping to overhaul us, knowing, as they afterward said, that we would be very hungry for some of the good salmon, and supposing that we had preceded them during the night, while they were asleep. But as their canoe was much the lightest, we were of course left far in the rear. We had some wind and tide in our favour; but when the night closed in upon us, we were ten or more miles from Vancouver. My colleague laid hold upon a paddle, and commenced, in addition to the weary crew, to propel our bark ahead with greater rapidity; and I, being a novice, was permitted once more to roll myself in my blanket, and lose my appetite for salmon in a state of unconsciousness. How or when we arrived at Vancouver I know not; but we were awakened in the morning by Dr. Tolmie, a gentleman of the company, and when I arose I found our rather queer bed-room hauled upon shore, and completely stowed with my associates, some covered with blankets, and others with none. Our appetites now returned with renewed vigour, and we remember doing ample justice to the excellent breakfast that was soon placed before us in the fort, in company with those we left, whom we found in health, which sweetened every other mercy.

This being the sabbath, we laboured to feed those with the bread of life who had, as good stewards, communicated to us in temporal things. We remained at Vancouver until the 26th, Mr. Lee engaged in packing and arranging some goods for his station at the Dalls, while I was making arrangements for the purpose of occupying the post assigned to me.

In the following week Mr. Lee left with two canoes deeply laden with necessaries for the Dalls, while I proceeded with my arrangements for our removal to Astoria.

CHAPTER XXI.

Account of the Dalls resumed—A cold-blooded murder committed—Encounter with Indians—Mission family suffer from sickness—Camp meeting—Mr. D. Lee's voyage from and to the Dalls—Journey to the Walamet station—Death of Mrs. Leslie—Birth—Marriages—Annual meeting—Building—Religious meetings—Death of Mrs. Jason Lee—Mr. and Mrs. D. Lee's voyage to and from Vancouver—Eruption of a volcano—Visit to Walamet Falls, and return—Religious state of the natives—Remarkable conversion—Mr. and Mrs. D. Lee sail for the United States.

To resume the account of the Dalls. After the writer had occupied about two months, from the 1st of June till near the end of July, 1840, in company with Mr. Frost, up and down the Columbia, as we have already stated in a preceding chapter, he pursued his way with his heavy-laden canoe from Fort Vancouver to the Dalls; where, after several days of hard and weary toil, and the usual rough and smooth of the journey, he arrived in safety, glad to meet Messrs. Babcock, Brewer, and Perkins, and their ladies, and Mrs. Lee, all in good spirits. We were happy to meet again, and thankful for the watchful care of Him who "encampeth round about his people." In my absence Mr. Perkins had been labouring among the people; and some difficulties and trials had arisen since my departure. Shortly after the camp meeting, a cold-blooded murder had been committed on the person of a leading man at Wishham, Cali-te-weet by name, who was regarded as a valuable Christian, and the most useful man in the village. A notorious villain, by the name of Chap-a-li, of the Wallah-wallah tribe, stole several of the man's horses, and he went after him to recover them. On arriving at his hut, the horses, it seems, were tied without, when he and those with him began to unloose them; and while they were doing this, the murderer aimed his rifle through an opening in the lodge, and killed the owner on the spot! This horrid deed of the reckless murderer awoke the spirit of revenge. A chief had ingloriously fallen—a relative, and he had many—and every

11

heart was moved; and it became an occasion of discouragement and declension. Up till now nothing had transpired so full of danger to the quietness and peace that had prevailed hitherto. The question would now arise, "What is the good of praying?" "Our brother prayed, but he is dead. If it will not keep us from dying, *why* pray? If we pray, we cannot revenge the death of our friends—we cannot fight our enemies. Those will suffer for our neglect of a sacred duty, and these will come and devour us." They were indeed "in a strait." So clearly did they see that prayer and revenge held no affinity. Mr. Perkins strove to restrain and preserve them from violence, and was successful to some extent; but a deep wound was inflicted that has never been healed. How true it is, "one sinner destroyeth much good!" Our hearts, pious reader, were filled with sorrow to see the souls of our care thus wasted; but we still hoped, and determined to labour for things that appertained to salvation.

The Indians were now all engaged in the salmon harvest, and we met with them in their salmon houses at the Dalls. These are only temporary, and are removed when the fishing season ends. Sometimes within, and at others we used to assemble them without, under the shadow of the elevated rocks. One sabbath, in the month of August, soon after my return from Vancouver, as above stated, taking horses, Mrs. Lee and myself rode to the Dalls, to meet the people for worship; and assembled them in the open air, where they sat upon the ground while they listened to the truths of God. Having held two meetings with them, in which we felt to say like Peter on the mount, "It is good for us to be here," we got upon our horses and set off for home. We had rode nearly half way, and were moving slowly along, when the tramp of horses behind apprized us that we were not alone; and looking around we saw five Indians galloping toward us. They soon came up, and several of them had muskets, and one reining his horse close to mine, laid hold of my bridle:

no sooner was his hold broken than it was seized by another on the other side. By this time it was supposed that war was the only alternative, and Mrs. Lee was directed to ride to the house, it being about a mile and a half distant. Now the relator was "alone in his glory!" "What is this?" said he, for he knew them, "What do you mean?" One replied, "We do not want to quarrel, but a talk. Our brother that lived with Mr. Perkins is dead, and our hearts are troubled; we want a blanket; Mr. Perkins (not truth) promised us one when you came back." "That is nothing to me; if Mr. Perkins has made a promise he will do it,—that is his business." Finding they could neither *lie* nor *awe* me into compliance, they left me a lone conqueror, and giving rein to their horses, they flew over the plain at the top of their speed,—and myself at their heels about three-fourths of a mile, to a divide in the trail, where they parted company, and left me to proceed alone to the mission house. Being aware of their intentions toward our band of horses, a man was sent immediately on my coming to bring them up.

And now for the rescue. Mrs. Lee had come post haste, and the news of the war had roused the martial spirit of Dr. Babcock and Mr. Brewer, and they had taken arms, and were ready to take the field, when the messenger came with news of victory! Our joy at this moment was soon a little abated; for the man arrived who had been sent after the horses, and reported that the conquered Indians had captured the best horse in the band! The boy about whose death this affair took place had been sent away from Mr. P. for bad conduct, and soon after he was taken sick and died. Mr. P. was with him and administered medicine to him in his sickness. He appeared to evince some grounds of hope in Christ, and requested his relatives not to trouble Mr. Perkins, after his death. If one who chanced to die had been in our employ recently, or died with us on a journey, they would try to make us pay for him: difficulties often grew from this cause, because we wholly denied any claim on this score, and we would not fix an annoying precedent.

Mr. Brewer took charge of the farm at the station, and had raised about fifty bushels of wheat; the season having been dry, it had suffered much from the drought. Dr. Babcock in his attention to the sick had lightened the burden of Mr. Perkins and myself very much, and we were anticipating pleasant days in each other's society and the efficient performance of our work in its several departments; but these hopes did not long shed their cheering light around us, as will soon appear. But before this, soon after my return from Vancouver, Mr. P. and his family had gone to the Walamet; and during their absence they were sick with the intermittent fever, and two of their crew of Indinas died at Walamet; while a third was left in the hands of the doctor. These trials delayed their return several days, and subjected them to many inconveniences; but having secured others in place of those whom they left, to work the canoe, they at length returned in safety to the Dalls in September. Previous to this, Dr. Babcock had gone to Fort Vancouver to give Mrs. Babcock the benefit of a journey for the improvement of her health, expecting to return in a short time. Soon, however, after reaching the fort, an express met him from Mr. Jason Lee, bound to the Dalls, directing him to remove immediately to the Walamet station, as his services were greatly needed among the sick. In compliance with these directions he hurried on to the Walamet. This movement, so unexpected, greatly thwarted our plans and expectations at the Dalls, and left us again without a physician. This was owing to the removal of Dr. White from his connection with the mission and his departure to the United States. At this time the intermittent fever prevailed at that station, and Mrs. Jason Lee was also attacked with the bilious remittent fever, which was near proving fatal; and from the effects of which she probably never recovered. The family of Mr. Parrish was visited in the removal by death of his oldest son. The prevalent sickness very much retarded the work which had been attempted, and the saw-mill which was being erected made slow advances. Messrs. Lee and Hines had explored the Umbaqua country, and found the establishment of a mission there wholly impracticable. Next month, October, Mr. J. Lee visited the Dalls station, the affairs of the Walamet having prevented his doing it at an earlier time, which circumstance operated unfavourably on the minds of the people, who had indulged a strong desire to see him, and expected he would have come to see them long before. A camp meeting was now held, and it was a time of blessed influence on many hearts—not more than one-third or one-fourth as many attended as at the first. The power and presence of God were in the midst, and his love was manifestly shed forth in enlarged measures. Evidences appeared to cheer our troubled spirits, and we " thanked God and took courage !" Some of the Wallah-wallahs among whom Mr. Perkins had been preaching were here admitted to baptism, and the Lord's supper was administered. Those days of labour and enjoyment will not soon be forgotten. Would that the good then apparent had continued and inceased, then had their peace been perpetuated as a river !

Our blessed meeting now closed, and Mr. J. Lee and myself returned to Walamet ; and my wife, who was going there to spend the winter, accompanied us. Having encountered the usual barriers of the voyage, the waves, and winds, and Cascades, and portages, and the like, we at length reached our destination in safety, thankful that none of the disasters of the journey had been of any serious character.

Here we enjoyed the social circle of our beloved ones for several days with much relish : and then, leaving Mrs. Lee and his friends here, the writer returned to the Dalls, taking up a cargo of supplies from Vancouver. The trip was performed with the share of difficulties common to this inclement season, midst drenching rains, high winds, and pinching frosts. Sometimes we were flying with our blanket sail before the wind, and again were compelled to land among the breakers, with canoe and cargo half under water. Having secured our lading above the reach of the waves, and hauled up our canoe, wet from head to foot, and our fingers stinging with the cold, we fly to the covert of the neighbouring rocks or willows to elude the freezing blast, and make a fire to dry our garments. Here we forget the dangers past, and quietly enjoy our good fire, not forgetting to keep our stomachs in an agreeable humour, till the fury of the wind abates so as to permit us to proceed. We are glad to come to our "desired haven," where, standing on the solid ground, we look back with wonder and gratitude upon the dangers we have escaped. It was now November, and the natives were all located in their winter quarters. This winter the number of the Indians at the Dalls occupied much of our time—meetings, and attention to their calls, and administering to their sick, which we did uniformly as far as lay in our power. Mr. Perkins also made a voyage to Walamet in December, and in the latter part of January it became necessary for the writer to accompany Dr. Babcock to that station. He had been on a professional visit at this place, and a daughter was added to Mr. Perkins's family on the 18th. There had been an unusual fall of snow, and a degree of cold seldom known in Oregon, the quicksilver falling to 18° below zero. The river was frozen half way down to the Cascades, and, to reach that point, it was necessary to make a journey over land twenty miles. It was important that the doctor should leave; but, being a new hand, it was thought proper for the writer to go with him on this new expedition. Arrangements were accordingly made, consisting of a small quantity of provisions, fire-works, an axe, a kettle, and our blankets. Snow covered the ground to the depth of several inches. We now bid our friends farewell, and started on our tramp, two whites and four Indians. We found the snow deep upon the hills, but fast melting; so that the hollows and runs were full of water, and little creeks were swollen into threatening torrents. Across one of these we felled a tree that stood on its bank, which served as a bridge on which some of us crossed, keeping our balance with a pole, resting one end on the bottom of the stream, while the rest seized the bridge with their hands, holding on to it till they had waded across on the lower side. Going on we came to the point of a rocky bluff that almost overhung the river, and so steep that we could scarcely hang upon it, not without fears that some misstep might precipitate us into the depths below. A little further we came to a deep gorge, and at first we thought that our only way now was to cut hazels and fasten them together, and drop ourselves down the precipice by them upon the rocky shore that now lay between it and the river; but on looking around, we discovered a way along the declivity, by which we descended in safety. Suffice to say, we reached our object, a river without ice; hired a canoe of the Indians; passed the Cascades in good order; encountered a field of ice above Vancouver without damage; stemmed the current of the Walamet to the mission, and then closed our journey in a hearty welcome to our families and friends.

Here a watch-night had been held at the close of the year, and a happy state of religious feeling prevailed. Several whites had been converted since the arrival of the last reinforcement. Mr. Hines was teaching the mission school with some success. Mrs. Leslie was fast failing, and died in February, 1841. She had been in Oregon between four and five years, suffered a large amount of sickness with patience and submission, and died a bright witness for God in the triumphs of faith, leaving five daughters, three of whom came with her to the country, and her husband, to mourn their loss. Her funeral sermon was preached by Mr. J. Lee, on those encouraging words, 2 Cor. iv, 17: "For our light affliction, which is but for a moment, worketh for us a far more exceeding and eternal weight of glory." There rests her dust, till the trump of God awake it to glory and immortality. "Blessed are the dead who die in the Lord!"

March 23d. Wilbur Fisk, son of Daniel and Maria T. Lee, was born. The writer will add that it was a day of gladness and thanksgiving to the parents.

About this time several matrimonial alliances were solemnized. Mr. J. L. Whitcom was married to Mrs. Susan Shepard, widow of the late Mr. Shepard; Mr. J. Holman to Miss Almira Phelps; and Mr. David Carter to Miss Orpha Lankton, all in obedience to that law which requires every son of Adam to wed a daughter of Eve.

On Monday, May 10th, we held our first annual meeting, which continued in much harmony nearly two weeks. Mr. Hines was appointed superintendent of the Oregon Mission Manual Labour School; Mr. Leslie to the settlement; Mr. Waller to the Walamet Falls; Messrs. Kone and Frost to Chenook; Dr. Richmond to Nesqually, and myself at the Dalls. The meeting ended, we were ready to return to the several posts assigned us, and soon prepared to leave. Mr. Carter had been hired several months at my station, and now returned with me, taking his newly-married lady with him. Taking an affectionate leave of our friends, we manned our two canoes for the voyage, and hastened back to our station. The Columbia was at its height, and the current very strong, and the sun poured its scalding rays upon us. The labour, and risk, and anxiety in passing the Cascades were immense. The cargoes had to be unloaded and reloaded not less than six times. In passing the canoe up the bad water, two men are in it, one at the stern and the other at the bow, having strong setting poles to keep it off the rocks; and a rope is fastened to the head, fifty yards long, which is manned by four or five men, and thus it is drawn up. But now, as it sometimes happens, we capsized one of our canoes, and damaged it on the rocks. We however soon repaired the breach, and moved on again. But with the Cascades we did not leave all our dangers, and Mrs. L., particularly, suffered much from fear. The winds were boisterous and the waves ran high, and at one time we were compelled to land in order to escape the fury of the blast, and the being dashed upon the rocks ahead; but we escaped with only a wetting.

Saturday, June 5th, we came in sight of the station at dusk; but the current was too strong for us to attempt the ascent with our cargoes without daylight. We now went ashore and encamped. After making all snug, myself and Mrs. Lee went on in our now light canoe, while Mr. and Mrs. Carter remained in camp, and reached our house before twelve o'clock, where we were gladly received by our friends, and were not a little thankful for our safe return.

On Monday Mr. and Mrs. Carter joined us, and now we were four families to bear ourselves up in our toils and trials, and

> Each to feel his brother's care,
> And each the other's burden bear.

Timber for a barn had been prepared by Mr. Carter; and now he put up the frame, assisted by Mr. Brewer and myself. This with the roof he finished during the summer, besides helping Mr. Brewer in harvest, and assisting in laying up a log meeting-house thirty by forty feet, which was much needed for winter. The farm produced this year a good supply of wheat, and a fine crop of potatoes; but to get our wheat ground we had to go to Fort Vancouver mill, a journey of seventy-five miles, and make two portages at the Cascades.

When we came back from Walamet, myself and family had yet a house to fit up for our accommodation. This could not be done the preceding year for the want of lumber; but during the winter we had procured the sawing of some. It will be recollected that our sawing here was all done with whip saws. Mr. Carter had done something toward the house previously to his going to the Walamet, and he lent a hand now to finish what he had begun. But, besides these, there were many things remained for myself and Mrs. Lee to do to make it, not to say comfortable, but as nearly so as we could. It consisted of a room ten feet wide by twenty long, having on one side a pantry and an entry, which occupied an additional space of five by ten feet, and on the other side a chimney and fire-place, with a closet on one side and a stairway on the other two and a half feet wide. Here we had to set up a small cook-stove, and then furnished our room with two stools which I had had made in earlier days; and besides this, the kindness of Mr. Perkins had supplied me with more than half a chair, which was repaired, and we esteemed it a great luxury. After this was added a table, and then a settee, and the room was used for a great many things, a kitchen, wash-room, parlour, bed-room, etc., etc. Over this was a chamber of the same dimensions, which was neatly fitted up for a sleeping-room. These rooms were lighted with two windows each. Mr. Perkins's family occupied the other part of the house of the same dimensions. This summer we received a visit from Mr. Jason Lee and his wife, who was in very poor health. They had before this been down to Clatsop station on her account, and hoped that the voyage to this place would prove beneficial and promote her recovery. She occupied our chamber, and we used every effort in our power to render her comfortable. During this visit he had a violent attack of the ague and fever, and my companion and myself strove to alleviate his sufferings. We felt thankful that we could do anything for those we so much loved. During their visit, Messrs. Clark and Littlejohn, Mr. Smith and Mr. Munger, arrived from Wallah-wallah, going to the Walamet; their wives were with them. Our interview with them was very agreeable, and while they tarried we enjoyed some profitable seasons of social and public worship; and when they resumed their journey our hearts went with them.

The time had now come when our beloved guests and relatives must leave us and return to the Walamet station. We felt it was painful parting, for it was very probable we were taking the last fond look, and so it proved in the case of Mrs. J. Lee. She was seated on horseback, and the writer walked at her side half a mile to the shore, where she was helped into the canoe; the parting farewell was exchanged, and soon they were gliding down the Columbia, and we returned, saying one to the other, She will meet us here no more!

Not long after this, Mr. Perkins and his wife set out for the Walamet. When they reached the falls, Mrs. P. remained at Mr. Waller's, and he went on to the upper station with Mr. Waller on horseback. Returning they had a severe time in ascending the Columbia, at the most dangerous and uncomfortable season in the year; but through the care of Him who tempers the wind to the shorn lamb, they returned in safety. Of the society of Mr. and Mrs. Carter we had been deprived some time, as they had removed to the Walamet. They were valuable Christian friends.

Our log meeting-house we were not able to finish. We once got up the rafters, but a high wind arose and they were blown down. We much needed a place where we could meet the people for prayers, and assemble them on the sabbath days; and the want of such accommodations kept many at their houses, and made our meetings small; and, to provide for these, an addition of a block of twelve by twenty feet was made to that part of my house occupied by Mr. P., which was fitted up for a place of meeting. Here we held prayers with the people morning and evening, and preached to them on the Lord's day. In general our time was so taken up in procuring lumber, building, canoeing to Vancouver and Walamet to bring up the necessary supplies and get our milling done, relieving the sick among the Indians, doing the work of servants in our own families, and in attending to the religious services mentioned above, as to prevent our performing that amount of itinerant labour which the wants of the people demanded. Besides these things, we devoted a part of our time to the study of the language. That we could not visit all the people as often as was necessary for their good, was a very serious disadvantage to them, and a source of affliction to ourselves; and among many it was the cause of disaffection, leading many to neglect to hear even when an opportunity was enjoyed. The Indian doctors resumed their practices, and a large proportion returned to their former vices. For our own benefit we had one discourse in English on the sabbath, and a prayer meeting in the evening; and in the week on Tuesday evening a concert prayer meeting with the Presbyterian missionaries, which was proposed by the writer soon after their arrival in Oregon, and in which we laid our common cause before the God of missions; and our class meetings on Thursdays. Mr. Perkins and myself took turns in preaching on the sabbath; and when we were visited by Mr. Jason Lee or any of the other preachers, we had the benefit of their instructions, which was a privilege we highly prized. Located, as we were, in the great thoroughfare from the interior to the lower country, we often had calls from the gentlemen of the Hudson's Bay Company as they were passing up and down in their boats, between fifteen and twenty almost every year. These boats are moved with oars, being manned with from four to six men, and take forty packages of ninety pounds weight each, besides the outfit and provisions of the crew. Those also emigrating to the Walamet Valley from the States and the mountains, all called here, and gave us an opportunity from time to time to remind them of a better and a heavenly country, to which their attention should be directed. Sometimes they came to us in want, and it was a great pleasure to us that we had the means of affording them any aid, worn out as they were with the toils and hardships of their protracted journey. We trust that some of them will praise God in heaven for the words of eternal life which they were permitted to hear while with us. One of these, who was, he said, "going to the Walamet to stay provided money grew on the bushes; but if not, he was going to California," was in a few months after brought to see that religion, not money, was the thing he wanted, and immediately he began to cry unto God in the disquietness of his soul, and continued many days in deep distress, till God spoke peace to his troubled heart. In the month of March, 1842, a daughter, an only child, was born to Mr. and Mrs. Jason Lee at Walamet; but this joyful occurrence was destined to be soon followed with deep sorrow; for in a few weeks the mother was suddenly removed by death. Thus were the fountains of grief opened again, before they were scarcely yet dried up, on account of a similar bereavement, in the bleeding heart of the stricken husband, smitten with breach upon breach. Did not the Lord uphold his servant; enabling him to say, "Though he slay me, yet will I trust in him?" We all deeply sympathized with him, and felt ourselves painfully bereft of a dear relative and sister. Thus did the Lord deal with his servants, giving tears in abundance; but blessed be his name! they were mingled with gratitude in the assurance we felt that she had entered into rest, and in the hope that we too should in due time follow her there, where "all is calm, and joy, and peace," and

"All the ship's company meet,
Who sail'd with our Saviour below."

February 29th, it became necessary for myself and Mrs. L. to make a voyage to Fort Vancouver. So leaving our friends at the Dalls we embarked in a canoe with a crew of four Indians, with our provisions, blankets, bedding, and all the etceteras, for a trip of weal or wo, sunshine and storm. The winter seemed past, so fine was the day, and the singing of birds had almost come. Having loaded in our baggage, we arranged a convenient seat as near the middle and bottom of the canoe as we could, and then seated ourselves side by side, facing the bow, with our little boy almost a year old in our arms, two Indians before and two aft. And now, the reader may see us gliding down the river, the white paddles as they are lifted from the water glistening in the sun, and hear their measured rap on the side of the canoe. Everything seemed to smile a pleasant voyage, and a quick return; but a few miles, and the winds arose, the waves ran high, the sky assumed a scowling face, and the turbulent waters threatened us with destruction, if we dared to proceed. Again and again did we escape their wrath by flying to the welcome shore for refuge; and when they had spent their force, and the wind made a pause for breath to blow again, we hastened from our hiding places, and hurried on. It rained copiously and long, rained till it snowed. There was a deep fall: when we made the portage at the Cascades it was a foot in depth, and more. When we encamped, we first scraped away the snow and set up our tent, and at the same time, some of the crew made a fire a little in front, and then, being provided with mats, some of them were spread down in the tent, and over them an oilcloth to guard our bedding against the dampness. Sometimes the rain would almost extinguish the fire, it fell in such profusion. In this way, after battling the elements nine days, we reached our destination in safety, a journey of eighty miles, and, through the blessing of God, all in good health and spirits. We were intending when we left the Dalls to visit Mr. and Mrs. Frost at Clatsop; but the length of time occupied in getting to this place prevented our doing it. At the fort we were received with the usual kind attentions, and after resting a little, and transacting the objects of our visit, we set off on our return; which we found more agreeable than our downward voyage. We reached our home on the night of the 18th of March, at twelve o'clock, having journeyed from the Cascades in one day, fifty miles, and enjoyed with our friends a mutual thanksgiving for our safe return.

March 21st, we held another camp meeting with the Indians. The number who attended at this meeting was much fewer than at either of the other two; yet it was attended with good to many. Some were powerfully reclaimed from a backslidden state. From all we witnessed at this meeting, our hearts were greatly encouraged to hope in God. There is not a Christian among us, had he been present, but would have said, "God is in this place!" More earnest prayers, the writer believes, were never offered, nor answers to prayers more evident than were witnessed here. A happy state of things followed for some time; till at length difficulties arose, and the love of most of those who had been blessed at the camp meeting waxed cold again. Thus were the spirits of the missionary band elevated with hope, and then depressed with disappointment, so frequent were the fair blossoms of promise cut off! Soon after the camp meeting Messrs. Lee and Leslie arrived from Walamet, now companions in sorrow. They had been husbands, but now no kind sharer of their joys and woes waited their return! We felt afflicted in their afflictions, and favoured in their ministrations of the blessed gospel. When they left, the writer accompanied them to the Walamet. As we passed along the Cascades, Mr. Leslie showed me the place in the rapids where he and Mrs. White so narrowly escaped drowning in 1838. The remembrance of that event almost chilled his blood, even at so late a period. We reached the Walamet in safety. Our second yearly meeting now commenced, and continued several days in much harmony. During the year, Mr. Kone had returned to the United States. Mr. Hines remained this year in connection with the Oregon Mission Manual Labour School, as superintendent, and preacher to the Walamet settlement. Mr. Frost at Clatsop, Dr. Richmond at Nesqually, Mr. Waller at Walamet Falls, and myself at the Dalls, and

Mr. Perkins, my colleague, as formerly. Mr. Leslie was left without an appointment in order to provide for his family, by putting his three elder daughters in school at the Sandwich Islands, or return with all his children to the States, or otherwise, as providence should direct. The writer now returned to the Dalls. During his absence Dr. Babcock and Mr. Raymond and their wives had come to the station from the Walamet, and a daughter had been added to the family of Mr. Raymond, and another to the family of Mr. Brewer, and Dr. Babcock had returned to the Walamet, leaving Mr. Raymond and family, who also followed soon after my return.

It was a great pleasure to meet my fellow-labourers again, and find them and my family well. Itinerating among the people employed most of my time during the months of June and July. Mrs. Lee accompanied me one week at the Dalls, where our time was employed in devotional exercises with the natives, in which they were often called together to preaching and prayers. Some appeared to manifest a good degree of religious interest, and our own souls were happy in the efforts we made to do them good.

In August went to Walamet with my family, to which a second son was added on the 7th of September. During our stay here Mrs. Lee suffered much from the fever and ague, as did our little boy Wilbur also, and myself. At the same time a blessed revival took place in the mission school, and a goodly number were powerfully converted, or reclaimed, and in its after progress some whites and several Owyhees were gathered in, and a very happy state of religious enjoyment continued to pervade the school throughout the winter following. Mr. and Mrs. Brewer from the Dalls, on a visit here, returned with us when we went back, and we were glad of their company along our liquid path. About the time we went to Walamet, Mr. Leslie, Dr. Richmond and family, and Mr. and Mrs. Whitcom and their children, left for the United States. Mr. Leslie took two of his daughters with him, leaving his eldest, who was married to Mr. Cornelius Rogers, and her two younger sisters in her care. They sailed from the Walamet River in August. In September a body of emigrants crossed the mountains from Missouri, consisting of one hundred and twenty-five persons, men, women, and children. Dr. E. White, formerly of the Oregon mission, came over with them, now sub Indian agent of the United States to Oregon.

In November the writer went again to the Walamet, and returned to the Dalls on the 30th, accompanied by Mr. and Mrs. Littlejohn and Mr. Geiger, going to the interior missions; and Dr. White, and Messrs. Cornelius Rogers and Thomas M'Kay, bound there on an agency to the Indians. The evening of our arrival there was an eruption of Mount St. Helen; and the next morning the ejected ashes were falling with a mist-like appearance, covering the leaves, fences, and stones, with a light, fine, gritty substance, in appearance like hoar frost, some specimens of which were collected. The volcano was over one hundred miles distant, due north from the junction of the Walamet with the Columbia, and west of north-west from the Dalls. In ascending the Columbia at this time we were much retarded by strong head winds, and an unusual degree of cold prevailed, and considerable ice formed along the shores. The men had to make themselves mittens. In three days we had not proceeded fifteen miles. We lay by over one sabbath, and had preaching and prayers; and every morning and evening we found it good to draw near to God. Our safe return again was a cause of mutual gladness. Here we were happy to meet with Mrs. Marcus Whitman, who spent the winter with us. Mrs. Littlejohn also tarried till after Christmas. Their Christian society was highly prized. Mr. Littlejohn, and the Indian agent, and Messrs. Rogers and M'Kay, came back from the interior before Christmas. It was an interesting sabbath-day. The Lord was in our midst. Next sabbath, New-year's, the Lord's supper was administered, and it was a season of refreshing to our souls. On Monday, 2d, Mr. Perkins's family received the addition of a daughter. Thus did the Lord in various ways manifest his love and kindness toward his needy servants.

The first and second sabbaths of February Mr. J. Lee was with us, and the preaching of the word and the holy communion were rendered a blessing to our souls. The name of the Lord be praised for the blessed privileges he permitted us to enjoy from time to time in that desert land! During his visit there was a remarkable fall of snow; and for many days the people were mostly confined to their houses.

One sabbath morning two men came for a coffin and a shroud to bury a child that had died the previous night; but as it was not in our power, nor our practice, to furnish these things, we refused their application. They wanted us to be at charges for them; and rather than to foot the bill themselves, they would have neither one nor the other. They would like to have their friends decently interred, provided we would do it, and it should cost them nothing. They were told that the thing was never known that strangers among any people should be required to bury that people's dead! and that the white men, and the Kinse and Wallah-wallah Indians, paid for coffins and grave clothes; and that it was manlike to do so, and mean to do otherwise. They now made a long harangue, to which a number that had collected around listened with mute attention; but no one seemed at all excited but themselves, and feeling themselves not very popular in the auditory, they brought their vociferating eloquence to a close, having exhausted their munitions and conquered their two warriors!

The snows were much longer in leaving us this year than usual, and the people were confined to their houses so long that it became the cause of much more sickness among them than usual. There was ice in the river till the 13th of March. On the morning of the

5th the quicksilver fell to 6° below zero. Four of the Hudson Bay Company's boats were eleven days in reaching this station from Vancouver; and here they were detained nine days more with the ice. Much of my time was employed in attention to the sick, some in the study of the language, to which Mr. P. devoted himself constantly. The usual meetings among the natives, and our English services, were continued.

Sabbath, 12th. The writer spoke to the Indians on the parable of the marriage of the king's son, Matt. xxii; and Mr. P. preached in English on "Let us search and try our ways."

Monday, April 3d. Mrs. Whitman, whose society we had enjoyed since October, left us to return to Waileptu. She had endeared herself greatly to us, and we regretted to part with her. But these things "must needs be," and we bend our will to the will that our heavenly Father appoints.

On Thursday, 27th, Mrs. Lee rode to the shore to visit a sick woman, and as she was crossing a creek into which the back water from the river set up, she suddenly found her horse plunged into water swimming deep, when she instantly dropped the reins and seized the mane, and thus escaped to shore, the distance being but a few yards. There were several paths leading down to the creek, and she took one too near the river. We were thankful that nothing more serious followed than a transitory alarm, and an unwelcome drenching. Early in May, Mr. Hines and Dr. White arrived from the Walamet, and Mr. P. went with them to the interior.

On the 9th, taking my family, we started to attend the yearly meeting at the Walamet Falls. Mrs. Lee's health had been suffering for many months, and only the preceding day she had a violent attack of the fever and ague, brought on by over-exertion in making the necessary preparations for the voyage. On our passage, at the Cascades, where we got next day at twelve o'clock, she was again prostrated in a violent paroxysm, and after waiting till it had somewhat abated at the head of the portage, she walked to the foot of the rapids, three miles. Next day we reached Vancouver, and ascended the Walamet about three miles, where we passed the night.

Friday, 12th. Pursued our way up the river. The day was very hot, and the sun scorched our heads as a blast from a furnace. To Mrs. L. the heat seemed scarcely endurable; the fever ran higher than in any previous attack, and while she lay in the canoe, scarcely able to raise a hand, we landed and made a bower over her to avert the beams of the sun, and thus secured a shade, which was a great relief. We reached the falls about 5 o'clock, P. M., when she was yet hardly able to go up to the house unassisted, which was but a few rods distant. Mrs. Waller received us very kindly, Mr. W. being absent. Here we were also glad to meet Mr. and Mrs. Frost, and Mr. and Mrs. Abernethy, and other friends. By the time our meeting closed, Mrs. L. had partially recovered from the ague and fever, and as soon as things could be put in train, we bid all here farewell, and set our faces toward the Dalls again.

The Lama, Capt. Nye, we found at Vancouver, having just arrived with new supplies for the Oregon Mission. To Capt. N. and his lady we were introduced by Mr. Leslie, who returned passenger with him from the Sandwich Islands, where he had left his two daughters at school. We now pursued our way to the Dalls, where, after traversing the river and the portages at the Cascades at the time of high water, and suffering the assaults of thousands of moschetoes, we were glad to arrive once more in safety, looking upon our return, as we had long been wont to do, as a great temporal salvation, so many were the dangers with which we were continually surrounded in the navigation of these waters. In these waters, the Columbia and its branches, we may record more than thirty deaths by drowning in five years preceding the writer's departure from Oregon. During this time, adding a few months, he has canoed twenty times up and down the Walamet, four times from Vancouver to Chenook, and thirty-two times between Vancouver and the Dalls, not less together than four thousand miles. If any one has reason to be thankful, he has more; and would here mark, and acknowledge the hand of God in his preservation.

As it regards the religious state of the natives at this station, the writer has aimed to give a correct though brief statement; and here he will add what he has to say further on this subject.

Of the mass it may be said that three-fourths and more appeared careless and indifferent about the teachings of the gospel, and many of these were even against hearing it preached, that they might go on in their heathenish practices, and in direct opposition to its commands, unrestrained. But they are not singular in this—would they were; for how many in this Christian land, reader, do the same? Why? Because they hate good and love evil, and that conscience may sleep over their sins! The remainder were those that latterly composed, for the greater part, our congregations; and among these some were found who continued to use the means of grace, and who, so far as could be known, were endeavouring to follow the light they had received; but against these some arose to laugh, and ridicule, and mock. Such was the state of the people at the time the writer left the country, in regard to the direct tendencies of missionary labour among them.

Doubtless the presence and labours of the missionaries there have also prevented bloodshed, and relieved many in sickness, and improved the condition of many by the introduction of better clothing. Many have been taught the use of the needle. A number of the girls were for a length of time weekly attendants at our house, where Mrs. Lee taught them this art. The cruel custom of flattening infants' heads still prevails, though some have in a few instances been dissuaded from it

Another case may be related more at length. It is that of Harriet Newell, of the Chenook tribe, sister to Wm. Brooks, who came to the United States with Mr. Jason Lee in 1838. She had been about seven years in the mission family, and first enjoyed peace with God at the revival in 1839. But after a time she lost what she had found, and lived in that state much of the time till the late revival, when she recovered her enjoyment, and never, it is believed, lost it more. She was intelligent, and read and spoke English fluently. But she had endured much suffering from that very afflicting diease so common in this country, the scrofula, for several years; and lately, for some months, it had preyed upon her lungs, and gave unequivocal evidence that her end was near. But now, as the lamp of life burnt low, she appeared to grow in grace, and to wait patiently and joyfully for her change. Her last words, a short time before she died, were, " All is well! All is well! All is well!" Happy for you, O reader, if, when your hour to die shall come, you too can exclaim, " All is well!"

The first camp meeting among the whites in Oregon was held in the Walamet Valley, Tu-al-a-tin Plain, in July, 1843. Of nineteen unconverted persons, fifteen professed to find pardon and " peace with God through our Lord Jesus Christ!"

Ride on, O Immanuel; from every heart the " clouds and darkness chase!" And let Oregon be saved! Amen! Even so come, Lord Jesus! And the glory shall be to the Father, and Son, and Holy Ghost!

It may be useful to relate here a remarkable conversion which took place at the Walamet Mission in 1840. The subject of it was an American, one of a family who were, it is believed, all pious with this single exception; and he had explored the region of doubt, read its musty volumes for years, and sat down in its gloomy shades. But the God of love undertook his case; and a wound received in his foot cutting an artery, which continued to bleed again and again, till he was reduced almost to a shadow, was the means of bringing him under religious influences, and saving his soul. The writer called upon him before this event, and it was clear, that though he was deeply afflicted, he yet saw not the hand that did it, that wrote over against him on the wall, "Weighed and wanting!" My visit was followed soon after by a letter, an answer to which I received from him soon after his conversion. An extract from it shall be here subjoined.

"*Walamet, January* 12, 1841.

"Having so far recovered my strength as to be able to ride to this place in two days, (meaning the Walamet Mission,) I arrived here in the same state of feeling as when you visited me. My mind was full of enmity against God and man. The world appeared to me a vast desert, in which was nothing desirable. Life seemed a curse, and I had no hope beyond it. Although weary of skepticism, I felt no disposition to believe in God, or in his word; at least, not until I had again investigated the whole subject. But through his mercy, and the prayers and exhortations of my friends here, my mind became powerfully exercised, and unbelief began to give way. I made an effort to believe in God. I called on his name, and I soon found a degree of peace of mind and love to him and all mankind, which I had never known before. I thank God through our Lord Jesus Christ for his mercy to sinners, of whom I am chief. Yours, &c.,

"ROBERT SHORTESS."

Did not the Lord's people know that he was with them? Every convert is a witness of God to his people of the verity of these blessed words, "Lo I am with you alway;" and a goodly number of such witnesses did he raise up from time to time, in the green vale of the Walamet. To his name be all the praise for ever! The mention of some happy deaths in the mission school at Walamet cannot but interest the pious reader. A lad of the Calapooya tribe, who had been named David Kilburn, and was living in the enjoyment of religion, was suddenly removed by death caused by a blow he accidentally received on his head, which so greatly injured the brain as to destroy life in a short time. This was in the winter of 1843, following the good work before mentioned. Another happy death was that of Emeline Porter: she was of the same tribe. She was converted in the beginning of the revival, and lived and died a Christian. She endured her sickness with submission, and died in triumphant peace.

Having returned to the Dalls, as before stated, it was soon found that Mrs. Lee, on account of her feeble health, required my attention nearly the whole time, and there was no good ground to hope that she would soon, or ever, recover, under the continuance of existing circumstances. She greatly needed a season of rest to recruit her prostrated strength, and which she could not have here, where the call for her labours was constant and imperative. Besides, her nervous system had also suffered material injury from the many exciting causes which had surrounded us for years here, and which continued to increase; and its improvement demanded a change of place, where medical aid might be associated with quietness and rest. For us to remain longer in the mission promised nothing advantageous to its interests, while at the same time it threatened our own with evils which we might well dread. To avoid them there appeared but one way, and it was believed that duty required us to embrace it. Therefore the resolution was made to avail ourselves of the earliest opportunity to return to the United States. A year has passed away since, yet no cause of regret has arisen on the account; but otherwise God has approved the course we have pursued. It was the last of July when we began our preparations to leave. Wednesday morning, August 2d, the writer preached to the little band at the Dalls, and then enjoyed with them the communion of the Lord's supper, in hope of drinking with them the "new wine of the kingdom," where our cemented hearts should no more be rent asunder. Precious to us were those dear ones with whom in sorrow and in joy we had so long been associated. Scarcely were ever heart-strings so strongly entwined together. At the dusk of evening we were all ready to embark in our canoe, which was to transport us on board the vessel in which we were to leave the country. We now took an affectionate leave of Mr. and Mrs. Perkins, and Mr. and Mrs. Brewer, and stepped into our canoe to make our last voyage down the Columbia; passed the Cascades with lightened hearts that we should be exposed to their toils and dangers no more; and touched at Fort Vancouver on business, and to take our last look at our friends there, to whose kindness we had been much indebted. Saturday morning went on board the bark Diamond, Capt. Fowler, from England, bound to the Sandwich Islands, where we had engaged our passage. Here Mrs. Lee remained while the writer went to the Walamet Falls, to close up his business with the mission. He reached there on Saturday night, preached on Sunday, and left again on Monday. It was hard parting with Messrs. Waller and Abernethy, and their wives, and other friends. Peace be with them! Sabbath, August 13th. The vessel had arrived at Fort George, and Mr. Jason Lee and myself preached at Mr. Birnie's. This was the last sabbath we spent together. While we were here the kind hospitalities of Mr. James Birnie's house were very generously served up for our entertainment. Mr. and Mrs. Frost, Dr. and Mrs. Babcock, with their families, were here, and with myself passengers of the Diamond. Mrs. Dr. Whitman was also here, having, with Mr. Leslie, accompanied me from the Walamet on a visit.

Tuesday, 15th. We took leave of our friends, and embarked on our voyage. In Baker's Bay we were detained till the following Monday, August 21st, when we crossed the bar, and sailed for California, where the bark was to touch on her way to the Islands.

> Farewell! Oregon, "Far West,"
> Land of my exile, may you ever be blest:
> Land of my toil, anxiety, pain;
> Land which my foot shall not press again;
> Land where mercy, kindness, love,
> In showers have blest me from above!
> Farewell, all ye tribes
> And aliens residing,
> Who down your smooth streams
> To eternity are gliding:
> Farewell!

CHAPTER XXII.

Voyage of Mr. Frost and family from Vancouver to Astoria—Murders committed—A body of Indians arrive to protect the settlement—One of the murderers is shot—Another of them is hung—Mr. Frost and others visit Mr. Smith at Clatsop Plains—Indian mother and her child—Mr. Frost visits Walamet Mission and returns—Barbarous act by the Indians—Indian trick—Mission family establish themselves—Extract from Mr. Frost's journal—His labours among the Indians—Salmon feast—Indian tradition.

HAVING received an invitation from Mr. Birnie at Astoria to bring my family down and take up lodgings with him until a house was furnished for our accommodation, and as we felt very anxious to commence our labours among the Indians to whom we had been sent, we got all things in readiness, and on the 3d of August bid adieu to our kind friends at Vancouver, who accompanied us to the river shore, where we embarked, with all our effects, on board of a row-boat which was furnished for the purpose by the kindness of Dr. M'Laughlin, and manned by two Canadians and two Hawaians, and set off for Astoria, leaving none but Mr. Abernethy and family, Mr. Raymond and Miss Philips, at Vancouver. These gentlemen were engaged in shipping the mission goods on board of the company's barge for the Walamet, and Miss Philips was in a feeble state of health, having fallen from a horse.

It was drawing toward evening when we commenced our voyage down the Columbia, and felt that we were now entirely separated from those with whom we had been so intimately connected for nearly a year, under very interesting and continually varying circumstances. This thought, in connection with the fact that we were now upon an expanse of waters in a frail bark, with no covering to screen us from the scorching sun by day, nor from the chilling damps by night, and not knowing what disaster might befall us before we should reach our destination, caused a momentary gloom to pass over the mind, not entirely dissimilar to that which broods over the lone orphan while the last loved relative is about entering the precincts of the dead. But recollecting that hundreds had preceded us upon the same track, even as far back as the days of Hunt, M'Kenzie, M'Tavish, and John Reed with his "tin box," all navigating the same stream, and who knows that it was not upon the same water, which, having performed its regular rounds over the face and through the bowels of the earth and the surrounding atmosphere, was now hastening in its downward course to mingle with the briny particles of the vast Pacific again—these thoughts, in connection with the consideration that our predecessors had passed here at that time when the very trees on the banks of the river must have appeared more wild, to say nothing of the savages of whom they were in continual danger, and that they were, in all probability, actuated by selfish motives only, while we were going forth bearing precious seed, though weeping, had the promise of returning again with rejoicing, bearing our sheaves with us— dispelled the clouds, and produced a serenity of feeling which can only be appreciated by those who enjoy it. We proceeded about eight miles when gray twilight had succeeded the setting sun, and Mount St. Helen, standing to the north-west of us, with her towering top covered with the snows of ages, appeared as though she had just arranged her white night-cap, indicative of her inclination to retire to rest. We too were weary, and directed our men to go ashore that we might prepare for repose, which was accordingly done; and we prepared our bed by laying down some mats in our department of the boat, which was square in form, placing thereon our bed, and when properly adjusted, our bed-room would have been by no means unpleasant, only for the want of a roof. But the sky was unclouded, and the atmosphere rather exhilarating, so that, after we were fairly stowed away, it was decided that a very comfortable night's rest might be reasonably anticipated; and our anticipations would have no doubt been realized, had it not been for an innumerable nightly band which soon came hovering over our unglazed window for the purpose of serenading. We listened to their music, but felt a little apprehensive that it might be their design to lull us to sleep with their plaintive, melting tones, and then, like a greedy gang of highwaymen, fall upon us pell-mell, and rob us of every drop of blood in our veins. We had scarcely interchanged a word in respect to the anticipated danger, when, all at once, we were pierced as with a thousand barbed arrows. Be not alarmed, dear reader. They were not the arrows of our Indian neighbours, but of a more blood-thirsty race, which are called by the savages "*oopoonoochickchick*," and in our less barbarous language "*moschetoes*." Our calculations for the night were now entirely broken up; and in order that the rest of the family might sleep, I engaged to sit up with a fan, and, as far as possible, keep these whining intruders out of the room. And if our fair readers find it as difficult at any time to keep themselves comfortably cool during a sultry summer's day in their parlours with *their* fans, as the writer found it to discharge his duty that night with *his*, he most sincerely sympathizes with them.

Night passed away, and with it our tormentors disappeared; and as we had a fine run the following day, we reached the lowermost of the Cathlamet Islands: here we tied our boat to a branch of a tree which extended over the water, and as it began to rain we rigged a temporary tent of sheets over us and enjoyed a good night's rest, the sea-breeze having confined the insect tribes to their marshy dwellings. The next morning we met with a cordial welcome from Mr. Birnie and family in time for breakfast. And, as I find it recorded in my journal, so we would here record our gratitude to our heavenly Father, for our safe arrival at the place which was to be the field of our future labour. We arrived on the 6th, and from this until the 9th we were engaged in arranging a few of our things for the present comfort of the family, as Mr. Birnie had kindly furnished us with a room for our present use.

On the morning of the 9th Mr. Solomon Smith arrived, with his family from the Walamet, for the purpose of settling near the missionary post that might be erected here. This was cause of joy on our part, inasmuch as he professed religion, and his wife was a Clatsop woman, and knew something concerning the true God, which was a ground for hope that they might prove subservient to the interests of the mission, besides augmenting our small circle of society.

This being the sabbath, I preached to the souls composing our three families, and one young man besides, from Job xxi, 15.

On the 10th Mr. Birnie, Smith, and myself crossed over to Young's Bay in search of a location where our neighbour Smith might make a farm, but returned without deciding upon any particular spot. 11th, commenced getting the Checalish and Chenook languages, and Mrs. Frost employed part of her time in teaching Mr. Birnie's children, of which he had six very interesting daughters living at home, and one little son, five of whom were capable of receiving instruction, which with our little son constituted the school.

On the evening of the 12th we had an eclipse of the moon, which was, by my time, at its height about 10h. 30m. in the evening. This eclipse, according to my Almanac, was at its height, in the latitude of Albany and New-York, at 1h. 51m. on the morning of the 13th.

Mr. Smith and family left us for the purpose of visiting the Clatsop Plain. Disturbance among the Indians. Several killed in their quarrels. 16th, preached from John xii, 26, my congregation consisting of Mr. B.'s family and my own; but we would not despise the day of small things.

At this time, one of the Canadians who came with us from Vancouver expressed a desire to go up to Pillar Rock, to see if all was well with the man at the salmon fishery, the same that had the goodness to tow up our canoe for us on a former occasion, and who at that time expressed much satisfaction in view of the prospect of having a missionary in the neighbourhood, and of being permitted to attend divine service on the sabbath, when the salmon season should close, and he return to Astoria. But what must have been our feelings when about nightfall, as Mr. B. and myself were walking on the platform, to behold the young Canadian, hastening up from the bank of the river, almost breathless, with horror depicted in his countenance, and as soon as he came within speaking distance, to hear him utter this thrilling sentence, "*M'Kay is murdered!*" M'Kay was the man before mentioned, as having charge of the fishery at the above place. He was a native of Scotland or the Orkney Islands. The young man stated, that when he arrived at the fishery, he saw no one, and all was silent, so much so that he suspected that all was not right. Being alone in a small canoe, he hastened to haul it on shore, and ran to the tent, and then, to his utter dismay, he beheld poor M'Kay completely perforated with a musket ball, and literally surrounded with a mass of coagulated blood! It appeared that the fatal ball passed through his body, entering the breast and coming out at the back, while his senses were locked up in sleep, depriving him of life, apparently, without any other struggle on his part but simply a contraction of the muscles. But this did not close the horrid scene: the young man thought of the little Indian boy who was with M'Kay, and, upon looking around, beheld the poor little fellow lying a short distance from the tent, dead also, having had his body ripped open with a knife ! Having finished these bloody acts, the murderers had robbed the tent of the property it contained, and made their escape. Fearing lest they might be skulking in the wood near at hand, the young man hastened to put the body of the murdered man, and the tent, in a large canoe belonging to the place, and made his way, with all speed, to communicate the sad intelligence to us, as above. We went to the water side, and had the corpse brought up and deposited in a room, according to the directions of Mr. Birnie, and on the following day, which was a dark day to us, and a gloomy commencement of our missionary work, we deposited the lifeless body in the tomb in accordance with the custom of our church. Thus was he, who hoped to enjoy the gospel privileges in time to come, cut off in the midst of his years, before his fond expectations were realized, and buried in a strange land, without one relative to weep over his untimely end. Reader, dost thou reckon upon long life, and anticipate the enjoyment of gospel privileges in days to come, but neglectest to make thy peace *now* with God ? Take heed : " Be ye *also* ready ; for in an hour that *ye* think not, the Son of man cometh."

Immediately after the body was brought down from the fishery, Mr. Birnie despatched a canoe with a letter to Vancouver, and another canoe to request Chenamas, the Chenook chief, who had proved himself a friend to the white man, to come over with his men to guard the house, lest it might prove to be a gang of Indians who had committed the murder, and being intent upon more blood and plunder, they might come and cut us off, as they had the devoted inmates of the tent.

Chenamas received the intelligence, and as soon as the wind and tide would permit, which was not until late at night, we heard the strokes of many paddles upon the sides of canoes approaching from the opposite side of the river and in a few minutes more the old chieftain, with fifteen or twenty of his warriors, stood upon the platform. They were each armed with musket and knife, and after being supplied with fresh ammunition, and abundantly regaled with biscuit and molasses, declared themselves, in the true spirit of their former chief Comcomly, whose bones were deposited near at hand, to be now ready, as he had been in years gone by, to protect this dwelling place of their white neighbours against the invasions of every anticipated foe. And that dark portentous brow, and fire-like flashing eye, exhibited by the brother of the chief while in consultation with the other warriors, with reference to the probable perpetrators of the cold-blooded murders, will never be forgotten by one who witnessed those scenes; if anything earthly ever indicated revenge, it was that fixed ferocious look.

The night passed away, while many a heavy sigh escaped upon the wings of the gentle sea breeze from our lodgment upon the spot where many anxious hearts and wakeful eyes had long since been enclosed within the stockading of the original fort, of which there was not a vestige now to be seen; and at length the morning sun returned, to remind us of the goodness of his Creator, who had watched over us, his feeble children, during his absence; and, as it were, pointed us to the promises of his precious Word, which shall all be as invariably fulfilled, in behalf of those who humbly trust in him, as the visits of this bright morning messenger.

All nature now put on a smile, and nothing among the surrounding objects of creation indicated the least unhappiness, save the pearly dew-drop upon the cheek of the blooming flowers, as though chaste Flora had gone forth at early dawn to weep over the wretchedness attendant upon human life, since the effect of man's first transgression manifested itself in the cries of righteous Abel's blood from the ground, for vengeance upon his devoted brother.

At the time of the above transaction, the brig Maryland, of Newburyport, was lying at anchor near Pillar Rock; but Captain Couch had no knowledge of these murders until he was informed thereof by a note from us: upon which he weighed anchor, and dropped down to Astoria.

On the 23d, which was the sabbath, I preached to my usual congregation, with the addition of Dr. Tolmie, who had arrived with a detachment from Vancouver, and several from on board of the Maryland: text, Psalm xvi, 8.

On the morning of the 24th a search was commenced for the murderers of M'Kay; and for this purpose a boat and canoe were manned and despatched for the vicinity of the fishery, where the murder had been committed, taking with them two squaws, the wives of two of the head men belonging to the clan which resided near Pillar Rock. These women had been taken, and were kept as hostages, and were to act as guides to the parties; it having been already ascertained that a slave belonging to the husband of one of these women was one of the murderers. About this time old Skumaquea, who, as has been heretofore stated, resided a few miles above the fishery, came down; and, as he had previously declared his innocence, and promised to use his best endeavours to apprehend the guilty, brought with him now a Quiniutle Indian, one of a tribe whose lands lay to the north of the Columbia; which Indian, and the slave above-mentioned, were declared to be the perpetrators of the crime. The Indian promised to remain at Astoria until the subject could be fully investigated, and Skumaquea returned to his home.

Dr. Tolmie, who went out with the party before mentioned, returned on the 26th, having seen nothing of those for whom they sought. And the prisoner above-mentioned, although he had expressed such a willingness to remain for further examination that Mr. Birnie was induced to leave him unbound, had embraced the first favourable opportunity, and made his escape.

Dr. Tolmie left again in the evening to join Dr.

M'Laughlin, who was on board of the barge from Vancouver, which was lying at Pillar Rock, having just come down.

On the morning of the 27th a canoe arrived from the party, bringing intelligence that the slave had been discovered by one of the Iraqua Indians in connection with the party, and shot through the head. Thus one of the murderers expiated his crime with his life. A bounty was now offered for the recapture of the Quiniutle Indian, the other murderer; and Skumaquea succeeded in apprehending him a second time, and delivered him over to Dr. M'Laughlin, who brought him down to Astoria on the morning of the 29th, being accompanied by a number of the Walamet settlers.

An examination was now instituted; and it was decided by all the whites present that this Quiniutle was one of the actual murderers, and that it was absolutely necessary for the prevention of further murders, and the commission of further depredations, that an example should be made of this criminal. He was, consequently, at one o'clock in the afternoon, hung up by the neck until he was dead. And the Indians present were made to understand that, while we were their friends, and desired to live in uninterrupted peace and harmony with them, yet they might expect that if any of their number were at any time guilty of the like crimes, they might expect a like punishment. And now we close this distressing scene.

Two of the company's vessels came in this morning, and are lying at anchor near the Maryland,—quite a fleet for this wild region.

Most of the gentlemen of the company, and the Walamet settlers, left for their respective homes; and the two Indian women who had been retained as hostages were permitted to go in search of their wandering husbands, being directed to say to them when found, that if they would come and make it appear that they were innocent with reference to the crime of which their slave had been guilty, they would be permitted to return to their home in peace. Mrs. Frost and our little boy have been afflicted with the ague and fever for some days, the result of living a short time at Vancouver, which is in the region where this epidemic prevails.

The 30th being the sabbath, I preached to our families and some of the officers and men from the vessels, from Psalm xcvii, 1. I would here transcribe some reflections recorded in my journal at that time only for fear of making this work too voluminous.

On the 1st of September I left Astoria in company with Dr. Tolmie and Mr. Calvin Tibits, an American settler from the Walamet, to visit Mr. Smith, on the Clatsop Plains. We had not seen Mr. Smith but once since he left Astoria, so that we felt anxious to know how he was getting along among his new neighbours. We crossed Young's Bay in a canoe, and went up a small river called the Skapanowin, which came into the bay from the south, and was navigable to within about a mile of the plain, at high tide. Here we hauled up our canoe, crossed the marsh, which was now nearly dry, and passed through a grove of timber to the plain; crossed the plain to the ocean, and proceeded along the beach until we arrived at the river that empties into the ocean near Cape Lookout. This stream is called by the natives Neacoxy, the water in which they take the fall salmon. Here we found the Clatsop Indians waiting for the commencement of their second salmon season, the season on the Columbia having closed in August. And here we found Mr. Smith, who had laid up the body of a log-cabin, about fifteen feet square, and was living in it without floor or roof.

We were now weary, having travelled about ten miles since we left our canoe : so, after having supped upon some very good elk meat, and talked over the news of the day, we laid ourselves down to sleep, and should have had a very good night's rest, but we were soon beset with an innumerable host of fleas, so that, instead of sleeping, we were obliged to fight all night. In the morning we took breakfast, and returned to the place on the plain where we had left our crew, and found that they had shot a deer, upon which we made a fine dinner, and then returned to Astoria.

Mr. Tibits had by this time about made up his mind to remove to this region; so we had a prospect of another white neighbour.

Sept. 6th. Preached from Isa. liii, 1. As Dr. T. and Mr. T. had left, my congregation was now reduced to but one man besides Mr. Birnie's family and my own. Nothing of moment transpired during the following week, and the next sabbath attended divine service as usual.

On the 14th, the owner of the slave, one of the murderers above mentioned, and his brother, came to Astoria, and gave assurances that they had had no knowledge of the designs of the murderer, and were entirely innocent with reference to that transaction. They then proceeded to Vancouver, continued there for some time, and then returned to their former abode.

Soon after this Mr. Smith left his family at Neacoxy, and called upon us on his way to Walamet in a canoe, for the purpose of obtaining a supply of bread-stuff, and other necessary winter supplies for his family.

On the 18th, we received letters from Walamet, by which we learned that several belonging to the mission were suffering with the intermittent fever.

For several days past, says my journal, there has been an Indian woman near this, on the beach, with a sick child. Last night the child died, and to-day it was taken to the place of interment; and in order that the Christian mother in the civilized world may be enabled to obtain a faint idea of the wretchedness of these wretched beings, let her imagine herself in the condition of this poor Indian woman: without house or home, for she was on a journey; her only child sick and at the point of death; but she has no food to administer to it, save a few crude roots and a little dried fish; she has no medicine to administer which might mitigate its sufferings; no bed on which to lay its emaciated body, and nothing but a miserable old rush mat with which to shelter it from the rays of the sun by day and the chilling damps by night; she sits by it on the ground, and watches it day and night, and wets its parched lips with water from an adjoining rill; and when it mourns, she weeps over it, and speaks to it in the most soothing manner. She does all she can for its recovery, but all in vain. Death is making his advances; he pursues his object with steady purpose, until he strikes the final blow. Is the Indian mother unfeeling at this crisis? Let her plaintive wailings testify. But this is not all. There is none to assist her in arranging the corpse for interment. She must roll it up in the piece of a blanket that covered its otherwise naked body while living. Over this she wraps the mat which constituted the house under which it expired; and, as it is their custom for the nearest relative to carry the dead, she slings it upon her own back, with a strap across her forehead; and thus she bears it away to some precipice on the bank of the river, to be devoured by some beast of prey, or to remain until Gabriel's trump shall awake its dust.

She now returns as she went, giving vent to her feelings in the customary notes of the loud, wild death-wail; shoves her small canoe from the shore, enters it alone, and, timing the strokes of her paddle with her notes of wo, she thus disappears.

Come, reader, let us now take a brief review of this scene. Here is the mother who fills the offices of the physician, the nurse, the night-watch, the hearse, the chief mourner, the funeral concourse, and the undertaker!

This is no fancy sketch on the part of the writer; it is a simple, matter-of-fact history of the condition of a portion of the human family. And who can reflect upon such scenes, while they enjoy the blessings of civilization and Christianity, and not find their hearts to overflow with gratitude to their heavenly Father, by whom they have been so highly distinguished? And who can meditate upon the exhibition of such wretchedness, and not feel their deepest sympathies aroused, and their bowels to yearn over the inhabitants of the dark portions of our earth? Many similar scenes of sorrow fell under our observation while in that region, but to relate them would take up too much of our room, and prove too painful to our feelings.

I wrote to the superintendent of the mission by Mr. Smith, requesting help to put up a covering for my family before the rainy season commenced; but as I received no answer, and as Mr. Smith did not return, I left my family at Astoria, and set out for Walamet via Vancouver, on the 28th, in company with a young gentleman from the ship Forager, which had just arrived from England, who was going to Vancouver in a boat.

We ascended the river as far as Cathlamet, where we met Mr. Smith, by whom I received a letter from the superintendent, stating that most of the mechanics were sick. Consequently, he knew not when help could be furnished me from that quarter, but that I had the privilege of employing Mr. Smith; but as the latter would be obliged to provide for his own family, it was evident that with what help he could afford, I should not be able to accomplish the labour of putting up a house that would screen my family from the approaching storms. So it was determined that I should hasten to Walamet in pursuit of further aid, while Smith should go down to his family, cover his cabin, and, if he had any spare time, commence cutting logs near the place where I had determined to build, which was about five miles from Point Adams, upon the Clatsop Plain. We supped together upon the bank of the river, and then pursued our voyages, Mr. Smith toward Clatsop, and we toward Vancouver, where we arrived on the second day after.

The next morning I engaged two Indians to take me in a small canoe to Champoeg, which was within fifteen miles of the Walamet Mission. In the evening we arrived at the Walamet Falls, where Mr. Waller was building a house for the accommodation of his family, as this was the place where he was to labour among the Indians. Spent the night with Mr. W., and prepared to resume my journey up the river; but my Indians had made up their minds during the night to go no further unless I would give them more than twice as much as they had agreed to perform the trip for when we left Vancouver: so here was a full stop, and as there were no Indians at this place that could be prevailed upon to take their place, it was doubtful whether I would get on unless their extortionate demands were met; and, seeing the strait in which I was placed, they held me to the point, and when they found that their avarice was not to be gratified, they set off for Vancouver, and left me to shift for myself as well as I could.

Mr. Waller now consented to let me have his man, a German, who was labouring with him in building his house, and we succeeded, after some time, in procuring an Indian, who had lost the use of his legs, to make the second man; and now, putting Jacob in the stern and the cripple in the bow, we proceeded up the river, and reached the Bute about sunset. Here we lodged in the cabin belonging to a Canadian, and in the morning I walked about two miles to Mr. Tibits. Here I took breakfast, and obtained a horse, and found my way to the mission by noon.

Found many of the members of the mission sick with the fever and ague, and the mechanics that were able to work employed on the saw-mill. Made known the object of my visit to the superintendent; and, after consultation, it was determined that the Rev. W. W. Kone should accompany me to Clatsop as my future colleague. And now we set about making preparations for the removal of Mr. Kone's family and goods, which was not an undertaking of small moment, as one hundred and sixty miles intervened between us and the place where we were to build our future dwelling. But no time could be lost; my family would be anxiously waiting my return; and in order to be shielded from the approaching rains, the trip must be made, and a house must be built from the stump in a few weeks. So, after enjoying the privileges of one more Christian sabbath with the brethren, we packed up Mr. Kone's goods on Monday, and on Tuesday morning obtained two Indian cañoes, and one white man, three Indians, and a Hawaian to navigate them; and on Thursday morning, having stowed in all the goods the canoes would contain, leaving small spaces wherein we were to sit, very much like men in the stocks, we placed two Indians and the Hawaian in the largest canoe, which contained the most of the goods; and our white man, Paddy, we took in the canoe with ourselves, making him helmsman, and one of the Indians we put in the bow to assist in paddling. We now commenced our downward voyage with a fair prospect of reaching Vancouver by the close of the following day; but, after running down several rapids in safety, we came to one which entirely knocked all our fond expectations in the head: for no sooner had the large canoe entered the swift water, than, through the bad management of the crew, it was borne down with rapidity against some snags, and, with a tremendous crash, went to pieces. As we were in the rear, we darted by them in a moment, and as we passed the fatal spot, there were trunks, barrels, pails, and bundles, and Indians and Hawaian, all jumbled together in strange confusion, every one apparently labouring to be uppermost. We ran our canoe upon a small island, leaped on shore, unloaded the cargo as soon as possible, and leaving Mrs. Kone in my charge, the canoe was immediately shoved off in pursuit of the floating cargo from the wreck. By this time the Indians and Hawaian had succeeded in towing several of the articles on shore, and were swimming after some of those which had not sunk, but were hastening down the stream.

It was near night when this unlooked-for disaster occurred; so that, when it became dark, many things were still missing, among which was Mrs. Kone's travelling trunk, containing a gold watch, and her most valuable clothing. I had lighted a fire, and as we could do no better, we set to work to get supper, and prepare for a night's lodging without a tent, as this very important article was also among the missing. We passed the night in safety, and sending Paddy and an Indian to the nearest white man's house on the river, which was eight or ten miles distant, for a canoe, the remainder of us went in search of the lost goods. We succeeded in finding the tent and a few other articles; but Mrs. K.'s trunk, pots, kettles, etc., etc., and our tool box, were irrecoverably lost. The remainder of the day was spent in drying the recovered goods, and when night returned we had a tent to lodge in.

On the following morning we loaded our canoe, and leaving Mr. Kone to take charge of the remaining goods, Mr. Hines, Mrs. Kone, and myself set out for Champoeg, and as the canoe for which we had sent arrived soon after our departure, we all met before night at the above-named place.

This being Saturday, we remained here until Monday morning, when, instead of being at Vancouver, as we had anticipated, we had the most part of our voyage still to make. We reached that place, however, on Wednesday at about ten o'clock, where we were entertained, as usual, with much kindness. Dr. M'Laughlin now furnished us with a boat, and we descended the Columbia, experiencing some rain and contrary winds, and arrived at Astoria on the following Monday morning, and were happy to find my family in comfortable health. Mrs. Frost was very happy to be put in possession of Mrs. Kone's society; and, notwithstanding all our former mishaps, we felt encouraged to go forward in our work with renewed energy.

But now the rainy season was soon to set in; therefore it was necessary that we should hasten to build a cabin to cover our heads. And as Mr. Smith had gone to his family to the southern end of Clatsop Plain, about eight miles by water and ten by land, immediately upon our separation at Cathlamet, as mentioned above, and having not been heard of since, we found it difficult to determine what course to pursue. But in the afternoon of the same day, as the Lord would have it, he came to Astoria with his canoe, having left his family in good health, and reported himself ready to assist us in making a house.

We now consulted upon the best mode of operation, and determined that we would leave our families in the care of Mr. Birnie, while we would proceed immediately to the Clatsop Plain and put up a cabin. So after arranging matters as well as we could, and packing up our tools, and provisions, and tent, which occupied our time until the next day, we bid our families farewell, launched our canoe, and steered our course across Young's Bay, entered the Skapanowin River, paddled up to the head of canoe navigation, and hauled our crazy bark on shore. We now made up our cargo into packs, loaded ourselves, as we had no beast of burden, and by a circuitous route, through the marsh and across the plain, upon which we forded two creeks, reached the place selected for our dwelling about sunset. Just before we reached the place we discovered a large bear near the spot where we desired to pitch our tent; this caused us, strangers to this description of inhabitants, to hesitate; but as Mr. Smith said, "I am not afraid of bears," and marched on, not even deigning to notice our new neighbour, we took courage, and as we approached, the bear withdrew, and retired into the thicket, so that we took possession of the place in peace, struck a fire, pitched our tent, and soon sat down to a hearty supper, which consisted of brown biscuit, pork roasted on a stick, and a cup of tea. We now united in prayer to Almighty God, imploring his direction and aid, that we might become instrumental in rearing the gospel standard in that wild place, where the enemy of all righteousness had from the beginning held unrivalled dominion. We now laid ourselves down and slept in peace and quietness until morning.

Mr. Smith thought it necessary to return to his family, to acquaint them with our arrival, and to make some arrangements to get Indians to assist us in carrying logs for our cabin: so after breakfast he left, and agreed to return on the following day, and we were, during that time, to fix on the spot where to set our building and commence operations.

Strange feelings were experienced by us that day: we were entirely alone, in a wild region, and upon a soil which had been seldom pressed by the white man's foot; surrounded by Indians who were ignorant, superstitious, and barbarous. And perhaps the reader will not think it amiss for me to turn aside from the main drift of the narrative, for the purpose of relating one of their barbarous acts, which was performed by them at Neacoxy, during Mr. Smith's absence to the Walamet, and which was made known to him by his wife, who was an eye-witness of the same, on his return.

The fall salmon season had not commenced, and as they are a most improvident people, never laying up enough during one season of plenty to last them until another, they were now entirely dependant upon roots, and came from the mountains for daily food; and as there were but two men in the whole clan that had the Elk "tamanawas," that is, the spirit of the elk hunter, of course, seeing that these two loved ease as well as any of them, their supply from the mountains was not very abundant. About this time one of the hunters went out and succeeded in bringing an elk into the camp; and, according to custom, the most of it was taken to the lodge of the chief. Here a feast was prepared and the whole clan invited to partake, and among the assembled guests there was an Indian who had been for some time in a declining state, who, after filling himself to his entire satisfaction, retired, previously to the breaking up of the party. The rest continued to feast and chat until a late hour. After the sick Indian returned to the lodge where he belonged, he stuck some pieces of meat upon a stick and set them up before the fire to roast; he then stretched himself out upon his mat for the purpose of recruiting strength sufficient to finish his share of the elk, when it should be sufficiently cooked; but contrary to his expectations, as it appeared, he fell into a sound sleep, so that when his sister, with whom he lived, and the other inmates of the lodge, returned, and found him in this posture, breathing hard, and sometimes groaning, caused, no doubt by having crammed his empty stomach with such a quantity of heavy food, and as they found that he could not be readily aroused from this torpid state, they all as one struck up the death-wail, and one ran to Mrs. Smith to borrow their shovel for the purpose of digging a grave for the man, whom they now pronounced to be dead. Mrs. Smith followed this messenger to the lodge, where she found the customary preparations for the interment of the dead going forward with haste; but as she found the man, to all appearance, not very near his natural end, she proposed to put off the funeral until the following morning, when, if the man was actually dead, they would bury him decently. This counsel was rejected with much spirit, they declaring that he was "*nowitka mamaluste*," that is, certainly dead, and without further ado he was rolled up in his blanket and mat, tied with a rope, and slung upon the back of a relative, and away they marched toward the place of burial, rending the air with their wailings. They arrive at the spot, lay down the living corpse, which uttered a pitiful groan; this was to them another conclusive evidence that it was high time he should be buried. Mrs. Smith expostulated. But they upbraided her with being regardless of their welfare; seeing that the salmon, which had just made their appearance, would all leave the river at once, if a dead body should be found above ground! The hole was hastily dug, and finding that she could not prevail, Mrs. S. returned to her house; but was told, by one that did remain, that after the body was put therein and some dirt thrown upon it, one of the men descended to tramp it down, which caused the poor half-buried man to groan aloud; but they persevered until his groaning ceased, and the "last sad offices" were completed. They now returned to the lodge, distributed the knife and such other articles left by the departed, among the present bereaved relations; and committed his elk meat, which was scarcely cooked before his burial and consequent death, to the flames, as it was against their conscience to eat anything which had been prepared by the dead. And as they had a great abundance of salmon that season, they were no doubt satisfied that they had performed a good work.

With this description of the character of those who were to be our future neighbours, in connection with the wildness of the face of nature around us, the reader will not wonder that we had strange feelings that day. But we were far from being discouraged, neither did we stop to look back. We selected the spot for our house, moved camp, dug a hole to obtain water, cleared a road from the plain to the timber, and returned a little before sunset to the tent. We now prepared our supper, and while we were eating, being seated in the door of the tent, our neighbour the bear made his appearance within a few rods of us: we immediately seized our guns and gave chase; but Bruin soon disappeared in the thicket, and we returned to complete our meal.

After washing our dishes, and arranging matters in the tent, we committed our families and selves to the care of our Father in heaven, and, being weary, soon fell asleep.

I should have mentioned, however, that before we retired for the night Mr. Smith returned, having obtained a promise from the Indians that they would come the next morning to assist in carrying logs.

We arose early in the morning. Mr. S. and myself entered the woods with our axes to cut logs, while Mr.

Kone remained to take care of the tent, and cook our breakfast.

The breakfast call was heard in due season; and our Rev. cook had done honour to his new and important office in preparing an excellent breakfast, which was served up in due form, consisting of cakes made of unbolted flour mixed with cold water, and baked upon a plank, which had been nicely hewn out for the purpose, and placed upon the clean embers before the fire; and fried pork, which, having been nicely browned, produced plenty of gravy in which to sop our bread; and an excellent cup of hyson, which our neighbour Smith declared to be a very pleasant and exhilarating beverage, desiring neither milk nor sugar to improve its flavour.

Kotata, the head man of the Clatsop clan, now made his appearance, in company with a number of his men. After we explained to him the object of our coming to settle among them, and the course we designed to pursue in all our transactions with them, he promised to use his influence with his people to prevent the commission of crime among them for the future, and expressed a desire to be instructed with reference to those things which pertained to their peace; and decided that it was good for us to build a house, and live among them. Six or eight of the men now went with us to the woods, and commenced carrying logs, while we continued to cut down the trees from six to ten inches in diameter, cutting them off at proper lengths; and before sunset we had all the logs cut for the body of the cabin, which we designed to be twenty feet long by eighteen wide. Being now fatigued, we returned to the tent, where we found a very inviting supper in readiness, consisting of brant, a species of the wild goose, and wild ducks, the roasting and broiling of which presented another evidence of the consummate skill of our excellent cook. The wild fowls were purchased from the Indians, who were exceedingly pleased at having a market so near at hand. After replenishing our stomachs with this welcome supply of fresh provisions, we attended family devotions outside of the tent, Mr. Smith praying in Indian, and interpreting a word of exhortation from us to our neighbours, to which they grunted assent; and then all hands lay down to rest,—we in our tent, and the Indians around the fire before the door.

The next day being Saturday we renewed our labour, and succeeded in getting all the logs upon the building spot. During the day a little circumstance occurred which led us to suspect that our new neighbours needed a little watching, notwithstanding their fair promises to deal honestly with us in all things; and by this transaction we also learned that these "untutored Indians" understood the "secrets of trade" quite as well as those of our own highly-cultivated nation. An Indian came into camp with a load of wild fowl, and, taking his word as to the number, I paid him down the established number of charges of ammunition for every one; but it was not long after this, when the cook came to overhaul the new stock for the purpose of selecting the finest for our next repast, that in so doing he found *one* fowl which presented a very unsavoury appearance. Upon this he called out to me, in a tone expressive of disgust, demanding to know whether it became his duty to cook *crows?* Being somewhat startled, and a little chagrined, I hastily inquired of the fowler why he had thus imposed upon me? To this the Indian replied, in such a manner as to show that he understood his business, by asking whether he did not say that he had brought so many fowls? Being answered in the affirmative, he then asked, Is not a *crow* a fowl? Of course this reply settled the business; and the laugh of all hands turned upon me, for having been so completely outdone by an Indian; and my highly-pleased associates decided that I deserved nothing but the crow for my supper.

The sabbath returned, and although we were far removed from the Christian congregation, we realized the fulfilment of the promise of that Being who dwelleth not in temples made with hands, in the refreshing and comforting influences of the Holy Spirit upon our hearts while we engaged in prayer and praise.

On the following morning we commenced laying up the square of our house; and in the afternoon we had a very unexpected visit from Mrs. Kone, Frost, and Birnie. And as they had come the distance of about fourteen miles, part of the way with canoe, and the remainder on foot, crossing the woods and plain, and wading two creeks, they were very much exhausted when they reached the tent; but they were soon refreshed with some wild fowl cooked precisely to their liking, and a cup of tea; in addition to which we had some light biscuit, of which they had brought a basket full from Astoria, having prepared it expressly for us, not thinking we had been faring so sumptuously. The ladies were quite well pleased with our location; but not more so than our little boy, who came with them, who thought the smooth prairie would be such a fine play-ground.

The next morning Mr. Smith and myself accompanied the ladies back to Astoria; and the next day brought over my cooking stove, and a number of other articles; carried the most of our cargo to the plain from the head of navigation, which was nearly a mile; and then, with a load, reached our tent about sunset, by a new route across the plain, which crossed no creek, and was one-half shorter.

Our worthy colleague was very happy on our return, having spent a very lonely night, as he had none but Indians for companions, with whom he could converse but little.

We were glad to get our suppers, and lie down to rest, as we were more than usnally fatigued with the labours of the day. Our loads had been very heavy, but were in such a form that we could not divide them, such as the bottom plate of Frazier's patent cooking stove, No. 4, a keg of nails weighing one hundred pounds, and several bags of flour of the same weight.

These we were obliged to carry one mile, and had then taken a full load through to the building place, which was at least two miles further.

Our Indians had succeeded in capturing our old neighbour the bear, which made them a splendid feast; and it was very amusing to witness the operation of cooking and eating. The bear was completely dissected, and the fire was surrounded with different portions of the body; and there the Indians were squatting around this circle of hissing and smoking flesh, devouring it as soon as it was cooked. A good night's rest succeeded a day of toil; and we arose next morning in health, and proceeded with our work; and were so successful as to finish laying up the cabin, and covering it with shingles, split out of a large fir tree about a quarter of a mile distant, at the end of two weeks. Put up our cooking stove, and felt that we were completely under cover.

We now determined to go for the ladies, while Mr. Kone would remain for the purpose of putting in a door and a window. Mr. Smith and myself set out in the morning, and arrived at Astoria by noon. Finding the ladies ready, and anxious to remove to our new home, we packed up our beds and bedding, and clothes for present use, leaving the remainder of our goods in charge with Mr. Birnie, loaded our canoe, and set off for the plain. We proceeded across Young's Bay, and up the Skapanowin to the head of navigation. Having been retarded in our progress in consequence of low water, we found the night closing in upon us, and concluded that it was not best to attempt to cross the marsh and forest in the night, but that we must make ourselves as comfortable as circumstances would allow until morning. Our arrangements for the night were as follows: we landed our cargo, and placed it upon the oars, one end of which was laid upon a log, and the other upon the ground, which was very wet. This done, we hauled the canoe ashore, and laid some boards, which were in the bottom, on the top of the cross bars;

on these we placed the beds, and thus prepared lodging for the ladies, and Emory, our little boy, and a little girl that Mrs. K. had taken to live with her.

We then struck a fire, having found a few sticks, which were very scarce within a quarter of a mile: and after some time we prevailed on the ladies to retire into their strange bed-chamber; but they found room to lie down; after which we rigged a pole over them, over which we stretched a pair of sheets, which formed a kind of tent; and now, supposing they would be tolerably comfortable, I determined to watch all night, while Mr. Smith, who was very weary, took a mat, and lay down in the grass, and fell asleep.

I remained sitting on a mat over the remains of our small fire, in company with the Indians. An hour passed away rather pleasantly, but then it commenced raining. This was a new and unexpected trial. I awoke Mr. Smith, who was shivering with the cold, having lain upon a frail mat upon the wet ground. We found ourselves in possession of two umbrellas, one of which we put over our flour, and the other we held over ourselves, while we hovered over our small remaining fire, which would afford us a little light and heat. That was a long night, bringing, as it passed away, many heavy showers. Becoming quite hungry, we got out some flour, and baked some dough cakes. This work was performed, not according to the most refined methods of domestic cookery, but sufficiently methodical to satisfy the calls of appetite. And we can assure our readers that if our old friend Smith should ever fall in with this volume, and read this paragraph, he would instantly recollect having pronounced those cakes "very sweet." We spent the remainder of the night in talking of almost everything that we could think of, in order to keep awake, being interrupted occasionally by the ladies, who would inquire very anxiously if it was near day. At length the eastern horizon gave indications of approaching light; and as soon as we could well discern the pathway that led to our dwelling, I took my little boy on my back, and was followed by the ladies, who were by no means dry, hoping soon to find a more comfortable place. We reached our cabin just in time to partake with Mr. Kone of a fine pair of roasted brant, which refreshed us much, and caused our unfloored cabin to appear more pleasant than if it had been a palace without food to replenish our wasting frames.

The sun had now risen; and after attending to our morning's devotions, and sending some breakfast to Mr. Smith, who remained with the canoe, I left the family, who set about clearing out the rubbish, and making arrangements for housekeeping, and returned to assist in bringing home our cargo. This was accomplished, with the exception of a few heavy articles, before night.

The rainy season had now commenced; and although that day proved to be one of sunshine, we could not expect but that there would be many of a different character soon. Therefore, after setting up our bedsteads upon the ground, and arranging some little necessaries in the cabin, it was determined that Mr. Kone and Smith should return to Astoria for a load of provisions, etc., and I should meet them the next day at the canoe landing, to assist in getting the cargo to the house.

I spent the following night very comfortably with the family; and meeting my associates in the morning, according to appointment, we succeeded in conveying to our cabin, with the help of a few Indians, a barrel of pork, which we had brought from Walamet, which was very near being lost at the time our canoe was wrecked, some molasses, a barrel of salmon, purchased from Mr. Birnie, eight hundred weight of flour, obtained at Vancouver, and a keg of butter.

Having now a cover for our heads, and a supply of food for some time, Mr. Smith set to work to prepare for his own family, which was still at the other end of the plain. Having obtained some plank from an Indian, which had been split out of a cedar log, I helped him to cut some crotches and poles, and assisted him about putting up a cabin about eight by ten feet, and high enough in the centre to permit a man to stand nearly upright. This we covered with shingles; and the next day his family came up, and took their lodging there, so that we had not only a house, but neighbours also.

Mr. Kone and myself now set about sawing off logs and splitting out "puncheons," or short plank, which an Indian carried to the building. We then put in some sleepers, laid down our plank in tiers, nailed them fast, and smoothed them as well as we could with an adze. In this way we succeeded in putting about two-thirds of a floor in our house, and having ceiled it within with rush mats, which we purchased from the Indian women, and calked it with moss without, we began to think we were quite comfortable. During this time Mr. Smith was getting out logs for a house for himself, and I helped him lay it up, which was fifteen feet square.

The month of December now arrived, and the southeast storms began to break upon our dwelling with tremendous force; and as we had not made calculations for such drifting rains when we shingled our cabin, we found the south side of the roof to leak like a sieve. This was a great affliction to us, as it frequently wet Mrs. Kone's bed; and the more than usual degree of dampness thus brought into the room rendered it unhealthy. But we trusted in God, and hoped for better things; and, notwithstanding all these embarrassments, and many which it is not necessary to mention, the hope of being instrumental in planting the gospel standard in this benighted region kept the heart whole, and proved a powerful stimulant to future action.

About the middle of December we found that our store of flour began to run low; so it became necessary to make another trip to Astoria. This we dreaded to undertake, as the path through the marsh and timber land from the head of canoe navigation to the plains had become exceedingly difficult from the vast amount of water which had already fallen; but our flour we must have, and other necessaries also. So Mr. Smith and myself set out again, with some Indian help, for the fort. On our arrival at that place we found that Mr. Tibits, for whom we had been looking for some time, had arrived, and a black man by the name of Wallace, who had deserted from the Maryland while she was in the river, in company with him. This was a source of joy to us, as we hoped to have another accession to our small neighbourhood.

After a short interview with our new neighbours, we loaded our canoes and returned to the Clatsop shore, being accompanied by Mr. Tibits. We proceeded about half way up the Skapanowin, and encamped for the night, and the next morning reached the old landing place. We succeeded in carrying all our effects through to the plain, but frequently sunk into the mire up to our knees, and were many times in danger of falling from logs, which we were obliged to cross, into the water beneath; and with much hard labour we reached our homes just at nightfall, leaving Mr. Tibits, who had become very much discouraged, to camp on the plain. This day's toil rendered our cabin a very desirable place, and a comfortable supper more refreshing to us than the most costly meal to the full-fed, indolent, gouty epicure.

Previous to this Mr. Kone and myself had succeeded in putting up a cabin, in addition to the one we occupied, in the form of an Indian lodge, for the accommodation of our Indian visitors, who frequently stayed all night and slept upon the floor in our house. We did not like to turn them out of doors in the storm lest they should become offended, but it was very unpleasant, as our bed-rooms were only partitioned off with sheets; and we were very happy when we were able to introduce our neighbours to the apartment especially set apart for their accommodation. We employed the coloured man who came with Mr. Tibits, whose help was very much needed at this time, as our strength was nearly exhausted.

Our time, which could be spared from daily labour, was frequently employed in conversing with the Indians about God and the Bible; but as we could not yet speak their language well, our means of communicating truth to them were very limited; but, to supply this want on our part, we frequently employed Mr. Smith and his wife as interpreters—endeavouring in this way to sow some of the good seed of the kingdom while we were labouring with our hands to supply the necessary wants of our families.

Messrs. Kone, Smith, Tibits, and myself set out soon after this for the shore of the Columbia in a northerly direction from our house, for the purpose of ascertaining whether we could not make a road to the river by that route upon dry ground, as it had become impossible to convey our furniture and further supplies from Astoria to our place by the old route until the next summer, because of the accumulated waters. After travelling about four miles in a direct line through thickets which were almost impenetrable, and across a wide salt marsh, we struck the river about half way between Young's Bay and Point Adams. Here we found a convenient place to build, but were satisfied that it was impracticable to open a road from that to our location on the plain. After much consultation, it was decided that it would be easier to construct a building here of sufficient size for the more comfortable accommodation of Mr. Kone's family and mine, and to which we could remove our goods from Astoria by water, than to remain where we were and labour to get our effects and provisions to that place while we remained entirely destitute of a team; especially as all our neighbours agreed to assist in building. And in addition to the above considerations, it was believed that it would be expedient for the future prosperity of the station, when we should obtain teams, for one family to remain on the bank of the river, where the missionary would have immediate access to the Indians during salmon season, as they would then be all on the banks of the river; and that the other should reside on the plain, where provisions could be raised for the support of the station without having to go to the Walamet for everything of this kind, and from whence the missionary from this place of residence could have access to the Clatsops at their winter residence at Neacoxy, and the Killemooks to the south during the rainy season.

We now returned to the plain, and after maturing our plans, we set out on the 24th of December for the place where we contemplated building. Mr. Tibits and Wallace, and an Indian, went by the way of the Skapanowin with a canoe, for the purpose of conveying our tools, provisions, tents, etc., while Messrs. Smith, Kone, and myself went by the way of the beach, and met according to appointment on the bank of the river. Here we pitched our tents, and after selecting a spot for our house, Mr. Kone and myself returned to our families, our men having engaged to proceed next morning to cutting logs. We now carried and cut wood sufficient for use during the sabbath, and then sat down to enjoy the comforts of home and the smiles of our families until the following Monday.

After this I spent a week in helping on with the building while Mr. Kone took charge of the families, and then he would spend a week at the building while I would remain at home. In this way we succeeded, with our help, to get up a log house twenty by thirty feet square, and one story high, covered it with shingles, and finished off our room with a floor above and below consisting of rough fir boards which we obtained at Vancouver, and which had been lying at Astoria since the time I came down with Mr. Kone's family, but which we had been unable to remove to the plain, and having calked this room with moss, we were ready to remove to our new dwelling on the 10th of February. We accomplished our removal by carrying Mrs. Kone on a chair the most of the way, as she was very feeble in consequence of having been very ill; while Mrs. Frost and children went on foot; and we reached our new dwelling before night, having made the tedious journey of seven miles on the beach of the ocean and river around Point Adams. The Indians now came up with our beds and some provisions, etc., and after preparing a cup of tea, we got some wood and made all the other preparations in our power to enjoy the sabbath, which was the following day.

During the next week we removed the remainder of our effects from the plain. And as soon as we were a little recovered from the effects produced by these labours, Mr. Kone and myself finished off the other part of the house, so that we now had each a room of fifteen by twenty feet in size, and a tight roof over our heads, and felt thankful that we were thus comfortably situated.

Mr. Tibits and Smith now commenced a cabin on each side of us, and before the salmon season commenced our two neighbours were enjoying the cover of their own roofs.

We had not enjoyed our new residence long before it was evident that Mrs. Kone's health was such that medical aid would soon be indispensable, and as it became necessary for Mr. Smith to go to the Walamet for supplies, a statement of her case was communicated to Dr. Babcock, our physician, and in about two weeks afterward the doctor and the Rev. Messrs. Leslie and Waller came down to make us a visit. We were happy to have the privilege of spending a few days with them. Finding Mrs. Kone still able to be removed, the brethren determined to take her to Vancouver. To this we did not object, although myself and family were to be entirely left alone, as Mr. Tibits had just gone to Walamet for supplies, and Mr. Smith had not returned.

After making the necessary arrangements, they took their leave, taking Mr. Kone and family with them. This left no civilized man nearer to us than Astoria, which was six miles distant across Young's Bay, and with this exception there was no other white resident on the river until we reached Vancouver, the distance of one hundred miles from us. But we considered ourselves safe while under the protection of our heavenly Father. On the following morning Mr. Smith returned from the Walamet. He had obtained a boat from Vancouver, and, with much difficulty, had brought down a pair of horses with which to commence farming on the plain, and we rejoiced very much in the prospect of being no longer obliged to supply the place of a beast of burden ourselves. That day Mr. Smith's family moved into one of our rooms. Mr. S. then left to take the boat home, and bring down his canoe loaded with provisions, and while he was absent Mr. Tibits returned; so we were not long without company.

The following extract from his journal will exhibit the writer's feelings at that time:—

"My cause is before the Lord, and I would fully confide in his wisdom and goodness, to preserve me and mine, although in an Indian country surrounded with intense moral darkness, and to guide us in the way that will be acceptable in his sight. O what degradation do we witness every day! What wretchedness have we seen since we have sojourned in this wilderness! Is not the time coming when this desert will bud and blossom? Is not the day hastening on when the peaceful reign of the Messiah shall be established here, where our fellow-men are now universally led captive by the devil at his will? O Lord, hasten to come and take possession of the purchase of thy blood! Turn and overturn, until the wickedness of the wicked shall come to an end, and when truth and righteousness shall universally prevail."

Mr. Smith removed his family to the plain in the course of a week, for the purpose of planting some potatoes and some garden vegetables; so that our only neighbour consisted of Mr. Tibits, and as he was a bachelor, Mrs. Frost had no female associate. While Mr. Kone's family were with us, and Messrs. Smith and Tibits were near us, we had quite a congregation to hear the word preached, and to unite in the worship of

God; but now my congregation consisted of Mr. Tibits, Mrs. Frost, and our little son, who were all that could understand English. To these I would preach the word on the sabbath, and when the Indians came in, which was very seldom, I would speak to them in their own tongue, which by this time we could speak very well, but we found it altogether insufficient as a medium by which to communicate to their dark minds the doctrines of the gospel. And as they had now come up to take possession of their summer residence, I used to go to their lodges to converse with them upon the subject of religion; and requested them to meet in the chief's lodge for the purpose of hearing me explain the Bible to them on the sabbath. This they promised to do, and the chief engaged to use his influence to get them together for that purpose. The next sabbath I attended the appointment, and found several at the lodge. I sung a hymn and prayed with them, and then read a portion of the Scriptures and gave such explanations as circumstances would permit, and closed the interview. They said that this was good, and that they would all attend the next sabbath. But when the next sabbath came they had scattered: some were shooting wild fowl, and others were fishing; so that I had none to preach to but the old chief and his wives and slave.

On the 22d of April an Indian arrived from Vancouver bringing a note from Mr. Kone, by which we were informed that Mrs. Kone had presented him with a son on the 18th, and that all were doing well. I received a note from the superintendent requesting me to attend the annual meeting at Walamet on the first Monday in May. We now determined to go up to Vancouver, where I would leave my family, and if Providence favoured the design I would go up to the Walamet, Mr. Smith having promised to come up from the plain and take care of our house and effects during our absence.

The following extract was recorded in my journal at

that time : "I find my health much impaired ; so much so that the cutting, clearing, and carrying wood for our fire, and attending to the other necessary jobs about the house, are attended with considerable pain ; but my hope is in God, and my desire for the salvation of the heathen is not abated. While I make this record, Mrs. Frost lies by my side on the bed sick with the headache, and our little boy is playing about the floor, jabbering to himself in the Indian tongue, which he acquires very readily."

April 24th. The salmon season has now commenced, and we were invited yesterday to partake with our red neighbours at Wasulsul's lodge, he being one of the head men and our nearest neighbour, living about half a mile from our house. We accepted the invitation ; and taking some knives, forks, and plates, bread, pepper, and salt, went up to the lodge, where, in the head man's department, a clean mat was spread for our reception. We entered and seated ourselves in good Indian style, and then witnessed the following operation. They had succeeded in taking four salmon, weighing from fifteen to thirty pounds each, which were lying side by side upon a mat, with their heads toward the west, and were covered with another mat. The wood was now brought in, and the women and slaves kindled a fire in the centre of the lodge about ten feet in length, over which there was a frame constructed something in the form of a large gridiron, made of round sticks, and raised about three feet from the fire. As soon as the fire commenced blazing, one of the men stepped forward with a knife and cut one of the salmon round the neck, then split it down the back each side of the bone, so that it was taken out while it was left attached to the head. The head and back bone were then laid on the frame over the fire to roast, observing to keep the tail toward the east, while an old man had some nice sticks prepared, by splitting them at one end and sharpening them at the other. In the split of one of these the broad-sides of the salmon, which were connected by the belly, were placed, and small sticks placed across the sides in an opposite direction, that it might not hang down or drop off when it became tender by cooking. The two parts of the stick were then tied together with some green grass which would not burn very readily; and being thus secured in a proper position to receive the heat on all its parts, it was set up before the fire by sticking the sharp end in the ground. In this way the four salmon were soon hissing and smoking, and sending forth a most delicious perfume throughout the lodge; and the slaves and children prepared the entrails for eating much in the same way.

While the salmon were roasting, the men related one of their traditions, which was of the following import: "A long time ago, Talapus," that is, one of their imaginary deities, "came this way from the south, in the form of the little wolf, and made all this land from Cape Lookout to Young's Bay; and finding the people very poor, and having nothing to eat but elk, and bear, and deer, and wild fowl, he made the salmon; and when they commenced to run up the river, he made a seine, and placing the snake on the shore to hold the land line, he went out in the canoe and threw the net. Then coming on shore, he and the snake drew the net to land, which contained a great draught of salmon. He now ordered them to be taken to the lodge and laid with their heads to the west until toward night, when the fire was prepared as above described: and Talapus learned their fathers how to cut the fish and roast them, and told them that for some time they must not eat only in the afternoon of each day, and that if any of them should touch a dead body, or eat vermin, until the strawberries began to ripen, the salmon would all leave the river, unless those who had thus defiled themselves should be prohibited from touching a salmon for a specified number of days; and that the same results would follow if their women, under certain circumstances, (who were also prohibited from enjoying the privileges of their houses, as it is their universal custom on such occasions,) should look upon a salmon net; and that until that time arrived when the berries began to ripen, which is about the first of June, they must cook the salmon in precisely the same way, and none of it must be taken out of the lodge in which it was cooked. But as soon as the specified time arrived, they were at liberty to cook the salmon as they might see proper, and sell them to whom they pleased."

The fact that they fully believe that this is a law imposed upon them by their deity, and that such distressing results would follow, namely, the removal of all the salmon, if this law should be transgressed, accounts for the most barbarous practice among them—of burying their people alive at the commencement of the salmon season, an instance of which has been already related.

The salmon was now pronounced well done, and it was taken down and placed in a shallow trough made of cedar, and our plates were filled with the choice pieces, and placed before us. We now divided our loaf of bread among the company, and all hands commenced feasting, except the man who prepared the fish for roasting, for Talapus had prohibited him from tasting a morsel for a certain number of days; and, notwithstanding this seemed to be a very self-denying work, as they had not had good fat salmon for a great many moons, our cook submitted with all cheerfulness, and made his feast upon bread and whale grease, of which they had had a great abundance during the past winter.

The feast was now ended, and as there was a part of our share left upon our plates, we were told that we might have it and come the next afternoon and finish it; but as we thought it would not be convenient for us to do so, the remnants were divided among the children, and the plates, knives, and forks were washed, so that none of the salmon might be carried out of the lodge; and then we were permitted to depart in peace to our home.

CHAPTER XXIII.

Mr. Frost attends the yearly meeting at Walamet—Manual Labour School—The Oregon Institute—Visiters—Extracts from Mr. Frost's journal—Exploring expedition—Messrs. Smith and Frost's journey to and from Walamet—Kilemook Indians—Mr. Kone and family return to the United States—Extracts from Mr. Frost's journal—Arrival of vessels—Immorality of seamen who visited Oregon—Reflections—Indians obtain ardent spirits, and proceed to murder one another—Some of the missionaries embark for the United States—Death of Rev. James Olley—Awful disaster—Return of missionaries to the United States, and conclusion.

We left home for Vancouver in an Indian canoe on the 29th of April, and tarried with Mr. Birnie at Astoria the following night. Here we had a conversation with Captain Varney, of the brig Thomas Pirkins, of Salem, Mass. The brig was partly freighted with supplies for the United States exploring expedition, which the captain assured us might be expected to enter the river every day.

On the following night we reached Oak Point, which was nearly half way from Astoria to Vancouver. Here we pitched our tent; and now it began to rain, so that it was exceedingly damp and chilly through the night. The next day, being sabbath, we did not design to move camp; and before noon Mrs. Frost was taken with a fit of the ague, symptoms of which disease had been hanging about her system since the previous autumn. And now we found ourselves in a very distressing situation, as we had no medicine; and as everything was so very damp, because of the rain, we hardly knew what course to pursue. But I directed my Indians to get what wood they could, with which we replenished our fire; I then heated a stone, which I put to Mrs. F.'s feet, and made her a cup of hot tea, which prescription had a tendency to relieve the pain in her head; and when the fit had subsided, and the storm abated, we determined to move camp a few miles to the mouth of the Cawalitz River, where we could obtain a supply of fuel, that we might get a fire sufficient to dry our clothes.

We packed all into the canoe, and set off; but had not gone more than a mile when it commenced raining again, and it poured down to that degree that we were literally drenched in a few minutes. We succeeded, however, in reaching the desired camping place, went on shore, pitched our tent, and in a few minutes the Indians kindled a rousing fire. The clouds passed off, and we dried our clothes and blankets, and lodged rather comfortably for the night.

We set out early in the morning for Vancouver; and during the day Mrs. F. had another fit of the ague, and as we were labouring to reach the fort that day, in order that we might obtain medical aid, she passed through the chill lying in the canoe, which was exceedingly distressing; and the succeeding fever reduced her strength to that degree that when we reached the landing place, at about sun-setting, she was scarcely able to walk to the fort. But as soon as we arrived the physician very kindly administered some medicine, which soon relieved her.

Finding Mrs. F.'s health improved, I left her on the following Wednesday with Mrs. Kone, at Vancouver, and set off for Walamet, and reached there on Friday, and was happy to find so many of the brethren in health. We had a very harmonious annual meeting, which continued its session nearly two weeks. During this session a committee was appointed for the purpose of selecting a location for the new manual labour school-house; and this committee afterward fixed upon a site near the mission saw-mill, where the school-house has since been erected.

A committee was also appointed with powers for the purpose of getting up a literary institution for the education of the youth of Oregon. This institution was to be denominated "The Oregon Institute." This praise-worthy design was carried so far into effect, through the efforts of individuals in the country, previous to my last visit to the Walamet, as to have erected a frame building of a very respectable size for the accommodation of the school, which building was then enclosed; and Mr. Gray and lady, formerly of the mission in the interior, were engaged as teachers.

On my return to Vancouver I had the pleasure to be made acquainted with the Rev. Messrs. Smith and Clark, and ladies, from the interior. These gentlemen were very much discouraged in view of the prospects of being useful in Oregon, so much so that Mr. Smith determined to leave the country, his lady also being in very delicate health.

While I remained at the fort I formed a very pleasant acquaintance with the Rev. Mr. Griffin also, of whom mention has heretofore been made.

We left Vancouver the next day after my return from Walamet, and proceeded to our station at Clatsop; and left Mr. Kone's family at the fort, as Mrs. Kone's health would not yet admit of a removal. We reached our home on the third day after we left our kind friends at Vancouver, and found all things in peace and safety.

During my absence from home the Vincennes, under the command of Lieut. Wilkes, of the United States exploring expedition, had arrived at Nasqually; and after arranging matters there, he came across the country to Astoria, being accompanied by Mr. Waldron, purser of the Vincennes, and another gentleman. Mr. Wilkes came over in company with Mr. Birnie, and dined with us in our log-cabin; after which we went down to Point Adams, to look out for the Peacock, another vessel of the squadron, which had been ordered to the Columbia, and which was expected before this.

On the 25th of May I crossed over to Astoria, where I had the pleasure of an introduction to Mr. Waldron, in whose society I was very much interested, and with whom I spent most of the day, Mr. Wilkes and the other gentleman having left for Vancouver. I will also mention here that during my absence from home the bark Wave, Capt. More, from England, arrived with a cargo of goods for the Hudson's Bay Company.

May 30th, sabbath. Preached from these words,

"Let your light so shine before men that they may see your good works, and glorify your Father which is in heaven," having my two neighbours, Mr. Smith and Tibits, and my family who could understand English, for my congregation.

On the 1st of June Mr. J. Lee, the superintendent of the mission, and lady, and Mr. Whitcomb and family, came down to make us a visit. Mr. W. came down for the benefit of the sea air, as his health was very feeble.

Mr. Kone and family also returned to their home with us; and as it had been decided by the superintendent that Mr. Kone might put up a frame-house for the more comfortable accommodation of his family, lumber had been sent down from Vancouver for the purpose, and a carpenter came from the Walamet to do the work. Thus the reader may discover that we were once more blessed with a good share of society; but this was no relief to our ladies in a temporal point of view, as the household labour was necessarily very much increased, and no help could be obtained. Our ladies considered it a great privilege, however, to wait upon company at all times, as far as our means and strength would permit.

We have also had a very pleasant visit with the Rev. Mr. Clark and lady, who came down in company with Mr. Kone.

Mr. Lee and myself spoke to the Indians, or as many of them as we could prevail upon to assemble for that purpose, who appeared to give some attention to the word delivered. But one of the head men said, when requested to attend preaching, that he understood how to steal, and that was enough for him to know.

I find an entry in my journal at this time which will enable the reader to enter into the writer's views and feelings when he recorded the same.

"You probably ask me, 'Watchman, what of the night?' All is dark. The wretchedness of the heathen is untold. The gospel *only* can ameliorate their condition. And O! how difficult to communicate one truth to their dark understandings. Yet we will continue to try. We will use the means within our reach, and leave the event with God, in whose hand are the hearts of all men!"

Mr. Lee and lady left us on the 22d of June, and Mr. Whitcomb's family have taken up their residence in Mr. Tibits' cabin for the present.

In the former part of the month of July the Peacock made her appearance off the mouth of the river, attended by the Flying-fish, a small schooner. Mr. Kone and myself manned our canoe and went down to the bay to meet her and welcome our countrymen to our wild shore and rustic home. But before we reached the bay, the Peacock struck the north breakers outside of the bar. We ascended Cape Disappointment, from whence we discovered that she was in a very dangerous situation; but as we could render her no aid, we returned to our homes at about sunset. The next day Kotata, the Indian chief, sent word to me that the ship had lost her masts, and that we must go and see her. Upon this we immediately rigged our canoe, and we had not gone far upon the river before we discovered that it was even so: the hulk of the vessel was to be seen in the midst of the breakers, which were light at this time, but her masts had entirely gone by the board. We hastened to Baker's Bay, where we were happy to find a part of the officers and crew, who had come ashore in the ship's boats, and the boats had returned to the wreck for the commander, and the remainder of the crew. We soon became acquainted with Mr. Speeden, the purser, and several of the other gentlemen. We had our tent pitched, and then waited anxiously for the return of the boats, and, to the joy of all, they at length returned, bringing every soul in safety to the shore. We were now introduced to Lieutenant Hudson, who had the command of the vessel, a gentleman much esteemed by his crew, and of whom we had subsequent evidence that he possessed the spirit, and practised the principles of the gospel of Christ. It would have been a great pleasure to us to have been so situated, that we might have afforded them comfortable accommodations when they reached the shore; but this was entirely out of the question. Our canoe, which we had despatched to the house for such refreshments as we had on hand, soon returned, and Mr. Birnie came down from Astoria with two tents and a good supply of provisions, so that we managed to give the officers a little refreshment, after which and some very agreeable conversation we retired to rest : the captain and some of the officers took up lodgings in our tents, and some under small arbours made of the branches of trees, and some I know not how; but we found ourselves all alive in the morning, and in tolerable health, and were thankful to God for his delivering and preserving mercy. We now returned home, and two of the gentlemen of the scientific corps accompanied us. The officers and crew soon took up their quarters at Astoria, and commenced surveying the river, and making scientific observations in the country. While they remained in the country we were favoured with occasional visits from the officers and gentlemen, which were very acceptable and gratifying to us. And Mr. Kone and myself had the satisfaction of preaching to them at Astoria on the sabbath, after the reading of the morning service of the Protestant Episcopal Church by Lieut. Hudson.

Mr. Smith and myself had for some time contemplated a journey to the Walamet by way of the Kilemook country, in order to ascertain the number of Indians in that region, their character, and the prospects of operating among them; and that on our return we might drive through a few cattle and horses, that we might have some milk and butter and beef for our family's use, and sufficient teams for the purpose of raising provisions for our own consumption. We accordingly set out on this tour, being accompanied by a sailor boy who had left the Wave, and an Indian as guide. We took with us one of Mr. Smith's horses to carry our provisions and tent. We accomplished this difficult journey, much of which had never before been travelled by a white man, in fourteen days. We passed down the coast to the southward for seven days, and then crossed from the coast to the Walamet Mission in seven days more. Here we attended to our business, obtained a few cattle and horses, and recruited our numbers by the addition of two men and one Indian, and set out to retrace our steps to Clatsop. This we found to be a difficult task; but we succeeded in accomplishing it in fourteen days. So that after an absence of thirty-six days, including the eight days we spent at Walamet, we reached our home in safety.

It had been reported that the Kilemooks were a numerous tribe of Indians, but they are like the most of the other "numerous tribes" in the country, very "few and far between;" these were so much so that we found, after passing through their entire country and seeing all their wigwams, that their number would not exceed two hundred, men, women, and children. Their character was, as far as we could ascertain, much the same in its general features as that of their neighbours at the north of them; and their country was perfectly in keeping with the character of the inhabitants. We saw no land, worth mentioning, that was fit for cultivation, after we left Cape Lookout at the southern extremity of the Clatsop Plain, until we crossed the mountains, which run parallel with the coast, and reached the Walamet Valley. The whole coast, as far as we travelled it, is made up of high rugged capes, which terminate in a very abrupt manner amidst the foaming billows which break in thunder tones upon the shore. We were obliged to cross all these capes but one or two, and then ford the rivers, which take their rise in the wide range of mountains between the ocean and the Walamet, and empty themselves in the Pacific, except some of them where we found Indians who ferried us over in their canoes. These valleys, through which the rivers found their way, appeared to be but little more than sufficiently wide to answer the purpose of channels through which the accumulated waters of the high lands were to find their way to their source. And none of these rivers appeared to be navigable, or at least no vessels could enter them from the ocean, as the breakers were seen to roll in across their entire mouths at any stage of the tide.

Having accomplished this exceedingly difficult tour, and having obtained the information for which we had been seeking, and the means in the use of which we might be able to procure, at least, a part of our future subsistence, we had new and more abundant grounds for thankfulness to our heavenly Father.

The month of October now returned, and it became necessary to make a trip to the Walamet by water, for the purpose of securing a store of provisions for the sustenance of our families during the rapidly-approaching rainy winter. Consequently but a few days were spent in getting a little wood, and in attending to some other little household affairs for the comfort of the family, and then I set out again in our canoe with a gang of Indians for the Walamet Mission.

We performed this trip of three hundred and twenty miles in an Indian canoe, besides procuring a sufficient store of provisions for the winter, and farming utensils, with which to commence operations on the plain as soon as circumstances would permit, in twenty-one days. The provisions, etc., we brought to the Walamet Falls, where they were shipped on board of a small schooner, which was built by a few Americans, during the previous summer, in the Walamet River, with the promise that the goods should be delivered at our station at Clatsop. When we returned I found my family in comfortable health; but Mrs. Kone's health had been failing since their return from Vancouver, and it became evident that her situation was such as to require a course of treatment such as could not be obtained in this country.

The Rev. A. B. Smith and lady, of whom mention

has already been made, had been for several days at our place on a visit, and were, on my return, still favouring our neighbourhood with their presence. Mr. S. was awaiting an opportunity to take passage for the Sandwich Islands, hoping to find employment in that very interesting missionary field, and a climate better adapted to the enfeebled health of his lady.

In November Mr. Smith, my old neighbour, removed to the plain, where he has no neighbours except our cattle and horses. In view of the unpromising prospects among the natives, and the continually declining state of Mrs. Kone's health, Mr. Kone made application to the superintendent of the mission for permission to return to the States, which was granted ; and as the bark Columbia, Captain Humphreys, of the Hudson's Bay Company, was ready to sail for Oahu, one of the Sandwich Islands, Mr. Kone and the Rev. A. B. Smith and families took passage on board of her : so that on the 30th of November, 1841, I found myself and family entirely alone, with the exception of a sailor boy and an Indian girl which he took to wife. These two we now employed as domestic helps ; and in addition to these, I supported an Indian and his family, who lived in a small lodge in the rear of my house, all the other Indian neighbours having removed to their winter quarters at the south end of the plain. Mr. Whitcomb and family had also returned to the Walamet, and had taken the carpenter with them, leaving the house designed for Mr. Kone partly framed.

The rainy season had fairly set in on the 1st of November, and the rain was now literally pouring down, being accompanied with very heavy thunder and lightning ; and it is worthy of remark, that it was a rare circumstance that we had any thunder at all, save at this time of the year, which was the early part of the rainy season.

And now that the reader may more fully enter into the writer's views and feelings at that time, when he had the best opportunity for reflection and consideration with respect to his peculiar work, and the circumstances of the heathen among whom he lived and laboured, he will subjoin some extracts from his journal, which were written at that time.

"It is acknowledged on all hands that the present prospects in respect to civilizing and Christianizing these natives are exceedingly gloomy. They are by a great majority fewer in number than they were supposed to be; and as each clan has a peculiar dialect or tongue, those who profess to be the best judges believe their language to be not worth reducing with the design of printing the same, and of making it the medium of communication. I am inclined to favour this view of the subject. And the prospect of teaching them the English language is no more promising. In respect to the adults, it would be the nearest thing to an impossibility. Their habits are formed, and they consider everything that has the appearance of work, that does not yield an immediate visible profit, as slavery: hence it is disgraceful, in their estimation, to labour. And as their organs of speech are formed, they cannot make our English sounds; for instance, I never met with an Indian in the country that could speak my name (Frost) properly: some would have it Mr. Plost, and others Floost, and the like; it seemed to be impossible for them to sound *fr*. And then, if they are taken when young, the prospect is but little better; for after they are cleansed from filth and vermin, and clothed, and fed, and taught for a few years, those of them that do not elope, preferring the liberty of the plains and mountains to the confinement, restraint, and labour of a school, suddenly drop into the grave in consequence of the most deadly and loathsome diseases which they inherit from their fathers and mothers. So that, at the time the writer left the country, there were more Indian children in the mission grave-yard at the Walamet, of such as had been taken by the missionaries and treated as above mentioned, than there were of such as were alive and in the manual labour school.

"Still I believe, if the proper means can be brought to bear upon them, at least some of these forlorn creatures may be benefited both for time and eternity. And will not the Lord and the church sustain those who continue in the field, and labour to accomplish this best of objects?

"At all events I am not yet satisfied that 'the Lord has nothing more for me to do in this land of darkness.' When I am fully satisfied of this, or that, in consequence of a broken constitution, I may be disqualified for the performance of the work assigned me, I will ask immediately to be removed to another field of labour."

We were now completely isolated from civilized society, save that of our own household. We have but two white neighbours, and they are seven miles from us—one on the Clatsop Plain, and the other at Astoria, across Young's Bay; and during the storms, which are now almost incessant, this bay cannot be crossed in a canoe without endangering life.

"December 26th. Since the 1st of November we have had but very few days without rain, and to-day it literally pours down. I have thought much of late of the privileges of my brethren in my native land, and especially of my brethren in the ministry, with whom I have travelled and laboured. How refreshing it would be to the spirit to enjoy an interview with them! But the same Lord who guides them in their labours of love is here, and the same Spirit which leads them into the way of truth and peace is hovering over us in this dreary region, and replenishes our hearts with daily showers of peace and mercy; and if it is the will of the Lord that we should remain here during the term of our natural lives, we hope at all times to be able to say, ' Thy will be done ;' and if we could see the way opened, and spiritual good being effected among these wretched heathen through our instrumentality, that we would rather be here in this lonely situation, surrounded with dense moral darkness, than in the city full, where all the comforts and conveniences of life are to be enjoyed with relatives and friends. And will not God extend the hand of mercy to these heathen through us as instruments? Or are they destined to fade away, and never be benefited by the gospel of peace? It certainly appears that if they are not enlightened soon, they never will be; for in a few years there will be none of them left."

"February 2d, 1842. The Indians are at this time coming up from the south end of the plain; and although there was an abundance of salmon last fall, they are now entirely destitute of food, except such roots as they can procure from day to day. The whale which usually drifts ashore, and furnishes them with food which they are very fond of, has been very scarce during the winter, as but a part of one came ashore. There are abundance of elk on the mountains, but they are too lazy to hunt only when hunger drives them to it. They have of late manifested a disposition to steal more than formerly; and they look upon a white man as a being altogether different from themselves, and all they expect by his being among them is *temporal benefit*, and the man that benefits them most in this way has the '*best heart.*'"

"I am quite confident, from all the observations which I have been enabled to make relative to their moral and physical condition, that there never will be anything like a permanent Christian church raised up from among them." "Their language is so defective, that thereby it is impossible to acquaint them with the true nature of *law;* and until they are brought to feel that they are condemned in consequence of having transgressed the law of God, how can they be made to feel the need of Christ, who 'hath redeemed us from the curse of the law, being made a curse for us?' Are they then without law? No, 'they are a law unto themselves;' and that law which the Spirit hath written upon their hearts has been very nearly obliterated by a persevering continuance in the practice of all manner of vice from generation to generation. Must they then be consigned over to irremediable destruction? We will leave them where we found them, if our efforts fail to ameliorate their condition, in the hands of a merciful God, who can have compassion upon the ignorant, and upon those that are out of the way."

"February 26th. But two children are now living out of ten or twelve that were born, to our knowledge, among the Indians of our neighbourhood, since last November, besides a number which were destroyed by their mothers in the earliest dawn of infancy. I saw several of those that died natural deaths, which were perfect masses of putrefaction before they expired, in consequence of disease which they had inherited from their parents." We could relate more horrid scenes than these, but delicacy forbids. It is perfectly astonishing to see with what composure the mothers will relate the many infanticides they have been guilty of committing. Mrs. Frost had a conversation one day with an Indian woman who called at our house with her little son, whom we used to clothe. This woman told Mrs. F. that she had destroyed her infants previous to this; and the reason why this, her little son then present, was living, was the fact that her husband had assured her that if she destroyed it he would kill her. And when asked the reason why she destroyed her infants, she said that as they had become very poor, and had no slaves, the drudgery all fell upon the women; and if they had many children they were prevented from doing their work; so that when their husbands came home weary and hungry, and found no fire and no roots to eat, they were angry, called them lazy, and beat and otherwise abused them. Therefore, in order that they might relieve themselves of much trouble and care, and escape abuse from their husbands, which made their hearts always poor and sad, they destroyed their infants as soon as they entered upon the stage of action!

I found myself at this time labouring under a severe attack of the bronchitis, so that it was quite difficult to attend to our family devotions. This disease had been increasing in virulence since the commencement of the rainy season.

"March 5th. Visited Mr. Smith upon the Plain, and found him very much discouraged. Surely he has difficulties to pass through of which those in the civilized world know nothing. O! how do those undervalue their privileges who are blessed with all the sweets of society, and all the privileges of a Christian community!"

March 14. Up to this time the rain had continued to descend as if the windows of heaven had been opened. I visited the Indian lodges, and talked to them about their hearts, and God, and the Bible; but they were exceedingly hungry, and wanted something to eat. I told them to come to my house, and they should have something. They soon followed me, and I divided a tierce of salmon, which I had purchased from them the previous summer, and salted for the use of my family, and gave each family from three to five. This, in addition to having fed several of them every day since the 1st of February, they said made their hearts very good, and caused them to like my talk very much; and they assured me that when the salmon came again we should not want.

A snow storm now ensued, and it became difficult for my sailor boy to get fuel enough to keep the room warm. So I called upon my Indian neighbour, Tawint, whose family I had nearly supported through the winter, and told him if he would help my boy get up some wood, he and his family should have an abundance of food every day until salmon came, notwithstanding his neighbours were near starving. To this proposition he assented with apparent good will, and helped some for the first and second days; but the third day my boy came in and told me that Tawint was lying on his back by his fire, and said that I was making a slave of him; for, said he, "other people get horses and blankets for working, but I get nothing but something to eat." I stepped into his lodge and scolded him for his ingratitude, and asked him if we were not rather the slaves? I had furnished him with the boards that had made a comfortable roof over their heads during the winter; and Mrs. F. had carried them food from our table every day. "O!" said he, "what of the boards? What do I do with them? They simply lie up there!" I then promised him that if he would not work he might starve; but my family would not see them suffer: so Mr. Tawint managed to get something to eat without becoming a slave. Besides being pestered for food, I am almost daily called upon by some of them for medicine, which I am not forward to deal out; for they are so extremely superstitious, that if one of them should die after taking medicine, they would be almost sure to attribute the death to those who gave the medicine, if they did not want to be paid for taking it if it cured them: as did an old Chenook squaw who went to Mr. Birnie with the fever and ague, and begged for some medicine. Her request was granted; and after she recovered from her sickness, she went to Mr. B. again, and said, "Seeing I have taken a great deal of your bad medicine, perhaps you will now give me some tea, and sugar, and something good to eat?" Of course the old lady's suit was not rejected, as my friend Birnie was a most liberal soul.

On the 2d of April I received a letter from the superintendent, which brought the sad intelligence of the death of his excellent wife, the particulars of which have already been given. I received a letter also from Mr. Kone by an American vessel, by which I learned that he expected to sail for the United States the 1st of this month. This vessel came for the purpose of trade. I boarded her in Baker's Bay, where I met with Mr. Birnie, who had reached the vessel before me; and as a part of the cargo was ardent spirits, we obtained a pledge from the captain and his first mate to the effect that no liquor should be sold or given to the natives, in view of the fact that if they should become intoxicated, bloodshed and murder would ensue; and in view of this pledge he was furnished with a house in my immediate neighbourhood, in which to trade with the Indians for salmon. During the day the vessel came to anchor in the river opposite to my house. Some barrels and goods were landed, and a man left to trade. My sailor boy entered on board of this vessel, and left his Indian wife with us, who by this time had become quite a help to Mrs. Frost.

On the 10th, another American vessel crossed the bar, which proved to be the brig Chenamus, Captain Couch, from Newburyport, Mass. On the 22d of April I received a letter from home, which brought us the first intelligence from my father's family since we bid them adieu in the autumn of 1839; and this letter informed us that one of my brothers, whom I left in health, had been called to leave his wife and little children, and appear before his gracious Judge. And about this time I received several letters from my old friends in the States. These were to us like cold water to a thirsty soul.

May 28th. Crime of every kind prevails among the heathen. This, however, is not so surprising, as they have no knowledge of God or of his laws, comparatively speaking. But what shall we say of those who come here from the civilized world, who were probably born of Christian parents, and as soon as they set their feet upon this dark shore, they lie down in all the abominations of the heathen ! And, while we are endeavouring to teach the heathen the law of God, how it mortifies us and puts us to the blush, when men, our own countrymen, coming even from the land of our "pilgrim fathers," tell the Indians that "there is no God," and that " all the missionaries tell them about such things are lies ;" and then commit such acts of licentiousness as to cause the Indians to say, " Hias nesika shame," that is, We are great ashamed. And, after talking of such acts, they have often said to me, " Hias peshock mika tilacum shicks," that is, Your people are very bad, friend. Well, who could deny it, if these were fair samples of our nation? Let it not be inferred from this statement of facts, that a similar course of conduct characterized *all* that came to this coast, for there were a number of gentlemen who came to this region both by land and sea, whose conduct gave evidence to all, and the Indians even were satisfied, that they were actuated by different principles. These gentlemen we used to point out to the Indians as examples of such as were guided by the principles laid down in the book of God, and the others as those who had rejected that book, because they hated its Author, and the course of righteousness which he required all men to pursue. I am aware that such guilty wretches have threatened to pour out their fury upon those missionaries who have, in their communications with the civilized world, made mention of the iniquitous course pursued by such creatures as soon as they considered themselves beyond the reach of civil power, and the restraints of civilized society.

One of these fellows told me, when I found it necessary to reprove him because of his brutal conduct among the heathen of my immediate neighbourhood, that "old Jason Lee," as he expressed himself, had, in some of his communications to the States, spoken of the disgraceful conduct of some American seamen while in this river at a certain time; and as he was an American seaman, and had been in the river before, he was determined to have revenge on Lee. This threat he uttered while his countenance gave evidence of the fiendish spirit that reigned within his heart. He was informed that we were not to be intimidated by the threats of the wicked, and that he and his associates in crime might rest assured, that, whether Mr. Lee had exposed them or not, such conduct must come to the light. He was then exhorted to turn his attention to that Bible which had been presented to him by a missionary, and make his peace with that God who would shortly bring every secret thing into judgment. But as he offered an Indian five blankets, a few weeks after this, to shoot Mr. Lee, while he (Mr. Lee) was making the writer a visit, and also talked of shooting the writer a few months afterward, it remained evident that he still meditated revenge, or rather that he was still led captive by the devil at his will.

In view of many peculiar circumstances which have transpired under the writer's immediate observation, two facts have pressed very heavily upon his mind, namely, the evangelization of the heathen world will be very much retarded, and the moral character of the heathen will be very much lowered, in consequence of the unhallowed influence exerted upon them by such as enter those regions from the civilized world, and refuse to be controlled and guided by the word of God. And that the *laws of civilization*, such as are founded upon the word of God, and *Christianity* must go hand in hand. God has ordained the one as well as the other, and if you will show me a country where *civil law*, of the above character, is not enforced, I will show you a country where the gospel makes but little if any progress.

I am aware that it has been very confidently asserted that if the heathen could be once converted, then civilization and domestic economy would follow among them as a matter of course; and the writer was once of the same opinion: but actual observation with respect to these particulars has caused him to change his mind; and he now fully believes, that *he*, whom God has ordained to be a terror to evil doers, as well as a praise to them that do well, must accompany the minister of reconciliation, in order that the work of the purification of the moral world be carried forward with success, in the use of such other means as are now in the hands of the church. And the writer will venture to state further, that the *Christian church* will never prosper among a people who are in a state of perfect *anarchy*.

From the above observations the reader cannot infer that the writer would favour the union of church and state; but rather that the church as a body, and all those who are without her pale, should be *equally* under the restriction of wholesome *civil laws*, founded upon proper principles.

And in view of what has just been stated with reference to the evil and destructive influence which is being exerted in heathen lands by the vast numbers of decided opposers of God and religion, who enter the dark portions of our earth from year to year, and from almost every point of the compass, should not the church redouble her exertions to Christianize the civilized portions of the world? Then when this is accomplished, our landsmen and seamen, when entering the heathen world, would hail the missionary as their brother and friend, and would hold up his hands, and cheer him on in his self-denying labours; nay, they would then be missionaries themselves, and would lay side and shoulder to the gospel chariot wheel, and the tide of mercy would, through such combined efforts, soon deluge the whole earth; and *He*, whose right it is to reign, would soon sway his sceptre over the whole moral world; and every knee would be seen to bow, and every tongue would be heard to confess that Jesus is Lord, to the glory of God the Father.

But those who are ready to chant the glories of their imaginary millennial morn, and others who are anxiously waiting to join the grand choir that shall attend the Messiah at his second advent, may as well hang their harps upon the willows, so long as the *devil* sends ten of his missionaries to the heathen world, while the *church* sends but one in the name of the Lord. And this state of things will never be materially changed, so long as the majority of the *wandering landsmen* and *seamen* who go forth from the bosom of civilized society are led captive by the devil at his will.

And now, in the further consideration of these overwhelming facts, what course shall the ministers of the Protestant church pursue? Shall they spend their remaining mental and physical strength in lashing each other, because of a few unimportant, not to say unmeaning, tenets which the different branches of the vast family adhere to? which great *family* is in possession *alone*, as an instrument in the hands of the great Head of the church, of that *power*, in the proper employment of which in a united capacity, the glorious day might soon be ushered in, when that portion of our earth which is now civilized would be universally subjugated to the reign of the Prince of peace; and when from this renovated portion of our globe such an influence would burst forth, like the flames from Nebuchadnezzar's furnace, and spread over and penetrate the habitations of cruelty, that the south would soon give up and the north would not hold back; and where now is heard naught but the wail of wo, songs of praise and holy triumph would be the burden of every breeze, and the echo of every hill and dale.

O when shall it once be when the watchmen on the walls of Zion shall see eye to eye, and when all God's people shall unite heart and hand, in carrying forward the victories of the cross? May the Lord hasten it in his own good time!

" June 16. I have just received intelligence that the Indians about two miles from me have this morning buried another of their men alive." I afterward talked to them on the subject, when they acknowledged the fact, but said that he was " cultis mischemus," that is, nothing but a slave! And when asked whether a slave was a horse or an elk, that caused them to treat him like a dumb beast and not like a man? they answered, "Wake shicks, cultus eliaty," that is, No, friend, nothing but a slave. But then their slaves are not *alone* treated in this manner, for when another instance of this kind, which I have mentioned, took place, it was a *man* that shared the same fate.

On the 17th of June the Rev. J. Lee, the superintendent of the mission, and Mr. Abernethy and Parrish, and families, made me a visit. Their arrival was hailed with much joy on our part, as Mrs. F. had not been favoured with the society of one of our ladies for better than seven months.

The American captain who had obtained a house near me for the purpose of trading salmon, sent down some ardent spirits by a worthless creature *from the States*, on the day that all our friends left us except Mrs. Abernethy and her two little children. A part of this liquor was dealt out among the natives, notwithstanding the pledge of the captain and his mate to the contrary; and the consequence was an excitement of the blood-thirsty spirit in the breast of the savages around us; and before night one Indian was shot through with a musket ball, so that he expired within two days afterward; and another was stabbed in five places with a knife; and one woman was shot through the mouth, cutting away part of her tongue; and two other women were wounded, one in the shoulder, and the other in the back of the head,—the wounds of these four did not prove mortal. But I ask who will be responsible, at least in a great degree, for the blood that was shed through the influence of that alcoholic draught? Surely the account of the vender of ardent spirits will be a dark one, and the succeeding results will be soul-appalling, unless he averts the blow by timely repentance and a hearty turning to the Lord. O my soul, come not thou into his secret!

The above transaction caused a dreg of bitterness to enter into our cup of joy, and our tears to flow afresh over the wickedness of those who had had their lives given them in a land of Bibles and prayers.

On the 15th of July Mr. Abernethy returned from the Walamet; and on the 26th Mr. Raymond and his family came down, having been appointed by the superintendent to take charge of the farming operations on the Clatsop Plain; and on the 27th Mr. Abernethy and family left us for their place of labour at the Walamet.

It was now probable that we should no more be left entirely alone while we should continue in the country; but much must be done before we could be comfortably housed upon the plain, where we hoped to be able to raise the most of our provisions after the next spring. The store that I had lain in during the preceding autumn had not, in consequence of the departure of Mr. Kone's family, become wholly exhausted ; so that, with the supply that Mr. Raymond had under way, we hoped to be comfortable until next spring.

And according to the directions of the superintendent we set to work immediately to prepare a house for the accommodation of our two families upon the plain. We in the first place took down some boards to the plain, which was done with comparative ease, as we had now a horse and cart. With these boards we finished out the floors in our original cabin ; and then Mr. R.'s family took possession of the same. Then Mr. Raymond and Smith removed the lumber to the plain which had been partly framed for a house for Mr. Kone previous to his departure from the country. I was able to render them some assistance, but as my constitution had been well nigh broken, I was not able to work as formerly. After this lumber was removed it was decided my family should also remove to the plain, in order that we might be on the spot to assist when our promised carpenter should come from the Walamet to put up our house. This removal was effected on the 18th of August ; and we commenced making shingles for our covering during the next rainy season.

On the 1st of September we were highly gratified with a visit from my old and tried friend, the Rev. Dr. Richmond, and Mr. Whitcomb, whose families were on board of the Chenamas, which was lying at Astoria, and on board of which they had taken passage to the United States. The doctor had become satisfied that the prospects of usefulness among the Indians would not warrant his longer continuance in the country. This I am fully convinced was the true state of the case : and, besides this, he had suffered much in consequence of family affliction. I should be very happy to have recourse to his journal, so that I might have the pleasure of laying before our readers some of the scenes through which he passed while at Nasqually, where I left him, just taking possession of the post assigned him, in the summer of 1840; but this privilege is denied me in consequence of the distance which now separates us. Mr. Whitcomb's constitution was entirely broken down, so that it was a matter of doubt whether he would live to reach home. By the last-named gentleman we learned that it was almost certain that we should get no carpenter from the Walamet to assist us about building, although there were but two months between that time and the rainy season.

This intelligence was altogether unexpected, as we had been expecting help every day; but if we were to have no help from a mechanic, there was certainly no time to be lost, or suffered to pass unimproved. So we set to work with what tools we had in possession, and with what help we could obtain from our neighbours; and their number had been increased, for Mr. Tibits had returned from California, where he had been on a tour with a party of the exploring expedition, who had gone across the land to that country. And Mr. T. brought a young man with him, by the name of Peter Brainard, who had assisted him in driving some cattle through from California to the Walamet, and from thence to the Clatsop Plain. And although none of us understood house building, yet by perseverance and hard labour we succeeded in getting our frame up, and our room finished off in a style peculiar to ourselves, and the size of fifteen feet by seventeen, so that I moved into it on the 6th of October.

I should have stated that the Rev. D. Leslie and his two daughters, and Dr. Baily with his family, had also taken passage on board of the Chenamas, which sailed for the Sandwich Islands in a few days after the above visit from Messrs. Richmond and Whitcomb.

On the 10th I received a letter from my brother who

resides in Ithaca, N. Y., which came across the mountains in the care of Dr E. White. By this we learned that our parents were living, and that the family was in usual health.

My own health had now become so much impaired that I was obliged to desist entirely from labour; the bronchitis, with which I had been afflicted for the past year, became much more severe, and I found my spine and liver to be much affected, so that there was continual pain in my side and back, and my nervous system became entirely deranged.

Mr. Raymond succeeded in finishing a room the size of the one I occupied, and took possession of it, so that we were able to keep ourselves dry and tolerably warm.

I preached in English to those who could understand me for a few sabbaths, but was obliged to desist.

December now arrived; but this rainy season so far was much milder than the preceding, as we were favoured with many sunny days, which were very pleasant. My throat now became so bad, and the pain in my side increased to that degree that I determined to go in pursuit of medical aid. I left home with my family on the 11th of December, and crossed over to Astoria and spent the night with Mr. Birnie's family. Here I left my family, and set out with my canoe for Vancouver, and on the following day as we were ascending the river, having Mount St. Helen in full view, we discovered a vast column of smoke ascending from the north-west side of the mount near its top, which proved to be a volcanic eruption, which has been mentioned already by my worthy associate. I asked my Indians, What is that? They looked toward the mountain, and replied, "What is that?" I said, Perhaps it is fire? They answered, "Perhaps it is fire." Seeing that I was not likely to make much headway by reasoning with them after this sort, I inquired if they had ever seen anything like it before? They said they had not; "but they had heard their old people say, that from the top of another mountain," which they call "Swalalahhost," which is situated to the south-east of Young's Bay, "where the thunder used to dwell," a like smoke used to issue forth. Upon the last-named mount one of the gentlemen of the exploring expedition found evidences of a former volcanic eruption. And the noise produced by that eruption, no doubt, caused the Indians to suppose that the thunder had taken up its residence there.

Near the evening of the second day after I left Astoria, having reached the Cawalitze River, we found the Columbia entirely frozen over. This entirely blasted all my hopes of being relieved from my temporal difficulties for the present, as our way to Vancouver was effectually hedged up. So I ordered my crew to "'bout ship," and steer for Astoria. And it was high time we did so, for the ice was closing in so rapidly below us that it was with difficulty that we forced our way through the sheets, which cut our canoe considerably; but we got all clear, and in the course of two hours we reached a fine camping place, where the Indians soon built a rousing fire of dry logs, pitched my tent, and cooked an abundant supply of salt salmon and potatoes, and large cakes of bread, made of flour unbolted, and baked upon a piece of bark, or a stone, or anything that came first to hand, which they set up before the fire, and some cakes they baked under the ashes. After selecting the nicest one for me, and filling my dish with the choice part of the salmon and some potatoes, and steeping me a cup of tea, we all set down to supper, and after doing the provided meal ample justice, my excellent crew stretched themselves around the fire and assured each other that no crew of Indians had ever had a better prospect of a finer night's rest than they had; and partaking of the same spirit, I committed myself to the protection of Heaven, and soon fell asleep.

At this time there were two canoes owned by two French settlers from the Cawalitze, who were going to

Vancouver with cargoes of wheat to be ground for the use of their families: they had ascended the Columbia about one mile above where we turned back, and were lying in the mouth of a little creek, where they were awaiting the removal of the ice. When the ice broke up they set out again, but had not proceeded far when one of the canoes was forced, by the floating ice, into the current, where it was broken to pieces, and the poor Canadian, who was labouring for the support of his family, was snatched from them in a moment by being drowned. If my memory serves me, the rest of the crew were saved after being badly frozen. The next day we reached Astoria, and although my health was not improved, we were thankful that I was not closed in with the ice, as were the poor Frenchmen. A storm now ensued, and we were kept at Astoria for several days, enjoying the hospitality of Mr. Birnie's family. The storm abated, and we arrived at our home on the 21st.

"On the 1st of January, 1843, I administered the sacrament of the Lord's supper to those present who professed to be the disciples of our Lord and Saviour Jesus Christ. The communicants consisted of Mr. Solomon H. Smith, Mr. and Mrs. Raymond, and Mrs. Frost. May we all surround our Father's table in his kingdom above."

On the 3d a man by the name of Cooper arrived from the Walamet, bringing the intelligence of the death of the Rev. James Olley, one of the mission family that left New-York in 1839 for Oregon. Brother Olley was beloved by all who knew him, and particularly so by the writer, who was very intimate with him during his voyage from New-York to Oregon, and believed him to be a worthy Christian. He was called to his reward by being drowned in the Walamet River on the 11th of December, 1842; and left a very amiable widow, who was now deprived of her second husband.

An opportunity now offered for me to go again in pursuit of medical aid; but as my wife was also in ill health, I determined to remain, and if our sufferings were to continue we would suffer together, and in the midst of our complicated difficulties we had abundant reasons for daily expressions of gratitude to our merciful Father in heaven.

Mr. Raymond left for the Walamet on the 10th, as the weather was very pleasant, for the purpose of getting some supplies, and some of his goods, and some farming utensils, and returned on the 14th of February, in the evening; bringing the heart-rending intelligence of a most awful disaster which took place on his return from the Walamet Mission to the Walamet Falls. The canoe containing his goods, and Mr. Crocker, from the state of New-York, a gentleman much respected, and Mr. Rogers, son-in-law to the Rev. D. Leslie, a young man of excellent Christian character, and of much promise, and his wife, oldest daughter of Mr. Leslie, a young lady much beloved by all who knew her because of her amiable disposition and Christian deportment, and her youngest sister, a child, and two Indians, were all swept over the falls, and in this awful manner were six souls ushered into the presence of their God, with scarcely a moment's warning. Mr. Raymond and Doctor White had but just stepped out of the canoe, and were making arrangements for the others to do so, when the canoe took a shear, and was caught by the rapid whirling current, and was carried down without a possibility of being stopped. I cannot dwell upon this awful event; for whenever I call it to mind, an inexpressible feeling comes over me, like unto that which seized my shattered nerves when the intelligence first reached me.

Doctor White came down with Mr. Raymond, and I was glad to avail myself of his help in my suffering state. He saw proper to operate upon my throat by cutting off the palate. This promised temporary relief, but the inflammation had become so thoroughly seated, that an immediate cure could not be expected. He also administered to our other difficulties, and remained with us until the 27th, when he left for Vancouver. By him I sent letters to the superintendent requesting my discharge, as I was now satisfied that my health was such that there was no prospect of my being able to render any more efficient service to the mission, and that a change of climate was necessary in order to my recovery.

"March 19. We have had most delightful weather since the 17th. I never saw anything to exceed it in the month of May in the United States. No material change in our health. My palate shorter, but throat very much inflamed, and severe pain in the side and back. Mr. Raymond getting out fencing stuff, and making preparations for farming. Some milk and butter from our cows, the fruit of our former toil. Received a letter from the superintendent, containing my dismissal from the mission, and commenced making preparations for my departure from the country."

Mr. Tibits built a cabin on the plain, and commenced preparations for farming. Mr. Smith put up another log house, which made him a more comfortable home. In this way the winter and spring passed away, and on the 1st of May Mr. Raymond planted a field of potatoes, and some garden vegetables, and Mr. Smith got in, in addition to potatoes and vegetables, some wheat and barley, oats and peas; and Mr. Tibits did the same. So that our little community began to present the appearance of civilization. Considering the very embarrassed circumstances under which we had laboured, it was acknowledged by those who visited us that a great change had been effected in this vicinity, which was, but about two and a half years previous to this, in an entirely wild state, when Messrs. Smith, Kone, and myself entered it with our provisions and a few tools on our backs, with which to commence operations.

On the 8th of April I left Clatsop for the Walamet via Vancouver. Attended our annual meeting at the Walamet Falls, where the Rev. A. F. Waller has been labouring for the benefit of the few Indians in this vicinity, and where, on the sabbath, he also preaches to the whites who reside here, among whom he has a class of church members. Mr. Abernethy, the mission steward, and his family, also reside here. The mission buildings at this place consist of a log dwelling, the one which Mr. Waller built for his own accommodation, and a frame dwelling occupied by Mr. Abernethy, and a very good framed store-house. Besides these, there are at that place two saw-mills and a flouring-mill, and about twenty-six other buildings, principally frame. I settled my accounts with the mission, and returned to Clatsop on the 8th of June, after making a very pleasant visit at Vancouver and Astoria. And as the company's vessel did not sail to the Islands until fall, we were obliged to wait until an opportunity offered by which we might take passage for home.

We continued to enjoy the society of our Clatsop friends until the 14th of August, when I obtained a passage for my family to Oahu via California, on board of the bark Diamond, Captain Fowler, of Scarborough, England. The Rev. Daniel Lee and Dr. Babcock and families have also taken passage with us. We bid our Clatsop friends adieu, and entered on board on the 15th, and dropped down to Baker's Bay, where we were obliged to lie until the 21st, waiting for a fair wind to cross the bar. During this time we were favoured with the society of Mr. Birnie, and Mr. Wilson, the clerk in charge of Mr. Cushion's trading establishment at the Walamet Falls, which was commenced in 1842, and for the successful prosecution of which a vessel was to be sent out annually from the States; and for two days before we left, Mrs. Birnie and children, a very interesting group, also favoured us with their company. The day before we left being the sabbath, Mr. Lee preached to us in the grove which skirts the bay. On the morning of the 21st the wind sprung up from the north, and as it was fair for us, we were all ordered on board; and now we took leave of our kind friends of Astoria, who with their canoes proceeded to their homes, and we weighed anchor and crossed the bar at the mouth of the Columbia.

The Rev. J. L. Parrish, my successor at Clatsop, had arrived with his family, and had taken possession of the mission house previous to my leaving; and the superintendent of the mission, and the Rev. D. Leslie, who had left his two daughters at Oahu at school, and had returned to Oregon on board of the Diamond, and Mr. Judson and family, were at Clatsop on a visit when I left that station.

Our vessel is under fine headway, and while my companions are beginning to pay tribute to " Old Neptune," I am taking the last look at the scene of my toil, which is rapidly fading from the view. Farewell, farewell, thou dark, wild shore, and may another messenger of mercy, more faithful and more prosperous than the one who is now returning to give an account of his stewardship, soon tread thy blood-stained soil! and may the day soon dawn when all those who float upon thy streams, and traverse thy forests, shall unite in ascribing praise and thanksgiving unto that great and good Being who hath watched over and most mercifully preserved us while we wandered in those wilds!

And now it may be asked, What good has been effected by the toil and sufferings of the three years and three months passed in Oregon, a brief relation of which is now closed? I answer, *Much*. Much crime has been prevented among the natives. Previous to our establishing that missionary post among them several murders were committed by them every year; but after our settlement there, there was not one murder committed among them until we left, except that which was committed while they were under the influence of *alcohol*, as has been already stated. And although none of them professed to be religious, yet my friend Mr. Birnie, who had an excellent opportunity of knowing, often told me that the moral character of the Indians of that vicinity was evidently improved. And besides this, it was no small consolation to the writer, and he thinks it will be the same to the Christian reader, to know that through the exertions of the church, the gospel standard has been reared on the shore of the *Pacific*, around which a civilized, and, in part at least, a Christian community is rallying, and will in all probability continue to rally until the consummation of all things, when Gabriel's trump shall summon the nations of the earth to come forth and receive their final destination. And the writer does not in the least regret that he embarked in that enterprise, although he now returns to his native land with but little hope of enjoying good health again in this life; he only regrets that circumstances were such that he was enabled to accomplish so little for the advancement of the Redeemer's kingdom while in that country.

We ran down the coast before a fine steady breeze; and on the 26th dropped anchor in the harbour of St. Francisco, on the coast of California. This is an extensive bay, and a most splendid harbour, and the surrounding country is well adapted to grazing, and much of it to the growing of wheat and other grains; but the country will never prosper until they have a very different government from the present. On the afternoon of the 29th we ran down to Whaler's Bay, and took in a supply of water; and on the 30th we set sail, and before sunset we lost sight of the coast.

At California we took three more passengers on board. The one was an elderly gentleman, a descendant of the Finlandish nobility, a gentleman of admirable qualities and of extensive research, well qualified in every sense to render society agreeable and happy, and above all he was a *Christian*. The other two gentlemen were formerly from the States; they were enterprising young men, and very agreeable in their manners. With this accession to our society, and the very kind and gentlemanly treatment which we received from Capt. Fowler and his officers, our passage to the island of Oahu was rendered very agreeable. My health was such that I was able to deliver one short discourse on this passage : on the other sabbath Mr. Lee officiated. We arrived at the harbour of Honolulu, Oahu, on the 16th of September, and obtained board for our families at the residence of Mr. John Colcord, a Christian brother. We were very happy to meet with our friends, who had treated us very kindly when on our outward-bound passage.

The inhabitants of these islands have been in quite an uproar for some time past, in consequence of some strange transactions by the French ; and from the fact that Lord George Paulet, commander of her Britannic Majesty's ship Carrysfort, had more recently taken possession of these islands in the name of her Majesty Queen Victoria, and had in a great measure overturned the government, which had a tendency to derange the business matters of the whole kingdom, and to impede the progress of the evangelization of the native inhabitants. But by the arrival of another British war ship, which took place not many weeks before we reached Oahu, the commander, Rear-Admiral Thomas, of the British navy, restored the Hawaian flag to its rightful owner, Kam-ahamaha III., king of the Sandwich Islands ; by which measure the prospect of tranquillity and prosperity was again brightening.

We found the elder of the two daughters of the Rev. D. Leslie, who had been placed by their father at school in this place previous to his return to Oregon, to be in a state of rapid decline ; and during our visit there she bid adieu to this world, and her remains were deposited near the graves of the late members of the Sandwich Island Mission who had been called to their reward.

We found the climate so debilitating that my health declined rapidly. This prevented my enjoying the society of our kind friends, the missionaries and foreign residents, as I wished to do. But still we found many things for which to be thankful, and shall never forget the many kindnesses we received from our friends there. Mr. Lee and myself engaged our passage to Boston on board of the bark Bhering, Captain B. F. Snow, of Boston; but she was not to sail until the month of November. At this time there were two American war vessels in the harbour, besides a number of merchantmen and whalers, but none of them that had accommodations for passengers were bound home. But the time passed away; and on the 18th of November the Bhering was ready for sea; and at about five o'clock in the afternoon of that day we weighed anchor, and sailed out of the harbour amidst hearty cheering from the shore, and from the vessels lying at anchor. Dr. Babcock remained at Oahu, designing to return to Oregon by the first opportunity.

The trade winds were very strong at this time, so that as soon as we had cleared the coral reef outside of the harbour we found ourselves in a very heavy seaway. This tested the strength of our nerves in the outset; and although I had up to this time boasted of having paid no "tribute to Neptune," I was now obliged, though very reluctantly, to cast up accounts, and square up all arrearages. This work was not accomplished on my part until the next day about noon; and I have no disposition to open accounts with the ocean god again.

On the 8th of December we had a view of Marua, one of the Society Islands, and on the 16th of January, 1844, we passed between the Diego Ramares, small, high, rocky islands, and Cape Horn, having both in full view at the same time. Here we found the weather somewhat cold, but with the exception of occasional squalls of snow, it was quite pleasant, and the ocean quite smooth. Four or five sail passed us in the morning, to the windward, on their outward-bound passage; but not within speaking distance. The sun set last night between *eight* and *nine* o'clock, and rose this morning between *three* and *four* o'clock ; and it was sufficiently light to read a plain print while sitting on deck at ten o clock at night. On the morning of this day we were gratified with a distant view of a splendid tornado, to the south of the Cape. On the 18th we had a furious gale : the appearance of the ocean was most wild and furious, and the seas so heavy that we were obliged to "heave to" in the afternoon. But by the next morning the wind abated, and we proceeded on our voyage.

On the 5th of February we spoke the brig Grace, of Newcastle, England, bound to the Cape of Good Hope, with a cargo of coal. We experienced nothing but the ordinary scenes at sea, until the 10th of March, when we were in latitude about 12° north. Our sails were now coloured red, with a sand or earth, which must have been blown off from the coast of Brazil or Africa, by a hurricane, which was nearly spent before it reached us.

After experiencing four heavy gales of wind, which were accompanied with rain and some snow, within the space of seven days past, we made Cape Ann on the morning of the 20th of March, and received a pilot from Boston at four o'clock in the afternoon, and at seven o'clock we cast anchor in the harbour. Thus ended our voyage of one hundred and twenty three days from Oahu. And we were very happy, after being confined on ship board during this time, to reach the land again, and felt that we had special cause for gratitude to our heavenly Father, whose unseen hand had upheld us during our voyaging, and travelling, and toils, since we engaged in the missionary enterprise. Since the autumn of 1839, my family had passed a little more than twelve months on ship board, having sailed about forty thousand miles. Our voyage from Oahu was rendered very comfortable and pleasant, by the very kind and gentlemanly treatment that we received from Captain Snow, his officers, and crew. Their kindness shall not be forgotten, and we pray that they may make the voyage of life in safety, and land at last in the harbour of endless rest.

We spent one night in Boston, and were cheered with an interview with some Christian friends residing in the city. We left Boston on the 22d, and arrived at New-York on the 23d.

The kind and most affectionate manner in which we were received by the Board of Managers of the Missionary Society, and by our Christian brethren and friends generally, has more than healed all the wounds that time and time's sorrows have made.

And now, in view of the foregoing general description of the Oregon Territory, which may be depended upon as being correct, we ask whether those do not make a *great mistake*, who sell off their possessions, and turn their backs upon the rich and wide-spread prairies of our western states, where they may be blessed with the protection of wholesome laws, and every facility for the accumulation of wealth and the achievement of honour, and spend the strength of their families, and the most of their substance, as many have done, in making a perilous, and, in many instances, a desperate journey across the Rocky Mountains, for the purpose of reaching an unsettled Indian country, that they may "*better their fortunes?*"

And, again, taking all the very embarrassing circumstances into the account, under which the missionaries have been obliged to labour, I ask the church and a candid public, whether as much has not been accomplished toward the evangelization of the inhabitants of that territory, as could reasonably have been expected?

And now in conclusion, we feel that we have done

our duty in preparing this work for the perusal of the public, and we hope and pray that it may have its designed effect, and that the blessing of the God of all grace may attend it wherever it may find its way, and that the writers and readers may employ those talents which have been, or may hereafter be committed unto them, in such a manner, that when the *Master* shall come to reckon with his servants, we may hear it said, with respect to us, " Well done, good and faithful servants ; ye have been faithful over a few things, I will make you rulers over many things : *enter into the joy of your Lord.*"

APPENDIX.

A SPECIMEN OF INDIAN DIALECTS.

KILLEMOOK DIALECT.

This clan inhabits a region of country to the south of Cape Lookout.

PRONOUNS.

I	Untsuh,
You	Unekeeh,
They	Hla ah at lah,
He	Ta at lah,
She	Hlah at lah,
Whose	Kah to keeh,
My	Un suttle,
We	Un a wahtle,
Ye	Cul a cula,
Their	Chun suns,
Our	Ne wahtle.

NAMES OF THINGS, &c.

Prairie or plain	Kolote,
Water	Clah ko,
Man	Ty yel a ho,
Woman	We clats,
Sand beach	Tes ah at lo,
Canoe	Atsy keetles,
House	Tes ne nowin,
Blanket	Clan a lats o,
Axe	Clah kyts ton,
See, to look	Ya hase,
None	Ke stow,
I do not understand	Cas kots canoya untsuh,
A man comes	Tyyelaho tasea,
They come	Hlahahatlah tasea,
Many people come	Clanatle stawat tasea,
Who comes?	Cato keep tasea?
Come ashore	Ocheahoh cheso,
Come ashore ye	Cheuku culacula cheso,
Go to the house you	Ahatlah tesnenowin unekeeh,

Where is that axe?	Chans keeh clahkytston?
I know not where	Nacahhah chans,
Whose canoe is that?	Cato keeh atsy keetles?
Make a canoe, you	Ahhunnah atsy keetles unekeeh,
Get your hat	Cannan unekeeh testeetka cotton,
Yonder it lies	Kah e stock,
It lies in the house	Stock tesnenowin,
I come	Untsuh tasea,
You come	Unekeeh tasea,
We come	Unawahtle taseeahtle,
When will you come?	Hunsey keeh coatseuse unekeeh?
By and by I will come	Eslany untsuh coatseuy,
Give me your hand	Chalsitsa isnucheachy,
What ails you?	Chas keeh ne keeh?
Whose is that boy?	Katokeeh cheuts?
Will you trade?	Cah see whyawhyatle?
Let us trade now	Cha kets whyawhyatle,
What do you want?	Tahi keeh hesuins?
I want a knife	Hoaktin skesuany,
How many knives?	Cahnucts kee hoaktin?
To-morrow I will give you a knife	Cowusks cachalsee hoaktin,
It rains now!	Kate cah loatle!
It will stop soon	Eslany cheatlah,
Now we will go and catch salmon	Eslany quocas howoyettle tusleuck,
Perhaps we will soon get plenty	Clanatle nacahah ocashowoyettle eslany,
To-night we will eat plenty	Huntul sohatleyatle clanatle,
To-morrow we will get more	Cowusks ocashowoyettle,
I love	Unsuh skesuany,
You love	Unekeeh skesuany,
We love	Unawahtle skesuanyatle,
They love	Chunsuns skesuins,
I go	Unsuka hatley,
You go	Unekeeh ahhatlee,
They go	Chunsuns cahhatle,
Go with me	Ahcahtsa untsuh,

I will go with you . . .	Untseeh cahcahtsee,
Will you go with me ? .	Unekeehee cahcahts unseeh?
My father	Untsuh allah,
Your father	Unekeeh islahhah,
Our father	Newahtle talieahtle,
Their father	Chunsuns lahahcus,
He speaks or talks . . .	Chenatle cheouins,
I have come a long way .	Ho tie tasee untsuh,
Make a fire	Ho kone,
Give me salmon . . .	Chalsitsa tusleuck,
I am hungry	Shotoyah untsuh,
My heart is now good .	Tohoatsnoyah teyinecas untsuh,
Long ago my heart was bad	Tehalatle tah til te yinecas untsuh,
Chief	Asahtshin,
An important chief . . .	Cas sesowahtle asahtshin.

An old Killemook man, whose son was drowned far from home, expressed his grief in the following manner: "Hatch e ki ah, hatch e ki ah, hatch e ki ah, hatch e ki ah; che kah, che kah, che kah, che kah," i. e. Oh my child, oh my child, oh my child, oh my child; my child, my child, my child, my child. And these expressions were attended with the tearing of his silvered locks, and the scratching of his body with his nails, and the smiting of his breast, and such expressions of the countenance as indicated the deepest anguish of spirit.

CHECALISH DIALECT.
The Checalish Indians reside to the north of Cape Disappointment.

PRONOUNS.

I or me	Ants,
You	Nauah,
He	Tesitnah,
She	Tesitnah,
We	Oshatlchihlah,
Ye or you	Alap,
They	Tsadinta.
Their chief deity . . .	Yeloput or Siloput,

Man	Steuh,
Boy	Stehoh,
Woman	Skaiklehl,
Girl	Skaiaklentl,
Young woman	Claledlintl,
The human body	Paitstitsa,
The head	Tematins,
Hair	Klikwatens,
Forehead	Taspotus,
Ear	Taqualant,
Eye	Tamose,
Nose	Tamakas,
Nostrils	Taslipahuks,
Teeth	Tayidents,
Tongue	Tahutsl,
Eyebrows	Tasoenteen,
Chin	Taskadlints,
Neck	Tachisp,
Throat	Silahome,
Windpipe	Tahokehoke,
Breast	Nawaiawhats,
Heart	Squadlam,
Shoulder	Hlakadinst,
Arm	Tashohemitsens,
Elbow	Matsa,
Thumb	Nawohatse,
First finger	Ahost,
Second do.	Anesonowaitsa,
Third do.	Ahitsoho,
Fourth do.	Tsohonu,
Thigh	Tsaispitsa,
Knee	Taadnst,
Leg	Tsotls,
Ankle	Mahamahas,
Foot	Stallash,
Fire	Machipe,
Make a fire	Pokochipe,
Put out the fire	Kwiakee,
Come in the house	Eselotstowatl,
Cold	Cleloh,
Warm	Whadlah,

Rain	Stolts,
Snow	Slahkok,
Ice	Sthoua,
House	Hash,
Horse	Stekeu,
Buffalo	Chuyewhalak,
Dog	Kahhah,
Potatoes	Tenneemas,
Bat or flying mouse	Patouksenitsa,
Racoon	Kwalas,
Musket	Tecletsenups,
Knife	Chano,
Fork	Sitssitstle,
Powder horn	Suchadlink.

CLATSOP DIALECT.

The Clatsops reside on the south side of the Columbia River.

PRONOUNS.

I	Nika,
You	Mika,
He	Yohka,
She	Ahka,
We	Elhika or nesika,
Ye or you	Mesika,
They	Klaska,
Ours	Nesika,
Yours	Mesika,
Theirs	Hlaska.

Man	Coatlalikum,
Woman	Cloachaman,
Brother	Ow,
Sister	Ats,
Slave	Eliaty or mischemus,
Pipe	Olomboh,
Tobacco	Kinutle,
The chief deity	Acarna,
The bad spirit	Exclahou,
Dead	Mamaluste,

To eat	Nohelholaboh,
I die	Nobuckata nika,
Breath, spirit, or soul	Yahanetty,
Heart	Esquamanahle,
I will take a smoke	Kinutle nohel holabah nika,
Salmon	Qunache,
Dog	Kamuks,
Deer	Mouits,
Elk	Molock,
Horse	Cuetan,
Cow	Moosmoos,
Bear	Atchhoat,
Wolf	Lalo,
Bird	Culacula,
Wild goose	Culluckalahbah,
Duck	Quahquah,
Wood	Tubits,
Finger ring	Quiaquia,
Sash	Oquivaquah,
Powder horn	Omuckwell,
Musket	Shuckwalellah,
Black	Kleloh,
White	Tekope,
Blue	Spuck,
Red	Pilpil,
Green	Petish,
Strawberries	Ommoty,
Whortleberries	Conespuck,
Cranberries	Sulumisha,
Gooseberries	Commosock.

I could give more extensive examples; but the above will be sufficient to show the difference between the dialects of the different clans that visit the Columbia River during the salmon season. There are perhaps five hundred individuals, the remnants of five different tribes, that fish on the Columbia, from the mouth of the river to the Cathlamet Islands, a distance of about twenty-five miles; and the dialects of these clans differ from each other as much as the examples do which I have given above.

The Far Western Frontier
An Arno Press Collection

[Angel, Myron, editor]. **History of Nevada.** 1881.

Barnes, Demas. **From the Atlantic to the Pacific, Overland.** 1866.

Beadle, J[ohn] H[anson]. **The Undeveloped West; Or, Five Years in the Territories.** [1873].

Bidwell, John. **Echoes of the Past:** An Account of the First Emigrant Train to California. [1914].

Bowles, Samuel. **Our New West.** 1869.

Browne, J[ohn] Ross. **Adventures in the Apache Country.** 1871.

Browne, J[ohn] Ross. **Report of the Debates in the Convention of California, on the Formation of the State Constitution.** 1850.

Byers, W[illiam] N. and J[ohn] H. Kellom. **Hand Book to the Gold Fields of Nebraska and Kansas.** 1859.

Carvalho, S[olomon] N. **Incidents of Travel and Adventure in the Far West; with Col. Fremont's Last Expedition Across the Rocky Mountains.** 1857.

Clayton, William. **William Clayton's Journal.** 1921.

Cooke, P[hilip] St. G[eorge]. **Scenes and Adventures in the Army.** 1857.

Cornwallis, Kinahan. **The New El Dorado; Or, British Columbia.** 1858.

Davis, W[illiam] W. H. **El Gringo; Or, New Mexico and Her People.** 1857.

De Quille, Dan. (William Wright). **A History of the Comstock Silver Lode & Mines.** 1889.

Delano, A[lonzo]. **Life on the Plains and Among the Diggings;** Being Scenes and Adventures of an Overland Journey to California. 1854.

Ferguson, Charles D. **The Experiences of a Forty-niner in California.** (Originally published as *The Experiences of a Forty-niner During Thirty-four Years' Residence in California and Australia*). 1888.

Forbes, Alexander. **California:** A History of Upper and Lower California. 1839.

Fossett, Frank. **Colorado:** Its Gold and Silver Mines, Farms and Stock Ranges, and Health and Pleasure Resorts. 1879.

The Gold Mines of California: Two Guidebooks. 1973.

Gray, W[illiam] H[enry]. **A History of Oregon, 1792–1849.** 1870.

Green, Thomas J. **Journal of the Texian Expedition Against Mier.** 1845.

Henry, W[illiam] S[eaton]. **Campaign Sketches of the War with Mexico.** 1847.

[Hildreth, James]. **Dragoon Campaigns to the Rocky Mountains.** 1836.

Hines, Gustavus. **Oregon:** Its History, Condition and Prospects. 1851.

Holley, Mary Austin. **Texas:** Observations, Historical, Geographical and Descriptive. 1833.

Hollister, Ovando J[ames]. **The Mines of Colorado.** 1867.

Hughes, John T. **Doniphan's Expedition.** 1847.

Johnston, W[illiam] G. **Experiences of a Forty-niner.** 1892.

Jones, Anson. **Memoranda and Official Correspondence Relating to the Republic of Texas, Its History and Annexation.** 1859.

Kelly, William. **An Excursion to California Over the Prairie, Rocky Mountains, and Great Sierra Nevada.** 1851. 2 Volumes in 1.

Lee, D[aniel] and J[oseph] H. Frost. **Ten Years in Oregon.** 1844.

Macfie, Matthew. **Vancouver Island and British Columbia.** 1865.

Marsh, James B. **Four Years in the Rockies; Or, the Adventures of Isaac P. Rose.** 1884.

Mowry, Sylvester. **Arizona and Sonora:** The Geography, History, and Resources of the Silver Region of North America. 1864.

Mullan, John. **Miners and Travelers' Guide to Oregon, Washington, Idaho, Montana, Wyoming, and Colorado.** 1865.

Newell, C[hester]. **History of the Revolution in Texas.** 1838.

Parker, A[mos] A[ndrew]. **Trip to the West and Texas.** 1835.

Pattie, James O[hio]. **The Personal Narrative of James O. Pattie, of Kentucky.** 1831.

Rae, W[illiam] F[raser]. **Westward by Rail:** The New Route to the East. 1871.

Ryan, William Redmond. **Personal Adventures in Upper and Lower California, in 1848-9.** 1850/1851. 2 Volumes in 1.

Shaw, William. **Golden Dreams and Waking Realities:** Being the Adventures of a Gold-Seeker in California and the Pacific Islands. 1851.

Stuart, Granville. **Montana As It Is:** Being a General Description of its Resources. 1865.

Texas in 1840, Or the Emigrant's Guide to the New Republic. 1840.

Thornton, J. Quinn. **Oregon and California in 1848.** 1849. 2 Volumes in 1.

Upham, Samuel C. **Notes of a Voyage to California via Cape Horn, Together with Scenes in El Dorado, in the Years 1849-'50.** 1878.

Woods, Daniel B. **Sixteen Months at the Gold Diggings.** 1851.

Young, F[rank] G., editor. **The Correspondence and Journals of Captain Nathaniel J. Wyeth, 1831-6.** 1899.